Understanding Project Management

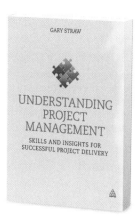

Understanding Project Management

Skills and insights for successful project delivery

Gary Straw

LONDON PHILADELPHIA NEW DELHI

First published in Great Britain and the United States in 2015 by Kogan Page Limited

2nd Floor, 45 Gee Street	1518 Walnut Street, Suite 1100	4737/23 Ansari Road
London	Philadelphia PA 19102	Daryaganj
EC1V 3RS	USA	New Delhi 110002
United Kingdom		India
www.koganpage.com		

© Gary Straw, 2015

The right of Gary Straw to be identified as the author of this work has been asserted by him in accordance with the Copyright, Designs and Patents Act 1988.

ISBN   978 0 7494 7055 5
E-ISBN 978 0 7494 7056 2

British Library Cataloguing-in-Publication Data

A CIP record for this book is available from the British Library.

Library of Congress Cataloging-in-Publication Data

Straw, Gary.
    Understanding project management : skills and insights for successful project delivery / Gary Straw.
        pages cm
        ISBN 978-0-7494-7055-5 (paperback) – ISBN 978-0-7494-7056-2 (ebk)   1. Project management.   I. Title.
        HD69.P75S7733 2015
        658.4'04–dc23
                                                                                    2015008798

Typeset by Graphicraft Limited, Hong Kong
Print production managed by Jellyfish
Printed and bound in Great Britain by CPI Group (UK) Ltd, Croydon CR0 4YY

CONTENTS

PREFACE

This is a generalist textbook for people involved (intentionally and unintention-ally) in the delivery of projects, as non-experts or experts. It is aimed to support learning in MBA, management and management-related master's degrees, and also for executives or management pursuing continuing professional development (CPD) schemes. It will also be suitable to support appropriate executive education schemes associated with projects, programmes or indeed portfolio management.

The book aims to provide an understanding of project management, help develop perspectives in application and enable the development of project management capability, at an individual, organization or project level. While retaining the rigour required within the higher education domain, content has been guided by practice.

The author has provided project-management-based courses for over a decade. This followed periods spent delivering projects in a variety of private- and public-sector markets. Within large multinational corporations and small businesses, whether managing the project or providing one part of a delivery solution, the challenges are often very similar; a set of generic principles underpin many of the project management activities and roles. Working with international students has provided additional insights into the challenges presented by learning style, person-ality and cultural basis. It has also provided significant motivation and inspiration.

Recent decades have seen some balancing in the content used as a platform for project management learning; the accumulation of a significant volume of technical knowledge and analytical techniques has been accompanied by a greater awareness of the need for approaches that are contingent upon the environment of the project and for insights into the appropriate deployment of soft skills. One example of this has been the increasing awareness of the significant influence of the stakeholder.

It is important to provide a depth of insight appropriate for a generalist course. While opportunities within project environments to apply techniques are potentially quite high, many students will need to understand why (and when) it is important to deploy a particular technique; they need to build knowledge and judgement rather than (or as well as) becoming subject experts.

Conveying such accumulated insights presents some challenges; if we introduced all the important project management topics in the first chapter, it would be the first and only one in the book. In order to manage projects effectively, we have to know lots of things; with an appropriate emphasis on practice and reflection within a real-world environment, topics are introduced in a layered-learning sequence. An analogy might be the playing of a game of cards. It may take time to understand the game; we might build a 'good hand' by picking up the right cards, putting down others, knowing when to play them, and recognizing that we might not always get the ideal set. We develop good judgement, which is fundamental within project environments.

Throughout the book there is an emphasis on balance: of introducing, understanding, interpreting and deploying project management knowledge in a business or organizational context, and recognizing the appropriate development of analytical skills. An ever-increasing proportion of projects have either transnational or cross-cultural dynamics. It is important to reflect not only this aspect but also the impact on global projects of the power of emerging economies. This comes in the form of approach, style and emphasis. Case studies are included to provoke discussion and reflection.

In order to help the student develop such an understanding of the subject, the book is split into four parts, each of three chapters. Part One, 'Projects in an ideal world', incorporates three chapters that mimic an often typical introduction for the novice project manager; the initial fundamental principles are followed by a consideration of projects at the conceptual stage, and the third chapter has an emphasis on planning. Each of these chapters introduces some relatively basic concepts that may be very familiar to a more experienced reader, but should be valuable to the inexperienced. The sequence of chapter topics should also provide a basis for those who need to study the subject in a more prescriptive project lifecycle-oriented mode.

Part Two, 'Projects in a real world', starts with a chapter that continues the project lifecycle theme, covering topics that are associated most strongly with the challenge of delivering projects; this in turn is followed by a chapter that considers the challenges associated with bringing a project to completion. The sixth chapter focuses on review and evaluation in project environments. This is intended to provoke the reader to consider that this is often the point at which the real-world project manager genuinely learns how to approach the next one. Encouraging reflection in terms of the potential gap between what we did and what we should have done will lead into the next set of chapters.

Part Three, 'Projects in a challenging world', increases the intensity of challenge. Chapter 7 focuses on projects as a business-as-normal activity, and this includes an exploration of forms of institutional or practitioner-based knowledge and support. The next chapter examines the many dimensions of aggregation within project environments; this provides additional challenges through the deployment of programmatic and portfolio-based activities. Attention turns to the global society in Chapter 9; many of the topics covered in previous ones are now considered within a broader set of challenges, associated with the international nature of projects, often faced by the practising manager or executive.

Drawing upon the themes developed in the previous areas of the book, Part Four, 'Developing a capability', aims to help readers to incorporate their learning in order to influence the successful delivery of projects, wherever they are based, whatever their role, whatever their cultural setting, or whenever they encounter them. Chapter 10 considers some fundamental aspects of management and leadership; this is followed by a chapter that encourages readers to reflect on team aspects and the spectrum of individual roles that comprise the project environment. This sets up the final chapter, which encourages the reader to adopt holistic and strategic perspectives and to expect continual change in many project environments.

Throughout the book the reader is encouraged to reflect widely on all of the areas covered and on their own experience, and to draw insights from adjacent and often unexpected knowledge or real-life experience. Likened to new journeys, projects incorporate anticipation, uncertainty, discovery, frustration, challenge and fulfilment. At the end we know where we have been. Enjoy the journey.

ACKNOWLEDGEMENTS

The motivation to write this book has largely come from frequent opportunities to witness the sometimes extraordinary achievement of ordinary people, each faced with their own mountains to climb. Be they in an early or later stage of their career, or whether they have limited or significant experience as a business school learner, they do great things. Sometimes this is achieved despite significant pressures in their personal lives.

I would like to express my thanks to those people; to the numerous friends and foes with whom I have worked and the countless students whom I have challenged and they have delivered. My thanks go to individuals from India, Pakistan, Sri Lanka, Ghana, Nigeria, Kenya, Russia, Poland, Canada, China, Taiwan, Japan, Vietnam, Germany, Netherlands, Spain, Greece, Belgium, Mexico, Venezuela, and several countries within the Middle Eastern nations.

It is important for me to make specific mention of the following people who helped with the process:

- Jon Whelan for a variety of initial insights;
- the external reviewers, Langes Supramaniam of Robert Gordon University and Steve Barron of Lancaster University, for reading and providing feedback on drafted chapters;
- Simon Dawkins, Stella Tsai, Peter Trumper and Mario Campoy for a variety of sector-specific or regional insights.

Many other people helped shape my perspectives by providing an opportunity for informal discussion and debate, including Trafford Feekins, Jules Cheung, Philip Squire, Claire Lin, and Richard and other members of the Straw family. Within my personal life and former business career, some have provided valuable insights into how to approach processes, things and people, including Peter Johnson, Julie Finch and the late Nia Williams.

By coincidence, the main delivery phase of this project started and ended in the accommodation and hospitality of the Tsai family, 6,500 miles from my home. Although we may think that our minds are open to new ideas and experiences, the extraordinary welcome I have experienced has provided great inspiration and motivation, both for the book and for the future.

This has, of course, been a challenging process, and I would like lastly and importantly to acknowledge the patient support and understanding of my family who have stayed with me during a challenging period. My parents have always been supportive; my sons David and Michael have often been an unusually useful source of anecdotes for the courses I have delivered. All together it makes us what we are – well humoured, resilient, genuine and passionate.

PART ONE
Projects in an ideal world

An introduction to projects and project management

01

LEARNING OUTCOMES

By applying the topics within this chapter you should be able to:

- gain insights into the challenge of characterizing projects and project management;

- reflect on initial considerations of the role of the project manager;

- explain the relationship between project management and risk management;

- evaluate and reflect upon risk within project management;

- explain the notion of project processes and project lifecycles;

- reflect upon the inherent complexity and fundamental role of the stakeholder.

Introduction

This book deals both with activities that can be identified more immediately as projects and those equivocal scenarios that might benefit from a project management approach. To start our exploration of the subject, it is useful first to consider activities that we can clearly articulate as projects and those that fall into a set that might sit elsewhere in the business management taxonomy, but that have some of the characteristics typical of a project. For those businesses or organizations whose success depends upon adopting and deploying the right approach for such activities, while clarity of definition might be challenging, this is insignificant compared with the need to ensure that objectives are met, deliverables are delivered, and success must not be through fortuitous endeavour. There are projects to be managed.

'Managing projects' and 'project managers' are expressions that we have become used to hearing in many areas of business and within ambitious societies. In fact, in a number of respects the language of project management has perhaps come of age. The terminology can be heard frequently. The word 'project' is used universally, sometimes with alacrity. With perhaps misplaced confidence, we might hear '… but I am the project manager!' asserted by individuals within a range of organizational scenarios. One example might be the hapless recruit in a reality entertainment show,[1] charged with organizing a marketing promotion to a diverse variety of clients, within an associated geographic location. As the process unfolds, it provides light entertainment to some, but mild irritation to real-life project managers, and a host of scenarios are acted out week by week. Are these really projects?

Within to an organizational setting, at the other end of the spectrum, a different individual will be tasked with putting together the activities for the construction of a hydro-electric power station that will result in the supply of electricity. This immediately seems a more obvious candidate for the project manager title. Yes, they are all projects. And yes, they are probably all project managers or are involved in the management of projects. Why?

Projects – initial perspectives

What activities constitute a project? What is it that I am doing that makes me a project manager? Table 1.1 includes five scenarios to consider these questions. In order to answer them, it is useful first to consider that there are a number of definitions for a project. The following have been drawn from a number of sources, within both the academic and practitioner areas. Considering these definitions helps to open our understanding of the field and also provides an insight into the types of 'expert sources' that might help support our journey through the project. We will first draw upon *Project Management* (2003), in which Harvey Maylor included the following definition for a project: 'A unique set of co-ordinated activities, with definite starting and finishing points, undertaken by an individual or organization to meet specific performance objectives within defined schedule, cost and performance parameters' (BS6079: 2000). A later definition from the Association for Project Management (2012) seems quite different; it is in fact a less detailed formulation of the concept: 'A unique, transient endeavour undertaken to achieve planned objectives'. The Project Management Institute (2013) definition encompasses much of the two previous statements, '… it's a temporary group activity designed to produce a unique product, service or result', but also muses '… so a project team often includes people

TABLE 1.1 Are these projects?

A	A language training company wants to introduce an e-learning platform
B	A company aims to improve the efficiency of material handling and processing by making improvements to its service and maintenance systems
C	The proposed partnership between two media production companies
D	A hotel wants to introduce a new customer loyalty programme
E	The construction of a new healthcare facility

who don't usually work together – sometimes from different organizations and across multiple geographies'.

Over recent decades, our understanding of project management has developed; the change in these definitions reveals the move in emphasis towards a concept that is more holistic in nature. Using either of these more recent definitions helps us frame the contemporary world of projects, but we might still encounter a scenario that doesn't quite fit, for example if we work on an activity that is almost unique but shares characteristics with a previous scenario.

We could argue that all of examples A–E in Table 1.1 are projects; the introduction of an e-learning platform appears to be a new activity in the language training company in example A. 'New-ness' also applies to the customer loyalty programme and healthcare facility construction in examples D and E. The proposed partnership between media production companies in example C also appears to be a new activity and will probably involve a project team composed of people who don't normally work together. Only in example B could we argue that the efficiency improvement activity is less obviously a project, but even then this is not a routine activity and a wise start position might be to approach it on a project basis. In fact, some organizations adopt this position (start by regarding the activity as a project) as a default approach to their work, as we shall see later.

A useful model that characterizes projects in terms of a relationship between volume and variety was mooted by Maylor (2003, 2010). The argument here is quite simple but very effective: the volume of activity process ranges from lower to higher, and similarly with the variation of activity. The resulting ellipse provides an understandable basis to fit our candidate projects. At one extreme (low variety, high volume) we could place the preparation of fast-food meals, for sale internationally – be they burgers, fried chicken, rice boxes, noodle dishes; there are a relatively small number of different fillings and they will be sold in high volume.

FIGURE 1.1   A spectrum of projects

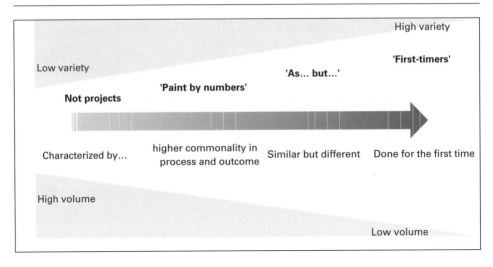

SOURCE: adapted from Maylor (2003, 2010)

At the other extreme within the ellipse we could place the exploration of the planet Mars (extremely low volume, high variety). Somewhere in the middle we could consider the 'paint-by-numbers' activities of some forms of regular housing construction or event management, and between these we might find an activity that we have delivered once before and we now need something similar but with inherent differences, such as a multi-venue entertainment tour. Of course, as examples these are in themselves extraordinarily different activities in terms of scale, complexity and risk. They nevertheless serve to demonstrate the variety of activities that could constitute a project, the degree of project, and the difficulty with finding an adequate definition.

For the purpose of characterizing projects in our discussions we will embrace this terminology, shown in Figure 1.1, throughout the rest of the book – 'Paint-by-numbers', 'As... but' and 'First-timer'. Although the terms are explained above, it is worth taking the opportunity here to highlight that this type of terminology can provide some challenges to learners who do not have English as their first language, notably the expression 'paint-by-numbers'. This is an aspect of a broader challenge faced in this particular learning and vocational area, and is a theme that will be explored further later in the book.

The project manager and project management

In our previous discussion we saw that it can be problematic finding an adequate definition for our project; if we now consider the person involved, this can introduce a further level of potential ambiguity. For example, we can argue that a project that is a first-timer project to you is not a first-timer to me. We therefore have an interpretation of the definition based on the perspective of the individual (or organization). We also see businesses that organize the delivery of their activities with a project management philosophy. So, if delivering an understanding of projects is difficult, how do we further comprehend the role of the project manager?

Returning to the definitions for a moment, some readers will need to apply one in order to classify the activity for which they are responsible. If the activity fits the definition well, it could be argued that the person managing it is a 'project manager' – for example, the appointment of a project manager to deliver the construction of a new hydro-electric power plant. Does this matter? Well, in other scenarios where the project is defined less clearly, the challenge may be to interpret the 'new-ness' or change aspects of the activity the project manager is charged with delivering; this may be sufficient to help the individual and/or the organization recognize that the activity is in fact a project, but unfortunately we often see a scenario where an individual takes responsibility largely unaware of this (hence the usage of the term 'accidental project manager' – those who do it but didn't realize or necessarily intend to do so).

Individuals responsible for the delivery of a project (however it is defined) might be classified as project managers, with associated job title and role definition; equally they may not, as they have been asked to undertake a task or activity but are largely unaware of the underlying challenges. At this preliminary stage we will define the project manager as an individual who has responsibility for an activity that fits one of the definitions of a project in the previous section. This will be developed further in later chapters.

Further, we will define 'project management' as the set of activities associated with the fulfilment of a project. This chimes with the Project Management Institute (2013) definition of project management as the 'application of knowledge, skills and techniques to execute projects effectively and efficiently'.

Project management is risk management

Risk. The very mention of the word provokes a reaction. In fact, it provokes many reactions, most often negative. Uncertainty, an alternative notion, evokes different emotions. Both could be deemed to be positive and negative: does this matter? Other reactions might stem from individual experience. To some, risk management is a 'necessary evil', a set of processes that they might feel rules their business-as-normal working world. Whether applied to educational visits, travelling, power generation or food production, the risk management processes are applied extensively:

- Will the students be in danger when they are travelling? Will a student suffer anaphylactic shock while enjoying third-party hospitality?

- What will happen if the plane flies through a cloud of volcanic ash? Will the engines stop working?
- Can a power-generating plant operate safely? What will happen if there is an earthquake?
- Is it safe to eat the food one day after the food advice 'use by' label? Is the food toxic?

There are many more examples that could be included for discussion. Notably, the interpretation (and view) of risk varies for the individual and also within and across societies; in some cultures the above examples indicate a move towards the expectation that all experiences should be provided incident-free. Why is this? Many of the reasons are obvious (such as safety) and others are less apparent.

Above all, any organization concerned by the issues included above will be aware that their reputation is constantly under threat. An educational establishment will take steps to minimize the chance of an incident during a study visit. An airline, whose primary concern is safety, should always take steps to minimize as far as possible any risk of an incident. Similarly for a power-generating plant; and of course a food producer will have similar concerns.

Understandably, therefore, risk is a key component of any organizational process. Risk is also a key component of any project. One difficulty often faced in our increasingly expectant world is the notion that society can prevent all the inherent problems and that someone will always be able to rescue a situation with little damage or harm done – that by invoking extensive risk management we will be able to manage anything bad happening. While this might seem particularly ambitious, in some areas it has some truth, as we can observe in the field of aviation safety.

It is worthwhile exploring our notion of risk and uncertainty (Table 1.2).

Of the five most common definitions for risk, four include the word danger. Uncertainty is concerned with doubt. We could argue that certainty can range from complete (100%) down to none (0%); I could state that 'I am 100% sure that...' or 'I have 0% certainty of something'. With lower levels of certainty we can correspondingly argue that the risk will be higher. Conversely, risks will be lower with higher levels of certainty.

Figure 1.2 draws out this point, and illustrates the progressive scale of 'riskiness' that we might encounter in the activities that we are managing. In fact, we could add the categories of projects from the previous section ('paint-by-numbers', 'as... but' etc) to the diagram.

Now we could be working on an activity with high certainty and low risk. However, if we are undertaking a new activity, the likelihood is that this will have characteristics of lower certainty and therefore higher risk. This can give us a problem: if, by definition, projects are new activities, or have degrees of 'new-ness'

TABLE 1.2   Most common definitions of risk and uncertainty
(*Oxford English Dictionary*, 6th edn, 2007)

Risk (noun)

1   Danger; possibility of loss, injury or other adverse circumstance
2   A chance or possibility of danger
3   A person considered a liability or danger; a person exposed to risk

Risk (verb)

4   Endanger, put at risk, expose to the chance of injury or loss
5   Venture on; accept the chance of...

Uncertainty (noun)

1   The quality or state of being uncertain; doubtfulness; hesitation; irresolution
2   A doubtful point
3   The amount of variation in a numerical result that is consistent with
     observation

FIGURE 1.2   Relationship between perceived certainty and
risk likelihood

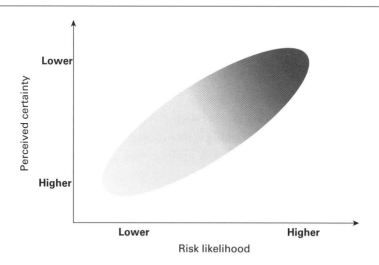

and therefore uncertainty, then project management has an equivalence to risk management. In other words, delivering projects is concerned with managing risks. With this understood, we must therefore ensure that our perspectives on – and response to – risk are maintained throughout the project, and we should also recognize the importance of carrying forward any associated risk considerations beyond the project itself.

For example, if our project is concerned with the development of a new visitor attraction in an isolated mountainous area with challenging access and climatic conditions, this might yield a substantial risk-related analysis that is fundamental to the project management process but also helps provide useful guidance for safe operation after the delivery period. Frequently the delivery of a project will reveal a host of risks; the knowledge generated from this is often carried forward to operational mode.

Learning point: risk is ever-present

In the world of projects, by definition there will be some risk. If we accept that projects have a degree of 'new-ness', there will be some uncertainty. If there is uncertainty, there will be some risk. As this is inevitable, we need to accept that this is a key feature of projects and therefore work with it. The area of risk and uncertainty is particularly important in project management. At this stage the emphasis should be on recognizing that risk is a natural element of projects; it should not be regarded as something evaluated once or at inappropriate times.

While it is important to distinguish between process and project risk, the continual presence of risk means that it should be incorporated 'as normal'; it should not be viewed as an isolated concept. Good project management incorporates risk as a project-wide concept, and this should help us to anticipate problems rather than react to circumstances when they have become problematic. As my boss once said to me: 'Gary, I don't like surprises.'

Within each of the following topics the reader is encouraged to reflect on the associated risks and develop an appropriate means of managing them. In order to do this, we need to extend our thinking beyond the first definitions of risk and establish a number of concepts. This includes the identification and assessment of risks, and most importantly the consequences resulting from our analysis.

Risk identification

What are the sources of risk? How do we evaluate this? Often a good step to take is to take one step backwards, to get a broad perspective of the project. We can define internal and external risks. We could 'frame' it from other perspectives, for example taking account of the stakeholder landscape; there may be other ways of framing that are appropriate to the particular context of the project or set out by an organization. For example, in a small-scale energy-generating project, a risk profile could be set out around the following headings (or risk 'areas'):

- **E**nvironmental
- **L**egislative
- **T**echnology
- **C**ontractual
- **F**inancial.

These were used for a particular project; for a different one, we would probably wish to add to or replace some of these.

The means of identifying risk can vary depending on our experience of similar activities or projects and on whether we spend time worrying or choose to pursue analytical techniques. As the following project management topics are introduced, risk will be discussed and appropriate techniques considered. In terms of assessing the level of risk, we need to consider likelihood and impact. These are two important risk assessment constructs; both can be difficult to determine as often we may not be able to do this with accuracy (and therefore confidence). For example, if we identify a risk relating to the poor performance of the project team, how can we determine the associated likelihood? It will be somewhere between 0 and 100 per cent. Similarly, in terms of the impact of this type of risk, the impact might vary depending upon the type and/or degree of poor performance.

One challenge we face here relates to the notion of risk and how we try to be scientific with it; we may make a subjective judgement that there is a risk, and then attempt to treat the likelihood in an objective way (expecting to give it a probability). Since we often have no basis to provide a numerical probability, often the best approach is to assign a number from a scale of 1 to 5 (1 = low; 5 = high). Of course, a similar train of thought can apply to 'impact'. We may be able to quantify this in the form of lost time or monetary terms, but again it may be appropriate to assign a number from a scale.

When this has been done, often the two values will be multiplied together to reveal the consequence or provide a further perspective of the scale:

$$\text{Consequence} = \text{Impact} \times \text{Likelihood}$$

TABLE 1.3   Example of risk-scoring analysis

Ref	Risk	Impact	Likelihood	'Consequence'
01L	Licence not obtained	5	2	10
02E	Pipeline routing causes damage	5	5	25
03T	Gradient causes back-flow	2	2	4
04	Next risk identified	I_4	L_4	$C_4 = I_4 \times L_4$
05	Next risk identified	I_5	L_5	$C_5 = I_5 \times L_5$

Table 1.3 shows an example of this type of analysis. This can also be used to prioritize, should that be required if the list is long. In this example, the risks have a reference code that includes a letter 'L', 'E' or 'T'. These refer to 'legislative', 'environmental' or 'technology', thus making a link with the risk areas identified.

Where time allows at the start of a project, it is good practice to give the team space and encouragement to consider the things about which they are uncertain or that could go wrong. In other words, they might be encouraged to worry. During a project which had a 'slow' start, a project director mentioned that the staff were doing some 'worrying', and that he was very pleased that this was taking place, adding that it was better to identify as many things up front as possible.

This is somewhat ideal, as for many projects the opportunity might be shorter; nevertheless, the activity needs to be undertaken. While this might generate a long list and be regarded either as trivial or as a 'tick-box' exercise, this may well help to reveal key risk areas. If a long list is generated, it can be prioritized. This should be revisited throughout the project.

Learning point: we need to acknowledge that it may be difficult to identify all project risks

Perhaps there are two initial things on which to remark with regard to this type of exercise: firstly, it is unlikely that every risk will be identified at early stages, and secondly, the process might include a risk that is regarded as so unlikely *it would never happen.*

With respect to the first of these, one example would be the recent development of visitor centres in the mountainous areas of the UK. Despite significant effort, several unforeseen risks emerged during the project deployment; these were associated with the nature of the construction process, which used sustainable materials, and while such hindsight is not uncommon in those types of projects, the team were not aware of this right at the start.

In terms of the second, almost every project could include a seemingly ridiculous risk that a meteorite might strike the Earth; on 15 February 2013, a meteor blast over Chelyabinsk that glowed 30 times brighter than the Sun injured around 1,500 people and damaged thousands of buildings (*National Geographic*, 2013).

Response to risk

Once the risk analysis is in place, we can consider the best way to respond to what has been identified. Table 1.4 highlights a number of options; we may wish to transfer, avoid, reduce, include a contingency and/or accept it. Managing this aspect of the process should be dynamic; the intelligent interpretation of this information will help an organization better understand the degree of reputational risk associated with the project. With this approach, it will be regarded as an integral component of project management rather than a reason not to do something.

We could apply the response strategy to each of the risks identified in Table 1.2 and determine a reduction of the consequence score. Some projects will use this type of extended scoring table to help manage risks through the project lifecycle.

TABLE 1.4   Risk response alternatives

Risk response strategy	Practical actions could include
Transfer the risk	Insuring against it, utilize subcontractors
Avoid the risk	Doing it a different way
Reduce the risk	Changing one or more aspects
Include a contingency	Add a buffer in terms of time or money
Accept it	Doing nothing

Project processes

One way of visualizing a new project is to compare the activity to a journey that has never been undertaken before, to a place that is completely unknown to us, and we don't know how we will get there, as in Figure 1.3.

FIGURE 1.3   Projects: an ambition to do something new

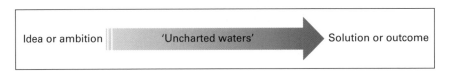

Drawing on the previous section, we introduced a range of project types, including 'Paint by numbers', 'As... but' and 'First-timers'. However we refer to different types of projects, can we characterize them all in terms of a project process? The Input–Constraint–Output–Mechanism (ICOM) model introduced in project management literature (Gardiner, 2005; Maylor, 2010) helps us; it reminds us of the mechanisms available (or that need to be available) and the constraints that help set the rules for the project.

Looking first at mechanisms:

People	bring capability, knowledge, experience, motivation and different character
Techniques/Tools	important but we may not have them in place at the start... or we could deploy a set of tools and techniques from a previous project scenario
Equipment	the requirement will depend on the type of project; this could vary widely
Organization	the means of organizing the project will vary depending on the context and setting; if taking place within a private-sector business, the organization will probably be different from a multi-party project hosted by a public-sector organization

A review of the constraints helps us to focus on some key components of project management shown in Figure 1.4; these set out emphasis and priority, and this helps to characterize the project. For example, within constraints we see time, cost, quality; these are often considered the core parameters, sometimes known as 'triple

FIGURE 1.4   Diagram developed on Figure 1.3 incorporating ICOM model attributes

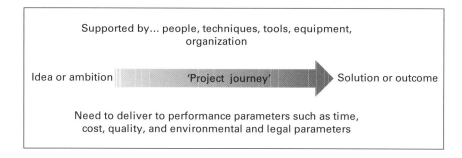

constraints', and are an immediate focus within the project. If the project is a sporting event, when are the key dates? If the activity is a research project, what is the budget? If the project is the delivery of a new aviation safety system, what is the associated system (quality) requirement?

We can visualize legal, ethical and environmental factors as constraints, but at the outset of the project we wouldn't necessarily know in what way. For example, we may not be aware of the type of contract required; we may not have fully realized the impact of our proposed new project on the environment and associated ethical issues. Additionally, the logic, activation sequence and indirect effects are often aspects that we understand better when we start to plan activities, or indeed sometimes when we come to the point of delivering the project.

CASE STUDY   Hafod Eryri: the building on top of a mountain[2]

... now tell me again, where is that?

Sitting on top of Snowdon, the highest mountain in Wales, Hafod Eryri characterizes many aspects of projects. Challenging to undertake for a host of reasons, concentrate first on the name – Hafod Eryri. Although the mountain gives its name to the famous area Snowdonia, the peak is in Gwynedd, an area steeped in history and legend, rich in tradition and culture, and one part of the UK where Welsh is the dominant language.

First, this aspect is significant: Hafod means, in Welsh, summer residence; Eryri is the area, Snowdonia. Many visitors, used to using English as their main or as a second language, may stutter over the pronunciation. The name immediately reveals that this project has taken place in the home of a bilingual society where cultures can divide or unite the populus. The stakeholder landscape may be as varied as the geography.

Secondly, Hafod Eryri is a story about building on top of a mountain. The project looks as if it is mainly about the challenge of engineering, environment and achievement. While that's true, it is really just one very important part, the final element in a protracted process that involved stakeholders, risk, financing, vision, creativity, perseverance, ingenuity – and lots of planning.

This could also be a story about awards and accolades, as the conferring of these has made the delivery team and parent organization proud of their achievements. It is also about commercial endeavour, as this project consumed £8.3m and included parties from the public and private sectors, whose interests are business based. In fact, it is a good example of almost every aspect of project management.

There had been buildings on the summit of Snowdon since the late 19th century. Increasing numbers of visitors provided an opportunity to establish the Snowdon Railway Company, but the weather was too severe for the existing wooden buildings. The visionary architect Clough Ellis Williams (creator of Portmeirion, an Italian-styled village developed in the same area) designed a building that was completed in 1935. Originally intended as a hotel, this served a number of purposes; improvement works were undertaken 1952–54 and other additions were made, but ultimately it became dilapidated.

In 1982, the Snowdonia National Park bought the building for a nominal sum and refurbished it with grant aid. The weather continued to do its work. With an average of 508 centimetres of rainfall annually, a temperature range of −20° to +30° and airspeeds up to 150 miles per hour (240 kilometres per hour) which would reduce the temperature by a further 30°, this presents a challenge not seen elsewhere in Britain.

A survey conducted in 1997 highlighted that over three-quarters of respondents thought that the summit building should be replaced. The first steps were taken in 1999: a partnership that included the Snowdonia National Park Authority (SNPA) and Snowdon Mountain Railway commissioned a feasibility study. Following progressive discussions and development of ideas with the appointed architect Ray Hole, planning approval for complete refurbishment was granted in 2004.

Funding was one of the first challenges; an appeal was launched, but ultimately funding was provided by the SNPA, the Welsh Assembly, EU structural funds, Visit Wales and the Snowdon Mountain Railway. With the appointment of the contractor Carillion, construction could start once the existing building had been demolished. At a ceremony well covered by the media, government ministers Carwyn Jones and Sue Essex struck the first symbolic blows.

The construction process was under way in 2007, establishing the site ready for foundation and steelworks. All of the materials and labour had to be transported to the top of the mountain using the Snowdon Mountain Railway train. This provides some logistical and commercial challenges: logistical in that the narrow gauge train, even with some conversion of its carriages, provided a limit on the weight, length, width and volume of material and equipment; commercial in that, while the train was being used to support transport logistics, it could not simultaneously be used to carry fee-paying customers (the primary business of the railway company). Also, as the summit station had been demolished, there was no business taking place there either. Interim commercial arrangements had to be put in place, regarded as a necessary element of the project budget.

The narrow working area at the summit provided a site defined by rock on one side and a steep incline on the other. This provided limitation of movement and, when combined with the logistical constraint highlighted in the previous paragraph, called for innovation and ingenuity in the working areas. One example of this was the twice-assembled steel framework – the first time as a rehearsal in a warehouse as it could not be altered once on-site.

Heavy snowfall in April 2008 caused the completion of the building to be delayed until September of the same year. The work had spanned two seasons having some of the worst weather remembered by many locally. The contractor's various attempts to overcome the impact of heavy snow were thwarted, and nature had its say in the schedule. This caused a knock-on effect for all of the parties involved, particularly the Snowdon Mountain Railway Company and the contractor, which had taken on the risk through the form of contract in place.

For a number of reasons, throughout the project the SNPA was concerned about stakeholder aspects. As one of three national parks in Wales, the SNPA has two statutory purposes, (a) to conserve and enhance the natural beauty, wildlife and cultural heritage of the area, and (b) to promote opportunities for the understanding and enjoyment of the special qualities of the area by the public. These two purposes highlight the diverse challenges presented by undertaking such a project. Stakeholders will scrutinize how the build affects these two purposes. Extensive consultation had therefore taken place prior to the construction phase. While some of this was challenging in terms of managing all expectations, it was a crucial part of the project. After all, reputational risk was at stake.

Stakeholders were encouraged to be a part of the project. For example the media were involved by reporting on the impact of the bad weather and being involved in the naming process (Hafod Eryri was chosen from over 500 suggestions canvassed by the BBC). Critics became advocates. No stones were left unturned. This provided a surprise for some who had expected a more traditional construction project management process and approach.

With the handover of the building, Hafod Eryri moved into an operational phase, opening its doors to the public on 12 June 2009: a triumph of vision, perseverance and effective project management. Time will tell how it performs and history will record whether or not it was as successful as the initial period.

Case reflection

Evaluate this case scenario, characterizing the project in terms of:

i   stakeholder groups and expectations;

ii style of project management;

iii risk profile;

iv the key stages or phases of the project;

v   likely complexities within the construction elements;

vi the reasons for the 'feel-good' aspects of the narrative.

Projects and lifecycles

Acknowledging first that a number of process activities may fall within the pool of definitions for a project, as we discussed earlier, each project will start at some point in time and there will be an end point. The end point might be associated with the fulfilment of objectives, depletion of project resources, be time-event related or even end through progressive abandonment. There are other scenarios: occasionally we hear the argument that the project 'doesn't really have a defined end point'. In some environments where a service is being developed, the time aspect may be open-ended. We will consider this aspect of ambiguity further, but at this stage we will regard projects as having a specific end point.

Lifecycle models

It is likely that our project will live through a number of phases. This provides the basis for contemplating the project lifecycle, another imperfect model that we often need to utilize or at least understand. A number of lifecycle models are used; some have four phases, others five and so on. This largely depends upon the specific activities that comprise the project. The model with four phases, dealing with conceptual, planning, execution and termination activities, is commonly used, sometimes with different labels. Hybrid models may also be required; this perhaps reflects the need to adapt or customize frameworks to accommodate the variety of circumstances – and emphasis – within a typical project environment.

For example, the Town and Country Planning Association (King and Shaw, 2010: 12) provide a guide for the planning, development and delivery of community energy projects in the UK, shown in Figure 1.5. Aiming to support planners and project

FIGURE 1.5   Typical phases within an energy project

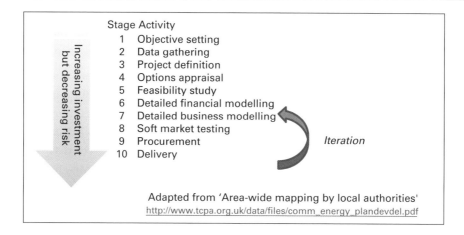

Stage Activity
1 Objective setting
2 Data gathering
3 Project definition
4 Options appraisal
5 Feasibility study
6 Detailed financial modelling
7 Detailed business modelling
8 Soft market testing
9 Procurement
10 Delivery

Iteration

Increasing investment but decreasing risk

Adapted from 'Area-wide mapping by local authorities'
http://www.tcpa.org.uk/data/files/comm_energy_plandevdel.pdf

developers, the guide usefully includes a flight path of a typical project within this area. This also illustrates in outline a project lifecycle that appears to have 10 distinct phases. We could argue that this in fact comprises several projects, or breaks key phases into phases in their own right. Either way, it is useful to reflect on this, since we may find that the adopted classroom model may need some moulding to fit the particular scenario of the project.

This guidance also highlights that the risk profile changes over the lifecycle of each project, as more certainty leads to a lowering of risk.

Lifecycle models: the ideal world and the real world

Within the ideal project lifecycle we would expect a number of activities to take place in a pre-ordained sequence. For example, activities relating to feasibility should take place early in the life of the project. However, in order for this to be true, we may need to assume that every project we take on is new and of the same type. In such an ideal world, we could adopt an unambiguous multi-stage planning and execution approach. In reality, we encounter projects in a variety of circumstances, where neither the project nor an expected component might be where we expect to see it. Projects that are the result of unexpected events (such as natural disasters) emphasize some of these aspects.

Where do we begin – at the start, in the middle or at the end? Most of us might be inclined to think 'at the start'. In the world of projects, many of us with a responsibility for them find that we might not start at the start. Some may find that they need to review a project that has (almost) been completed; some may be involved in developing the initial idea; others may be given a project to execute, wrestling with the process of converting someone else's idea into a finished product or service. Some may be responsible for analysing the value of an initial idea, seeking to convert thoughts into numbers that quantify benefits to canvass for the project to take place. Others may even have the sometimes onerous task of evaluating a situation and recommending that the project stops. There are, of course, many other possibilities.

Not only may we start at different places in the project lifecycle, but our roles are likely to vary, even if we are all called project managers or are fulfilling the role. As we discussed earlier, there are many scenarios where individuals are involved in a management activity, discovering that their activity is a project and that they are undertaking a role of project manager or have a strong participatory function in the delivery of a project. Does this happen in other worlds, such as accounting or medicine? Perhaps; but when we use the terms 'project' and 'project manager', we may not always be entirely clear about what is meant by these expressions nor what to expect.

In an ideal world, the concept of the project would be universally understood, the project well defined and the project manager would have full control of the process in order to deliver the expected outcome. The expression 'expected outcome' further reveals the challenges inherent within projects: what expectation, whose expectation? This discussion is intended to make us think; even if we have many years of experience, it is sometimes worthwhile taking a step back from the activities or intensity of the project. What is our role, and where is the project in the lifecycle?

In some project scenarios, much of what has been said above could be turned into generic sets of instruction. For example, some areas of construction or event management lend themselves well to the four-stage lifecycle model. Furthermore, where the degree of repeatability is relatively high, the project management process can be likened to that required to build a model kit – open the box, take out the instructions and parts, and build each stage to complete the model.

However, one of the problems we face in the world of projects is that many do not come in a box. Rather, they can be undefined and ambiguous – may start with a picture that is in our minds. We don't know what is in the box, the shape of the parts or the number of stages, and the instructions do not exist yet. We may have to design every part of the process, from start to finish. And, of course, the picture in the minds of two people could be quite different.

Projects and gates

Having introduced the notion of a project lifecycle and then discussed some difficulties we might experience in application, we further need to be aware of 'gated processes'. For some projects, there is no certainty that they will go through a full lifecycle as we have initially described them; there will be an associated sequence of gates through which the project must pass. For example, a study might reveal the positive feasibility of a proposed activity, leading to the need for funding. The case for funding might not be guaranteed. Additionally, the feasibility analysis might have revealed the need to revise aspects of the proposed project, leading to a redesign. A successful redesign might then lead to a similar case for funding. At this stage, the project might stop because it is not possible to secure funding. Of course, this could have happened at the feasibility phase.

Such a scenario is not uncommon in a number of areas, such as start-up projects, scientific product development and heritage projects. Figure 1.6 shows the fall in numbers of potential pharmaceutical products at each stage or gate within the discovery or approval process (*The Times*, 2006). The detail is not necessarily as important here as the awareness that it is likely that considerable effort and expenditure is likely before a drug gets to market. A project of this type can look elongated diagrammatically, with timeframes that are quite different from projects in other sectors. There are many other areas; indeed, the whole notion of a business case development process is a further example of this characteristic. These projects have stage gates; the outcome of the evaluation at each of these could be 'proceed', 'stop', 'redesign' or 'recycle', and there are other possibilities depending on the context of the activity.

Above all, this raises a number of issues in terms of the management of the project. When we investigate the feasibility of a potential project, this might return the advice 'STOP' (do not proceed further for reasons revealed in the analysis), 'GO' (yes, let us proceed) or 'MAYBE' (more information is required). The stop/go/maybe nature of feasibility, business case and other processes can be the norm for these types of project, and we may need to consider the management of these quite carefully. This aspect will feature in a number of discussions regarding projects.

Projects: ingredients and early insights

Ingredients

Building on our earlier discussion, if we consider the hypothetical footprint of a new project, this will help to reveal the empirical ingredients that comprise a project process; these in turn will become the building blocks of those projects that we encounter within our working and domestic environments. The next chapter will utilize this approach to develop detail, since it will focus on the activities that often take place at the conceptual stage of a new project. Later chapters that contemplate particular contextual challenges will refer to the ingredients; these could also be

FIGURE 1.6   Drug development and approval gates

Fence / Gate

Start	1	2	3	4	5	6	7	8
Potential drug	Discovery of effect	Pre-clinical development	Phase I clinical trials	Phase II clinical trials	Phase III clinical trials	Licensing	Authorization for NHS use	Easy availability on the NHS
Natural substances – plants, fungi, etc.	Sort out potential pharmaceuticals from useless chemicals	Drug development process (lengthy)	Drug tested – whether safe and behaviour in humans	Drug tested – whether effective and dose level	Test of drug potential – large trial with ill patients	Permission to sell – Application (c. 100 A4 ring binders). Can take up to 10 years	Approval from PPA (and equivalents). All drugs scrutinized for supply/demand/ pricing	Affected by NHS budgets. Guidance from NICE.
Survivors at each stage	0.2%	5%	66%	50%	66%	95%	99%	99%
Failing	99.8%	95%	33%	50%	33%	50%	1%	1%
Millions	2000	100	70	35	23	22	21	20

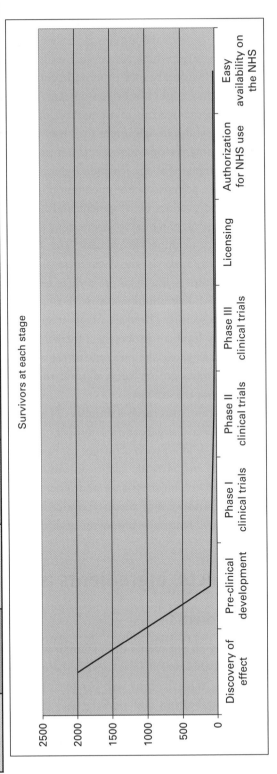

Survivors at each stage

2500

2000

1500

1000

500

0

Discovery of effect | Pre-clinical development | Phase I clinical trials | Phase II clinical trials | Phase III clinical trials | Licensing | Authorization for NHS use | Easy availability on the NHS

SOURCE: adapted from: The Times (2006) Thrills, spills and pills regarded as the algebra of project management. This has an appeal both to those who want to develop or adapt more formalized approaches and to those who prefer to work in a more scientific manner.

If we regard the ingredients of our project as simple algebra, perhaps through learning and the development of our own experience we can then understand how the challenging project is a complex combination of this. In turn, this will help us to use the right combination of more scientific methods and soft skills, guiding our future intuition and approach to manage a successful project. This will be explored in some depth in later chapters.

In the earlier section we introduced the ICOM model, in which there are an input, an output, a number of mechanisms and associated constraints. Following our discussion above, we could argue that a successful project outcome is the successful output from the ICOM model and represent this as follows:

Successful project outcome = function (Input, Constraints, Mechanisms)

In other words, a successful project depends on the ingredients of input, constraints and mechanisms, but at this stage we do not know the actual composition or emphasis. To use a cooking metaphor, although we can visualize the final dish, we are not sure of the precise ingredients, nor do we know the quantities, emphasis, timing, among many other things. While this might appear quite a strange comparison, the reality is that for a novice chef, creating the perfect dish can be a significant challenge. The parallels with the challenge facing the novice project manager are strikingly similar. We can extend this metaphor, as the project might have many parts, just as the chef is faced with producing the meal, a composition of many dishes. Satisfying the tastes of the consumer of the meal might finally parallel the challenge of meeting stakeholder expectations. Perhaps at that point the comparisons end.

It is often experience that helps us to determine the aspects of input, the management of constraints and mechanisms; at this stage we need to understand which elements are important and initially how we might manage them.

Early insights

At this stage it is appropriate to introduce two additional insights, since we will refer to them progressively throughout the book. Firstly, we need to be aware of the 'bodies of knowledge'. Bodies of knowledge are a complete set of concepts, terms and activities that make up a professional domain (APM, 2012: xvii). There are a number of international organizations that can help with our understanding here. For example, the Project Management Institute exists to 'serve practitioners and organizations with standards that describe good practices, globally recognized credentials that certify project management expertise, and resources for professional development, networking and community' (PMI, 2014). This includes the provision of specific knowledge and vocabulary, and for some these bodies can also support the development of careers.

Secondly, the term **project** is often used interchangeably with the word **programme**. At this stage we will regard a programme as a collection of more than one project (connected formally or not), or a combination of projects plus other organizational or project-like activities. The definition will be refined in the second half of the book, when we consider the vocabulary of strategy and the role of projects as a key part of the delivery of associated objectives.

Projects are complex; stakeholders; change

Complexity

Building on our earlier discussion, it is also worth considering that projects are not only inherently built on risk, they also tend to be complex activities. What do we mean by complex? A couple of definitions usefully highlight some aspects of the problem (Table 1.5).

The first definition highlights *many different and connected parts*; this is central to the challenge often faced in managing a project. Although the second is normally associated with mathematics (to help solve a problem such as 'what is the square root of −25?'), it could equally be applied directly to many projects where budget and costs are exceeded... 'denoting or involving *numbers or quantities containing both a real and an imaginary part*'. For some projects this is an apposite expression.

Do we need to understand the level of complexity within the projects we manage? This can certainly help in terms of ensuring that the management approach adopted is appropriate for the scale of challenge it will present. For example, in a public-sector multi-partner project where there may be considerable ambiguity in terms of

TABLE 1.5   Most common definitions for 'complex'
(*Oxford English Dictionary*, 6th edn, 2007)

Complex (adj)
1 'Consisting of many different and connected parts; not easy to analyse or understand'
2 Mathematics – 'denoting or involving numbers or quantities containing both a real and an imaginary part

stakeholder ambition, objectives, structure and roles, among many other aspects, understanding the complexity might help to determine whether to adopt an appropriate formalized project management approach. Conversely, if the complexity of the activity is lower, we may be over-managing the project if we utilize similar approaches.

This is not an exact science and there is no universal model to derive complexity. For example, it is expressed as a component or contributor to technical risk through the numbers and interrelatedness of steps (Nicholas and Steyn, 2012: 354); in large engineering projects it has been expressed as a three-component technical–organization–environment framework (Bosch-Rekveldt *et al*, 2011); project complexity has been identified as a key variable affecting risk management (Thamhain, 2013). Thamhain (2013: 23) also highlights the different streams of research that discuss complexity of projects from a project organization and environment perspective, and a second characterization of complexity within projects. A final comment sums up this challenge – 'research about the concept of complexity has been conducted for years, but there is little consensus on what project complexity is' (Chronéer and Bergquist, 2012: 22).

Whichever model or framework we might utilize to help frame our understanding, the important part is to recognize that complexity is inherent within projects. This perhaps provides a justification for committing to undertake sufficient analysis, to accept additional formality in management processes when appropriate, and to understand that for some projects a quantity, such as budget, might contain both real and imaginary parts!

Stakeholders

While discussing complexity above, we mentioned stakeholders; arguably this is one of the most fundamental components of any project. With some similarity to risk, the stakeholder topic is a recurrent theme through all of the chapters of the book. At this stage, we need first to explore what is meant by the term stakeholder and apply this to project environments. By setting out an understanding of this aspect we should then be able to explore the impact of stakeholders and develop approaches to manage the associated processes. A word of caution: this area can be one of the most difficult areas to 'manage'.

Firstly, without any stakeholders, there is no project. Why? Because stakeholders include people within and outside the project; some of these will have requested the project, or will finance it, or benefit from it, or have been annoyed by it or helped to deliver it. There are, of course, many other affecting- or affected-stakeholder groups we could consider. Secondly, many of the stakeholder groups will be outside the direct control of project management. The effect of this can be underestimated.

FIGURE 1.7   Incorporation of stakeholders into project process

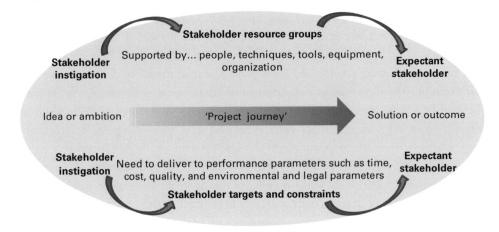

Figure 1.7 shows the potential incorporation of stakeholders into the project process diagram; the project sits in a stakeholder envelope. Now who's in charge here?

What do we mean by project stakeholders? A common understanding of stakeholders in this context is that they are groups or individuals who affect or are affected by the project. Freeman, Harrison and Wicks (2007: 6) define the stakeholder as 'any group or individual who can affect or is affected by the achievement of a corporation's purpose'. This is interesting, because the authors go on to reveal that 'many critics of the idea of managing stakeholders suggest it encourages business leaders to focus their attention on non-business activities'. They argue that this is untrue; a similar challenge may be present in our projects. The project may be affected by powerful interest groups, so if we don't manage this aspect of the project (it could be regarded as the non-business part), the project might fail.

Stakeholders can be grouped as 'internal' or 'external' (Freeman, 2010: 216), 'primary' or 'secondary' (Cleland and Ireland, 2002: 176–77); they can be classified as organizational stakeholders (Mullins, 2010: 714–15), including employees, providers of finance, customers, community or government. External stakeholders can also be divided into economic, socio-political and technological (Johnson, Scholes and Whittington, 2008: 153–55) types, each with their associated expectations and conflicts.

Whichever way we classify project stakeholders, it is vital to undertake sufficient analysis and put in place appropriate mechanisms to manage different aspects throughout the life of the project. Indeed, some projects might provide a surprise in terms of the large amount of time and effort we need to devote to the stakeholder groups to achieve success in the project. A final point: we may need to consider the stakeholder perspective well beyond our initially defined project timeframe.

The decommissioning of a nuclear reactor is an example of this; an unknown long-term health impact of an inhaled product developed for consumers is a second.

We should revise our formula for success:

Successful project = function (Stakeholder, Successful project outcome)

Change

While in the last topic we have considered the potentially successful project from a stakeholder perspective, we must also temper any optimism with the realism that accompanies the effect of a project. The idea for the project may come as a desire to change something, a situation or a scenario. The need to improve a process, penetrate a new market or develop a new market all equate to changing something.

Change is a key theme; it is impossible to undertake a project without causing this effect. In this respect, its relationship with project management has strong similarities to risk management, and it is worth highlighting that a 'show-stopping' risk may have the same effect on a project as unwelcome and resisted change; a project may be stopped, altered or regarded as unsuccessful because of this. Chapter 4 will have a focus on change as something that has to be managed within the project; Chapter 6 will highlight that it will often be unexpected; Chapter 12 will consider change from the perspective of leadership.

Summary

In this chapter we have taken the opportunity to introduce the notion of projects and project management, and also to consider the person who is involved in this, often but not always known as the project manager. The underlying models of project lifecycle, process and complexity have been introduced. We have explored the persistently important aspects of risk and stakeholder within project environments, developing some detail in approach before encouraging the reader to apply these concepts within future chapters. Accompanying the introduction of topics, the reader has also been encouraged to consider the potential gap between ideal and real dimensions of project management, and to expect the unexpected.

We have been introduced to the world of projects.

Notes

1 Entertainment programmes such as *The Apprentice*, TV programme, BBC, London, first shown 7 May 2005.

2   This case study draws upon information from the following sources:

Architecture Today (2009) Ray Hole Architects: Hafod Eryri – Snowdon
  Summit Building, Gwynedd, 1 July, retrieved on 4 August 2014 from
  www.architecturetoday.co.uk/?p=1332

The Independent (26 May 2009) Makeover for 'highest slum in Wales', retrieved on
  4 August 2014 from www.independent.co.uk/news/uk/this-britain/makeover-for-
  highest–slum-in-wales-1690633.html#

Snowdonia National Park (2009) Hafod Eryri: a new building for Snowdon Summit

Snowdonia National Park (2010) Eryri Snowdonia 2010–2011

Snowdonia National Park (2010) Cynllun Rheolaeth Parc Cenedlaethol Eryri

Snowdonia National Park (2010) Success again for Hafod Eryri, retrieved on 4 August
  2014 from www.eryri-npa.gov.uk/park-authority/newsroom/press-releases-2010/
  2010-10-19?SQ_DESIGN_NAME=print

Snowdonia National Park (2009) New summit building, retrieved on 4 August 2014
  from www.eryri-npa.gov.uk/visiting/hafod-eryri/new-summit-building

Snowdonia Active (2008) Mass media on Snowdon, retrieved on 4 August 2014 from
  www.snowdonia-active.com/news.asp?newsid=601

Snowdonia Society (nd) Hafod Eryri: what's your verdict? Retrieved on 4 August 2014
  from www.snowdonia-society.org.uk/news.php?n_id=99

References

Association for Project Management (APM) (2012) *APM Body of Knowledge*, APM, Princes
  Risborough, Bucks

Bosch-Rekveldt, M, Jongkind, Y, Mooi, H *et al* (2011) Grasping project complexity in
  large engineering projects: The TOE (Technical, Organisational and Environmental)
  framework, *International Journal of Project Management*, **29**, pp 728–39

Chronéer, D and Bergquist, B (2012) Managerial complexity in process industrial R&D
  projects: a Swedish study, *Project Management Journal*, **43** (2), pp 21–36

Cleland, I and Ireland, L (2002) *Project Management: Strategic design and implementation*,
  McGraw-Hill, New York

Freeman, R E (2010) *Strategic Management*, Cambridge University Press, Cambridge

Freeman, R E, Harrison, J S and Wicks, A C (2007) *Managing for Stakeholders: Survival,
  reputation and success*, Yale University Press, New Haven, CT

Gardiner, P (2005) *Project Management: A strategic planning approach*, Palgrave
  MacMillan, Basingstoke

Johnson, G, Scholes, K and Whittington, R (2008) *Exploring Corporate Strategy*, 8th edn,
  Financial Times Prentice Hall, Harlow

King, M and Shaw, R (2010) Community energy: planning, development and delivery,
  Town and Country Planning Association, London

Maylor, H (2003) *Project Management*, 3rd edn, Pearson Education, Harlow

Maylor, H (2010) *Project Management*, 4th edn, Pearson Education, Harlow

Mullins, L (2010) *Management and Organisational Behaviour*, Prentice Hall, Harlow

National Geographic (2013) Russian meteor's air blast was one for the record books, 6 November, retrieved 23 May 2014 from http://news.nationalgeographic.com/news/2013/11/131106-russian-meteor-chelyabinsk-airburst-500-kilotons/

Nicholas, J and Steyn, H (2012) *Project Management for Engineering, Business and Technology*, Routledge, London

Project Management Institute (PMI) (2013) *A Guide to the Project Management Body of Knowledge*, PMI Inc., Newtown Square, PA

Project Management Institute (PMI) (2014) [Online] retrieved 12 November 2014 from www.pmi.org/en.aspx

Thamhain, H (2013) Managing risks in complex projects, *Project Management Journal*, **44** (2), pp 20–35

The Times (2006) Thrills, spills and pills, 8 April

Projects at the conceptual phase

02

LEARNING OUTCOMES

By applying the topics within this chapter you should be able to:

- explain the notion of the conceptual phase of a project;

- explore the role of feasibility and business case;

- reflect on the initial drivers of project requirements;

- evaluate and reflect upon the role of stakeholders during this phase;

- approach this phase through asking a set of fundamental questions;

- reflect upon the inherent assumptions that will inevitably be present.

Introduction

Chapter 1 introduced some general concepts associated with projects and project management, setting the scene for our exploration of the subject. We discussed the notion of project lifecycle, acknowledging that while it is an imperfect concept, in generalized form it is a useful basis to develop our understanding; often a project lifecycle is most apparent when the activity is viewed retrospectively, as the ambiguity in sequence and focus is clarified. All projects must therefore have early pre-delivery phases.

This chapter will consider the first of these and introduce the activities that we might encounter at the 'conceptual' phase. At the same time as introducing some fundamental frameworks in an 'ideal' project scenario, the reader is also encouraged to be reflective and critical. For example, it is useful to acknowledge that, while there will be a start point for our idealized project, our entry point to the project might be in quite a different place, perhaps at a later phase within the lifecycle. This is pertinent, since we might inherit a situation that is quite difficult to manage, or indeed may need to reapply work that might often take place at a conceptual stage.

We will start our exploration of the conceptual phase by considering how the project might have been born. Although parallels will be drawn between the emergence of a project, birth, parentage and other analogies as relevant, much of the terminology adopted will be found in project management literature, professional training handbooks and guides.

One further thing to consider at this stage, before we move into the chapter topics: acknowledging the existence of the project lifecycle provides a basis for us to 'isolate' and bound a particular stage that we have labelled 'conceptual'. This chapter will be followed by one that is concerned with planning activities. This segmentation is somewhat artificial, as in the world of practice we will find that often the phases seem to overlap, and many of the topics often sit in slightly different places, or in all of them. Nevertheless, we will explore the topics in this sequence, as it will enable the process of 'unfolding' projects.

Conceptual phase

Let's take a hypothetical project and start at the start. Where does the project come from? What is the project seeking to deliver? In fact, what is the project? The answer to these questions could be manyfold. Some projects will be born from a response to an emerging opportunity, a problem, an aspiration to do things in a different way; rightly or wrongly, some might simply be described as 'my boss's idea'.

Doubtless, for all there will be a reason or rationale. In some cases this will be the result of a strategic planning process, for which significant expenditure and resources may be expended. All will take place for a reason; a business case may exist, but the scale of the case made will vary. Another thing to consider is that all projects are likely to cause some form of change.

Projects arise for a variety of reasons; some examples are shown in Table 2.1. Where the activity follows from an intended strategic planning process, projects could include new product or new market development, in any sector or industry. A change of political climate might open a new market for an existing product; new technology offers opportunities to provide an updated product.

In scenarios where a project emerges as a response to a change or problem, this could include examples that have an already-established rationale (such as a change of environmental standards) and others that take place in a more reactive style where the justification is determined within a similar timeframe. Responses to unexpected events such as difficult-to-predict natural disasters are particularly acute examples of this latter type.

TABLE 2.1 Sources of projects

Source	Examples
New opportunity	New market for existing product; new product
Need to overcome a problem	A building is 'obsolete'; a system does not work well enough
Response to change	Activities caused by a change of government, recession, environmental standards, public perception
New idea	Could combine characteristics of above examples; a completely new idea or concept originating from creative source

The notion of a new idea often combines elements of these previous situations. In our ideal project, idea, feasibility and business case are early-stage activities. In reality, the particular context of the project (in terms of type and organizational setting) will determine the precise form of demonstrating rationale or reason. Let us consider a generic lifecycle model. We have asserted that idea, feasibility and business case are early-stage activities, shown in Figure 2.1.

Furthermore, the point at which we get involved varies for different individuals. For example, as per our ideal project, we could develop an idea (our own, or originating from someone else), explore the feasibility of an idea, or develop the associated business case. Of course, there are other scenarios that have the above components. While this chapter is focused on the activities associated with conceptual elements of the project, it is also worthwhile recognizing that, for some of us, we might 'join',

FIGURE 2.1 Entry points

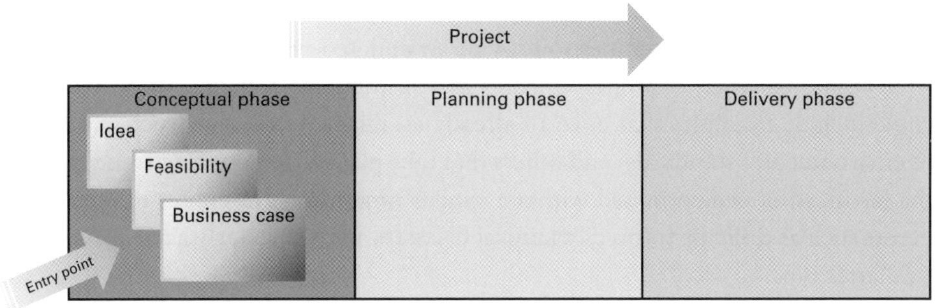

'manage' or 'lead' the project at the planning, implementation or even at the review stage. In some scenarios we may even take lead responsibility in response to problems or difficulties within a project. This complicating aspect has some characteristics comparable with our previous discussion (in Chapter 1) highlighting that a first-timer project to me may not be a first-timer to you. Here the concern is with adapting an ideal approach to learning about projects; often the reality is not like this.

Entry points

Entry point: Idea

Developing the discussion from above, our entry point to the project could be the idea itself, and we may subsequently develop and deliver the whole project. An entrepreneur would exhibit these characteristics; it is their idea, they explore the feasibility, build a business case, undertake the planning and start the business.

For some projects the nature of the activity may require high levels of creativity at the initial stages. This type of activity may be difficult to manage, as applying a management process may inhibit the creativity itself. We will say more about this in Chapter 7 in relation to the adoption of the most relevant project management approach; at this point it is important to recognize the value of this in the project deployment process. Hence the project might start with an idea, or a process intended to stimulate the production of ideas.

If an output of the creative phase is the generation of a number of ideas that need to be considered for feasibility or business case development, this could be the entry point for some project managers. An example will help develop our thinking: in contrast with perhaps more traditional types of project, let us consider the challenges associated with providing support to a potential commercialization or spin-out opportunity within a higher education department.

The goal of the project is a successful business venture; our role is to provide project management in the form of supporting the business planning and venture development process. This encompasses working closely with relevant academic and support staff, modelling their vision, ideas and products, opportunities and capabilities into a business plan… and identifying areas missing (or gaps) from the business plan required for potential start-up investment purposes.

This is a focused early-stage activity. Considerable time is spent modelling the ideas into plausible business planning. One of the problems we encounter is that the key academic is quite brilliantly creative. Why does this pose any difficulties? In a process of converting ideas into formal planning documents, the degree of flexibility required to satisfy the producer of ideas does not match very easily the rigidity required by the accountant who is generating the financial analysis part, the profit and loss, cash-flow and balance sheet forecasts.

The strength of the idea creator is a challenge for the modelling needs of the project process, and is not an easy problem to deal with. Of course, it depends on the context of the activity – we could argue that this is not the best way to invest in a new start-up of this type. It nevertheless provides a good example of the contrast between the fluidity of the conceptual phase and the needs of planning, something we will explore further in the coming chapters. This type of project management role often requires a particular behavioural style and approach that may be difficult for some project managers to enact.

We need also to consider the coherence between the background or underlying strategy and the project itself. In other words, is organizational strategy a driver in this project, or is the project a driver in the deployment of organizational strategy? Or is it both? This is another important area for us to understand. The word 'organization' could be interchanged for others, depending upon the context of the project. It could be organization, multi-organization, departmental or individual. Other vocabulary is often adopted.

In fact, the range could reflect any organizational classification such as those in the public, private or 'third' sector. This discussion also reminds us that the project could originate from anywhere on the planet where people initiate something. With this in mind, we will introduce an entity as the 'project parent'. This aspect will be developed further; at this stage it is important to recognize the value of having support from the parent for the activity, wherever the start point. Without this, there will likely be problems and in some cases it could lead to the failure of the project.

Figure 2.2 shows the potentially different start points within the conceptual phase of the project with the corresponding type of support ideally offered from the project parent in order to ensure that the activity takes place on a rational strategic basis.

Entry point: Feasibility evaluation

Within some scenarios, the early stages of the project need to be undertaken with a particular approach as part of a formal management process. For some, it will be essential to complete a full feasibility analysis with business case. What do we mean by checking early feasibility? Organizations have adopted a number of different ways to undertake this. A study might include the analysis of possibility, practicality and viability. There could be a focus on potential problems, an evaluation of alternatives with costs and benefits. Evaluating these sufficiently will help to engender confidence and provide a form of assurance for the project parent (or 'sponsor'). The specific approach adopted varies, depending on the context and setting of the potential

FIGURE 2.2   Strategic alignment and start points for the project
management

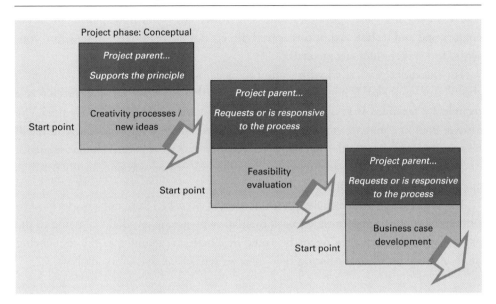

project. Scope and detail of content, focus and style may be prescribed or developed
as any evaluation work is undertaken.

The following points are based on the helpful framework introduced by Gardiner
(2005: 83) for developing a feasibility study:

- Determine the problem.
- Evaluate alternatives, potential, cost-effectiveness and feasibility.
- Analyse technology requirements.
- Assess capabilities.
- Evaluate the risk.
- Undertake analysis of trade-off constraints.
- Identify success factors.
- Generate preliminary estimates for time and cost.

For example, within the Severn Tidal Power Feasibility Study (BERR, 2008), the
terms of reference focused on four areas:

i   Cost, benefit and impact.

ii   Identification of preferred project.

iii Consideration of how to fulfil regulatory requirements.

iv On the basis of alternative options, decide whether and on what basis to support the project.

The feasibility study incorporated six areas of work – environment (exploring impacts), engineering and technical (options appraisal), economic, regional, planning and consents, and stakeholder engagement.

The questions associated with testing the feasibility could reveal that the project should not go ahead. It might also reveal that further information is required – is it technically feasible? If yes, we may need to demonstrate this; if no, why not? The answer could be maybe, in which case we will need further information. There will be an associated risk profile, and things to consider such as impact. A similar sequence of questions will also be asked regarding whether the project is economically feasible, as per the points made above.

The sequence in which these questions should be asked may not always be self-evident. It might be appropriate to ask them in sequence, in parallel, or, owing to the nature of the activity, they might be asked in a heuristic manner, as the sequencing might depend on the information that emerges within the feasibility analysis.

Entry point: Business case development

While developing the feasibility analysis, it may be appropriate to develop an associated business case. The precise form of this will depend on the specific context. If this is the route adopted, or indeed if the preferred route to take is to develop a business case, there are a number of formats that organizations tend to adopt; some will have a template for this, others will not. The APM (2012: 94) defines a business case as 'a justification for undertaking a project or programme; it evaluates the benefit, cost and risk of alternative options and the rationale for the preferred solution'. This might typically include:

- strategic case/strategic fit/objectives;
- options appraisal;
- expected benefits/consequences;
- commercial aspects – costs/affordability/achievability;
- uncertainty and risk appraisal.

This can be a useful starting point if there is no readily available template, and the resulting documents should be used at key review stages (or 'gates', introduced in Chapter 1) throughout the project. For the PMI (2013), the business case has a stronger focus in terms of relationship with feasibility study and as a subsequent basis for the authorization of project management activities. Although subtle, this difference may indicate the preference for a style that is appropriate for the specific project context.

Both feasibility and business case will be revisited; once we have established the core elements of a typical project management process and associated vocabulary in the next chapters, we will be able to consider the specific challenges associated with getting the early stages right. Nevertheless, throughout the project lifecycle it is worth asking the questions: Is there a business case? However benefits and costs are measured, are the benefits greater than the costs involved? Or, is Benefits – Costs > 0? Sometimes these may be difficult questions to answer, since the benefits are often both difficult to predict and awkward to quantify, and the costs are often difficult to quantify and awkward to predict. Also, the interpretation of these will vary in the eyes of stakeholder groups.

Introduction to business case analytical methods

The presentation of business cases can be a challenging exercise, and demonstrating that realistic benefits are greater than likely costs can be difficult. An uncomplicated example is shown in Figures 2.3 and 2.4; this is based on a project scenario whereby the purchase of ice-cream-making machines forms the basis of a new (or extension) business venture. Figure 2.3 includes a payback analysis for three options (1: 'Counter ice cream machine'; 2: '3 in 1 ice cream machine'; 3: 'ice cream blending machine'). The payback for each is calculated by dividing the implementation cost by the annual profit. The corresponding rate of return is calculated (doing the reciprocal calculation ie annual profit divided by implementation cost).

This reveals that scenario 3 has the shortest payback period and highest rate of return. It also requires the highest start-up capital; it is likely that an entrepreneur will have funding limits, so this will be a consideration. Crucially, the time value of money is not reflected in the analysis; that is, we are comparing an implementation cost in the present time against future profits, and inflation will erode these in real terms. The effect of this can be significant for large projects, and inflation (or the cost of capital) has to be factored into the calculation, as shown in Figure 2.4; to keep things simple, the analysis focuses on scenario 2. This shows that the breakeven point is delayed, from the end of year 3 into year 4, when we take into account the time value of money. It is important to note that during periods of low inflation (and low borrowing costs), the effect of this is considerably different from periods of high inflation and high borrowing costs.

While it is important for the project manager to be familiar with the terminology and general principles, this may be an area for the introduction of specialist support. It is also worthwhile highlighting that the estimation of both costs and benefits can be very difficult. The benefits associated with system implementation projects or hosting a mega-event (such as the Olympic Games) are examples of this.

FIGURE 2.3 Business case example of payback approach

Project: Set up ice cream retail business	No sites = 2		Payback analysis	Rate of return analysis
Alternative scenarios			Payback period = implementation cost / annual profit	Rate of return = annual profit / implementation cost
1 *Counter ice cream machine (cost)*	€	4,000		
Implementation cost	€	8,000	years	
Annual profits expected	€	2,400	**Payback period = 3.3**	**Rate of return = 30%**
2 *3 in 1 ice cream machine (cost)*	€	3,600		
Implementation cost	€	7,200	years	
Annual profits expected	€	1,800	**Payback period = 4.0**	**Rate of return = 25%**
3 *Ice cream blending machine (cost)*	€	6,000		
Implementation cost	€	12,000	years	
Annual profits expected	€	4,000	**Payback period = 3.0**	**Rate of return = 33%**

Limitations: The best scenario (3) has the highest initial project costs; more funds to raise
   The analysis does not take account of profits made after the project costs have been met
   Crucially the 'time value of money' is not accounted for

FIGURE 2.4 Continuing the example

Scenario 2

	Year	1	2	3	4	5
Expected profit	Annual	€ 2,400	€ 2,400	€ 2,400	€ 2,400	€ 2,400
	Accumulated	€ 2,400	€ 4,800	€ 7,200	€ 9,600	€ 12,000

If we do not account for inflation then the payback gives us an answer

Without accounting for the time value of money it looks like payback period is at the end of year 3

Cost of capital		5%	5%	5%	5%	5%
Net present value	Annual	€ 2,400	€ 2,286	€ 2,177	€ 2,073	€ 1,974
	Accumulated	€ 2,400	€ 4,686	€ 6,863	€ 8,936	€ 10,910

We need to calculate the net present value (NPV)

$NPV = Value / (1 + cost of capital)^{n-1}$

7200

Payback period is in fact during year 4

CASE STUDY   Changbin and Taichung Wind Project[1]

We might not like it but we have to do it

Located on the west coast of Taiwan, the Changbin and Taichung Wind Project consists of two separate sites with 62 wind turbines (climatefriendly.com). It provides approximately 500 gigawatt hours of electricity to the state electricity authority Taipower, which is enough power for around 110,000 households. This is an increasingly important contributor to the energy supply in Taiwan, since nearly 98 per cent of consumption is provided through imported fuels such as coal and gas.

Set therefore against an economy which is facing significant energy security challenges, the opportunity to deliver power from renewable energy generation schemes is especially welcome. But how welcome was the scheme, and how was this developed and presented as a business case?

The project has been assessed and accredited as 'Gold Standard Voluntary Emission Reduction' (verified and certified as per the requirements of the UNFCCC methodology ACM0002, version 07, 14 December 2007). The project was developed from the outset with Voluntary Emission Reduction (VER) uppermost in the strategy; the revenue opportunities presented through the sale of VERs often make a difference to the feasibility/viability of this type of project, and this aspect features strongly in the business case established at the start of the project.

The 'Project Design Form' (Southpolecarbon.com) sets out seven key areas that need to be fully documented:

- general description of project activity;
- application of baseline methodology;
- duration of project activity/crediting period;
- application of monitoring methodology and plan;
- estimation of greenhouse gas emissions (GHG) by source;
- environmental impacts;
- stakeholder comments.

The general description, or project overview, explains the scope and specification, and summarizes the project's contribution to sustainable development. These are arguments that support the case being made; this reminds us that the project will contribute to a reduction in greenhouse gas emissions, will be producing energy that does not contribute to global warming, and provides 'clean' electricity to the equivalent of 110,000 households.

It also highlights opportunities for employment creation and technology transfer and the contribution it makes to the reduction of other pollutants.

The case was presented strongly, but economic viability was a problem; aside from achieving the right price for the electricity generated and sold from the project, without the mechanism to sell VERs (carbon credits) it does not reach viability. Financial viability is one of the project's early risks, and VER revenues improve the feasibility sufficiently to attract investors. As such, this is a crucial part of the project development process.

A key step in the process was to define alternatives to the project activity; these ranged from doing nothing, doing the project without VER credits, to looking at power generation using alternative fuels (hydro, photovoltaic, biomass, fossil fuel). The investment analysis concluded that the proposal would not be attractive without VER revenues, so the proposal sought to ensure that this was achieved.

The process included an environmental assessment. This spanned assessing the physical, chemical and ecological environment, reviewing sociological and economic factors, and considering the impact on tourism and culture. Stakeholders were consulted regarding the process and invited to public hearings. Two were held, one each for the Changbin and Taichung wind farms, raising the following main items:

- noise concerns and views (in terms of sight) affected by the connection of the line to the national grid;

- that building might require the cutting down of 'trees in the windbreak forest';

- concerns that the project owner is not the state electricity authority but an independent power provider;

- whether the turbines would stop during a typhoon.

Responses were provided to reassure people on these points and to other comments received during the overall consultation process.

The timeline detailed a start in 2000 with the opening of an office in Taipei; after 'proof of early consideration', bank finance was secured in September 2006. This date also marks the establishment of the contract and becomes the 'project start date'. Following the establishment of cooperative agreements between appropriate parties, construction started on Changbin Phase I (December 2006) and Taichung Phase I (December 2007); production started from Changbin Phase I in June 2007 (+6 months) and Taichung July 2008 (+7 months). The report notes the positive impact on the project made by working with South Pole Carbon, who, as the first 'carbon consultant present in Taiwan (2007)' established the contract within two months.

The project had proceeded; construction had taken place; the wind turbines produce electricity. The project development process had been successful. In part, success stemmed from having the right geographic location on the windy west coast; notably, the Changbin site was located in the area of a dedicated industrial park, with few people living there. This scenario is not always typical, as wind energy projects – with their attendant transmission cables and stations – have been a great source of discontent with increasingly vocal stakeholder groups. This continues to be the case. The pressure on energy supply might slow, but it will not abate; we might not like it, but we have to do it.

Case reflection

The challenges faced in this case scenario are commonly experienced in similar project environments:

i   Evaluate likely feasibility issues for this type of project within a range of territories; consider stakeholder consultation aspects.

ii Determine the key aspects of the business case and associated, more general, presentational and communication challenges.

iii Propose a strategy for working with stakeholders based on the topics in this chapter. Consider the paradox in these scenarios: we need electricity but we don't seem to like the idea of generating it. How do we deal with this?

Sometimes elements of this process will be undertaken a number of times, with no guarantee that the project will ultimately take place. The feasibility analysis could reveal an aspect that needs to be modified; it might highlight a need for additional funding; there could be many other outcomes that result in revision and resubmission. This may also be true for the development of business cases, especially in public projects where political drivers are prominent. For example, an *Economist* article regarding the proposed HS2 (UK High-Speed rail) project highlighted that 'on October 29th the government made a better case for the railway' (*The Economist*, 2013). What had they got wrong? It discussed the difficulty associated with quantifying economic benefit, how some items had been mistakenly counted twice, and that some original assumptions were flawed as technology had changed during the same period (examples included the provision of wi-fi services on trains and the wide-scale adoption of personal computing power). A further interesting aspect to this example is that the article also mentioned that 'few alternatives have been looked at in depth', highlighting a scenario where business case and feasibility work takes place concurrently rather than in sequence.

Early-stage feasibility might also be affected by the outcome of interaction with stakeholder groups. This involvement of stakeholders can provide unexpected challenges to the management of the project, especially when potentially affected stakeholder groups are as capable in management processes as the project-hosting organization. Sometimes this can spawn a host of lengthy activities, such as the consultation processes that take place in relation to concerned stakeholder groups affected by the siting of wind turbines or along the route of a proposed high-speed railway line as per the previous example.

This is a universal project management challenge. A recent scenario in the coastal resort of Arcachon, southwest France, has seen the *Sud Ouest* newspaper (2014) reporting on a public enquiry regarding the University of Bordeaux proposal to develop a Pôle océanographique (Centre for Oceanography) near the harbour/marina area; the headline was '27 247 signatures contre le Pôle océanographique' (27,247 signatures opposing the Centre). We can find examples on every continent, highlighting both business case issues and the likelihood of a response to change caused by the project.

As with many projects causing change, stakeholders have concerns and wherever possible these need to be managed. It is worth linking this discussion with that in Chapter 1 regarding gated processes: at early stages of many projects there is no certainty that the project will follow the anticipated course, design or path, and an associated lack of certainty that the project might stop can feature prominently in the minds of those responsible for the project. Furthermore, considerations of success may also feel premature; gates are ever-present on the path of the project. These are all issues that could be affected dramatically by stakeholders as well as considering the outcomes from feasibility and business case analyses.

In other situations, projects start without these feasibility processes taking place in a formalized way. Sometimes reflecting an individual personality style, this does not necessarily mean that the feasibility or rationale-building activities have not taken place; often it is a default management style. However, this could be a more problematic approach to adopt if the project management process is weak, if the original concept is flawed or if the stakeholder aspects have not been considered at this conceptual stage. There are risks associated with starting a project that has not been adequately thought through.

Some important questions

Wherever the entry point for the person looking after the project, it is helpful to bring together the different early-stage strands by asking the following questions:

1 Who is asking for it?
2 What do they want? (What is it?)
3 Why do they want it?
4 How much will it cost?
5 When do they want it?

Learning point: prompts, not prescriptions

Sometimes we might be criticized for being too analytical; alternatively, we often realize that we should have spent longer evaluating a situation before taking action, as we got it wrong. The list of questions above is not exhaustive, and answering one of these may prompt others not listed here. This is about using your brain – the most important tool of a potentially successful project manager.

Answering these questions helps to inform development of frameworks that might need to be adopted to ensure that processes are in place to manage the project. Wise project managers will identify this as a key stage and apply a suitable tool; the inexperienced may not realize the importance of this activity. Some organizations will have a template for their staff to use. Others will have nothing. We can look towards the bodies of knowledge for help here, and will find phraseology such as 'Project Charter' (part of the vocabulary used by the PMI) or 'Project Initiation Document', among a number of others. The principle is important here; whether we choose to apply an 'off-the-shelf' framework or develop one ourselves, the important aspect is to deploy something that is appropriate to the needs of the project.

A project document at this early stage is potentially valuable. For example, in relation to a scenario in Chapter 1 that mentioned unforeseen risks, in that particular situation one of the key mechanisms that helped to resolve the emergent problems was to utilize the formal project management document at the centre of recovery tactics. An ultimately successful process was pursued with stakeholders – a revised project specification was developed that would deliver a comparable visitor attraction; the project parent negotiated for an enhanced budget with internal and external stakeholders who had been fully informed of the project, in no small part helped by the development and circulation of the project management document. The stakeholders knew about the project and were aware that it was a new activity with associated challenges.

It is worthwhile reflecting on language used in the questions posed; in four out of the five, the words 'who' or 'they' were used – persons, parties, organizations or groups were associated with nearly all of the questions. Think *stakeholders*. Let us now use the questions to develop our own thinking, as this will help us gain important insights at the conceptual stage of the project.

Who is asking for it?

Understanding this better will start to clarify whether the project has an external or internal focus (or 'driver') and indicate commitment levels and motivation, among many other things. This can be further broken into a number of areas by also asking 'whose expectation?' and 'who will have influence?'

At the conceptual stage of the project, we need to consider the 'who' part quite carefully, but the potential intensity of associated analysis might well depend upon the type of project. Are we talking about clients, customers or users? Are these the same? Is the person who requests the project the one who benefits (sometimes a different word may be used, not always positive) from the outcome of it? Are these inside or outside the organization?

In order to answer this, we need to understand:

i   who the project stakeholders are;

ii what their needs are; and

iii what their expectations are.

We could further investigate their interests, try to understand their position on the project and their importance, and also seek to predict how they might behave over the course of the project lifecycle. This area, concerning stakeholders, has become increasingly important within the whole area of project management. At this stage, let us undertake a preliminary stakeholder analysis. Later we shall see that greater depth is often beneficial and, in many cases, it is valuable to review this throughout the life of the project. Several of the examples used so far in this chapter have high-lighted the scrutiny of the project by stakeholder groups; anyone involved in the promotion of a project of this ilk may feel the heat of that scrutiny. It is as if, in Figure 2.5, the project is going through a stakeholder oven.

FIGURE 2.5   Stakeholder oven

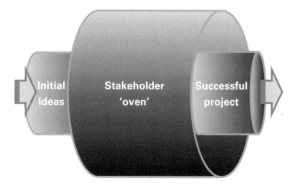

We have already defined project stakeholders as those who can affect the project and those who are affected by it. Stakeholders could be represented as a space through which the project must travel; succeeding with the stakeholder groups will help to yield success in the project, though success cannot be guaranteed. How do we approach this vital aspect of the management of the project? It is helpful to work through this in a sequence of steps. We need to identify the stakeholders, undertake the associated analysis and determine appropriate conclusions, in order to set out a strategy. We should then act on the results of this work.

Identify

It is helpful to bring forward the alternative classifications of stakeholder groups from the previous chapter, as we need an appropriate framework to help identify the stakeholders within each group:

- internal or external (Freeman, 2010: 216);
- primary or secondary (Cleland and Ireland, 2002: 176–77);
- organizational, including employees, providers of finance, customers, community, or government (Mullins, 2010: 714–15);
- economic, socio-political and technological (Johnson, Scholes and Whittington, 2008: 153–55).

Although these frameworks will help us, the exercise may still provide some difficulties, since at this early stage we may not be fully aware of the impact of our new project or understand enough about the parties we need to satisfy in order to deliver specific aspects of the project. It is important to get to know your stakeholders.

Analyse

Following the identification of the stakeholder groups, we need to understand their impact on the project. Ask the questions mentioned earlier (What do they need? What do they want? What are they expecting?) and also pursue any other aspects we consider potentially valuable. Why? There are considerable associated risks here. We can also incorporate the questions associated with risk that we introduced in Chapter 1: Where is the uncertainty? What is the risk? Can we identify the likelihood and impact? Do we understand the consequence of this? What is our response? A lot of questions have been raised. If we don't do our best to address these queries, they will be answered in due course, at a significant point or stage of the project, sometimes with potentially disastrous consequences.

A popular approach to this type of analysis is to adopt one or more stakeholder grids, based on the terms above. A commonly used model is the power–interest grid.

FIGURE 2.6   Stakeholder power and interest

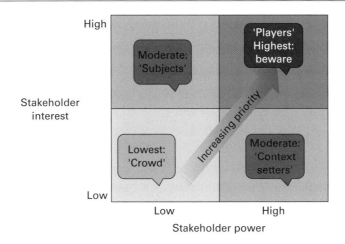

SOURCE: adapted from Ackermann and Eden (2011)

The analysis logic is quite straightforward – establish the relative level of their interest in the project against their relative power and assign the results to quadrants. Figure 2.6 shows a grid adapted from Ackermann and Eden (2011) that includes the terminology 'crowd', 'subjects', 'context setters' and 'players', representing different types of stakeholder.

The movement of stakeholders within this grid is almost as important as the picture presented from the first analysis, on which the management processes might be established. There is a risk of complacency; if we undertake the analysis once only, the impact resulting from the movement of a stakeholder from low to moderate could be significant. For example, the rise of political movements such as the UK Independence Party in 2013/2014 has some of this characteristic; originally regarded as a party of protest, the relatively strong performance in local and European elections in 2014 put pressure on mainstream political parties, resulting in a shift of policy focus. The situation was emulated across many of the European states, and some international cross-border projects that had been conceived on a 2009 basis would have to be revised in the light of issues arising from policies intended to restrict immigration. This highlights the combined aspect of stakeholder shift, political response and policy change with the resulting change in underlying project environment. The risk profile would have changed as well.

A second set of examples is provided by the scenarios that have emerged in the US tobacco industry. In July 2014, *The Washington Post* reported a case that involved punitive damages worth $23.6bn (*The Washington Post*, 2014). A key stakeholder management point related to this case is that 'smokers and their families need only prove addiction and that smoking caused their illness or death'. The power – interest position of smokers will have changed over the decades since they consumed their first cigarettes.

Conclude

Although this may be the first part of a more exhaustive investigation of stakeholder drivers, it is important to draw together the analysis. Often the use of an approach such as this can be challenging, and can lead to difficulty with either the placement of a particular stakeholder (we might want to put them in different places on a grid) or the reaching of consensus in terms of the information produced. Perhaps the best way to deal with this aspect is to undertake to repeat the process at appropriate times. Note that we need to ensure that such exercises add value; otherwise we should ask ourselves whether valuable time is being wasted.

Assuming that we are able to complete the analysis satisfactorily, our conclusions will help to inform the next activity, which is to draw together a high-level stakeholder strategy.

Stakeholder strategy

The stakeholder strategy should be both optimal and efficient, that is, we should seek to ensure that it is optimal in terms of value to the project process, and practical and efficient in terms of (opportunity) cost. It should also be proportionate. We could also argue that this work should be reflected as both a cost and a benefit to any business case developed. Of course, both of these aspects might be difficult to quantify, for different reasons: for cost, we may not know how or when we will conduct the exercise; for benefit, this might both depend on the success of the activity and be unquantifiable in terms of actual benefit.

Cleland and Ireland (2002: 273) introduced a 'project stakeholder management process' comprising the following five points:

- Collect information about stakeholder capabilities and options.
- Identify probable stakeholder strategies.
- Determine how these might affect current project interests.
- Continuously monitor and provide comprehensive information about probable actions in the project stakeholder environment that might have impact on the interests of the project.
- Organize the collection, analysis and dissemination of stakeholder information for the project team.

This is a helpful framework that can be adapted to the particular circumstances of the project. One final point to consider here: as we are considering this during the conceptual phase of an ideal project, we need to conduct this initially at a high level (as we will not have the insights that will be gained further into the project lifecycle). This is one of several reasons why it is important to revisit the stakeholder analysis work. We will, of course, return to the stakeholder theme during our discussion of planning, which is covered in the next chapter.

Learning point: travelling to Ystradgynlais

In a former business development role I found myself travelling to a place called Ystradgynlais in south Wales, once every three or four weeks. Accompanied by a wise, experienced member of the team, the journey there and back was always well humoured; aside from meeting prospective or existing clients, the time spent there seemed to be based around spending time 'on a more social level' with a senior member of a local government organization; the discussions were also well humoured, wide-ranging and generally productive, but I sometimes found it difficult to account adequately for all of the time spent during these working days.

I was largely unaware of the value this would provide until, after a change of role, my work involved the delivery of a challenging multi-party project, of which one party was the organization that I had visited, and got to know, every three or four weeks. The value of accidental but effective bridge-building cannot be underestimated. During the planning and delivery phases, these types of stakeholder relationship can be pivotal. If we get the opportunity to do this, do it. This is likely to be well understood in a number of cultures, as we will explore later.

Act

We need to put our stakeholder strategy into action. Picking up the point made at the end of our discussion of the last step, as we are at an early stage of the project this may constrain our ability to put this in place fully; it makes sense to implement this initially at a high level, with further detail developed at later stages of the project.

Review

Although it might seem premature to review the outcome of our stakeholder management process at the conceptual phase, considering it here also has a value in terms of thinking forward: over the life of the project, stakeholder groups can change – their position within our analysis might change; so too might our information and knowledge. It would be unwise to undertake this only once and assume that it will continue to underpin the delivery of our project. After all, wouldn't that be risky?

At the conceptual phase, our information will be incomplete, so we will therefore have uncertainty, and in turn this means that there will be risks. Whatever the profile of our project (and some will be high profile, for example the delivery of a healthcare product), we need to remember that the project could put at risk our reputation, as individual, organization or other entity. Reputational risk is a key consideration for any organization, large or small, public or private, and provides additional justification for understanding stakeholder management activities.

Why do they want it?

Although we have already considered this aspect earlier, if our entry point does not include involvement in the feasibility/business cases, it is important to pursue this sufficiently. We need to understand the rationale for the project and strength of motivation. This might also reveal where problems might lie. It is difficult to propose a generic approach here, but often a good way into this is to follow the why question with another why question; we seek the information that will inform our perspectives on the proposed project. Sometimes we will be able to offer some associated diagnostic support too, especially if the proposed project is similar to one in our own experience.

What do they want?

This is a very important aspect of the initial framing of the project. Determining what is required can be difficult to achieve in certain project environments, such as systems development. If there is ambiguity of requirement, it will be difficult to deliver against such an expectation. What is it?

- A bridge, building, vehicle, ship?
- An energy strategy, energy supply, transmission system?
- A conference, a sporting event?
- A new management scheme?
- A new educational scheme?
- A new health service?
- A political manifesto?
- A new information system? An app?

Whatever it is, it will have some specific characteristics. In some cases these can be articulated reasonably clearly; in others it can be particularly difficult to establish exactly what will be delivered. Information systems projects typify this. Projects that are based upon the exploitation of creative thinking (or involving creative thinkers) can also present some significant challenges; after all, if the objective of the project is to produce something fundamentally new, trying to anticipate exactly what it will look like might have some characteristics of fortune telling. This does not mean that defining 'what' should not take place. Rather, it reveals the potentially disastrous impact of not articulating sufficiently the scope of what we are expected to deliver.

Note the introduction of the word 'scope'. It is a particularly important project management concept to embrace. Scope has been defined by the APM (2012: 120) as 'the totality of the outputs, outcomes and benefits, and the work required to produce them'. Within this section we will adopt the Oxford English Dictionary definition, 'the extent of the area or subject matter that something deals with or to which it is relevant', and focus on the extent of the area and the term 'relevant'. Again we should pose the question: 'What is it that you want?'

Establishing the 'what' could comprise aspects such as specification or outputs. Using scope is an intelligent approach that helps establish boundaries; in turn, this will help to ensure that we deliver what is required, avoiding a grilling by the media (often seen in public-sector environments) or, for many organizations (in the private sector), ensuring that we make a profit.

Even if we can determine the scope of our project quite clearly, our inexperience or individual character type sometimes contrives to make this problematic, in turn having a corresponding impact on the project. The two following examples are provided to help explain this.

Our first example is in an academic research environment. A higher education institution such as a university provides, in theory, opportunity to develop collaborative links with industry, and we might see a member of staff who has expertise of potential commercial interest 'consulting' for an external client. After a meeting between the university and client, the researcher undertakes to explore agreed items A, B and C. One month later, at the next meeting with the client, the researcher provides insights on A and B, doesn't cover C, but has added D and E. The researcher felt that this was relevant to the exercise (but was not asked for by the client).

In a different example, a very capable member of the organization has been deployed to manage a project that involves the construction of assets X and Y in readiness for the subsequent use of these in operational mode (Z). A well-constructed project document has been developed, but there is a problem unseen by the project manager: developed on the basis of an original application for external funds, the document sets out the project to include all the components X, Y and Z, whereas the project focus is on delivering just X and Y. Z should have been excluded, since this was the focus and target for the subsequent operational phase.

Both examples unintentionally included items that should have been 'out of scope'. When we realize what we have done, it seems very obvious, but we will make mistakes such as this. Experience (or training) will sharpen our focus, and such things are unlikely to happen next time. Both of our examples convey scenarios which are quite tangible. System development work can be fraught with scope issues, given the nature of projects in that area. Contracts are often seen to help mitigate the impact of ambiguity of scope, but these can be difficult to utilize during a conceptual phase. We will discuss this further.

When do they want it?

Sometimes this may be an easy question to answer – for example, the start date of major sporting events is normally known years ahead. Other projects may have a timing component that is agreed with appropriate stakeholder groups; some projects with clearly articulated stages may have dependencies, for example with the availability of key equipment; in certain areas, projects may have a lower time-emphasis, and in some projects the time aspect is open-ended. Of course, the project manager might need to provide input as to what would be feasible as a delivery time, and for some projects this is in fact a difficult question to answer.

How much will it cost?

This may not be known, and an answer to the question might be to state an upper limit. The question might be rhetorical, as the person asking it (the project manager) might need to work out the costs and resources required. On the other hand, the budget may already have been agreed, and the task is to deliver the project within this limit. Often the starting point for the budget is somewhere between the two scenarios.

How will we do it?

A further challenge for some; for others this may seem, initially at least, straightforward. 'How do we do it' might also become 'what will we need?'… people, equipment, money, commitment, innovative designs,… not sure? This is a key area where strong analytical skills can be particularly valuable. It may be appropriate to try to rehearse this in our minds, individually or with members of the project team. And by rehearsing the answer to this question we start to recognize the likelihood that how we do it will depend on people, teams, and the other 'soft' stuff.

What assumptions will be needed?
What constraints will there be?

While undertaking this process we are going to have to make some assumptions, and it is a good time to explore whether there are any specific constraints and start to build a risk profile for the activity. Each of these may be difficult to ascertain, but at a conceptual stage of the project these most likely will contribute to the success or failure of the project.

An example that could usefully provide some context for this would be the consultant who eagerly responds to an invitation to tender (ITT) for a small piece of work, perhaps of 10–15 days duration. The ITT might be quite brief and ambiguous, reflecting the instigator's own lack of knowledge about the project. The consultant wants to win the work, but the lack of clarity in terms of definition makes it difficult to estimate whether the project will actually take between 10 and 15 days or indeed whether it might take longer. This is a fairly typical scenario that might face a small-scale business and has a direct impact on profitability. How should the consultant respond to the ITT – decline to bid, request more information or bid on the basis of the information provided? Often any further information received does not clarify sufficiently the areas of concern or the likely effort required to deliver the project. What are the problems here? The consultant will probably want to evaluate the risk profile and reflect any remaining uncertainty with some cleverly worded 'small print' that highlights assumptions required, any potential constraints or issues of scope.

Summary

In this chapter we have introduced the activities that are often associated with the conceptual phases of projects. This has been stimulated both by considering the early entry points into projects of idea, feasibility and business case, and also by posing a number of questions that seek to reveal all of the insights that help us to prepare for the planning of the project.

Important but challenging concepts such as scope have been discussed, and a strong stakeholder theme runs through almost all of the topics. We discover that there are a number of aspects associated with the nature of early phases in the project lifecycle, largely concerned with uncertainty; this will be examined further within the next area, which focuses on planning.

The answers to the questions posed above help us to draw together a basis for the planning of the project; in some areas this will be enacted as a project charter or project initiation document. While we acknowledge that this is a sound approach to take, we also recognize that projects may start in a different style, and we have started to consider the early-stage instinctive aspects of the person who is involved with the project. We will next consider the planning aspects of projects.

Note

1 This case study draws upon information from the following sources:

Climate Friendly, Changbin and Taichung Wind Project, retrieved on 3 August 2014 from www.climatefriendly.com/Projects/Projects/Changbin_and_Taichung_Wind_Project/

Climate Friendly, Changbin and Taichung Wind Project: Increasing Taiwan's energy security, retrieved on 3 August 2014 from www.climatefriendly.com/.../ Changbin_Taichung_Wind_Project_Profile

RWE, GS VER project Changbin and Taichung Taiwan, retrieved on 3 August 2014 from https://www.rwe.com/web/cms/en/600048/rwe-supply-trading/industrial-customers/ commodity-solutions/commodities/gs-ver-project-changbin-and-taichung-taiwan/

South Pole Carbon, Changbin and Taichung wind power, Taiwan, retrieved on 3 August 2014 from www.southpolecarbon.com/public/projects/0190.pdf

Visit to site on 3 November 2013

References

Ackermann, F and Eden, C (2011) Strategic management of stakeholders: theory and practice, *Long Range Planning*, **44**, pp 179–96

Association for Project Management (APM) (2012) *APM Body of Knowledge*, APM, Princes Risborough, Bucks

Cleland, I and Ireland, L (2002) *Project Management: Strategic design and implementation*, McGraw-Hill, New York

Department for Business Enterprise & Regulatory Reform (BERR) (2008) Severn Tidal Power Feasibility Study, retrieved from http://webarchive.nationalarchives.gov.uk/ 20090609003228/www.berr.gov.uk/files/file43810.pdf

The Economist (2013) High-speed rail: accounting trips, 2 November

Freeman, R E (2010) *Strategic Management*, Cambridge University Press, Cambridge

Gardiner, P (2005) *Project Management: A strategic planning approach*, Palgrave MacMillan, Basingstoke

Johnson, G, Scholes, K and Whittington, R (2008) *Exploring Corporate Strategy*, 8th edn, Financial Times Prentice Hall, Harlow

Mullins, L (2010) *Management and Organisational Behaviour*, Prentice Hall, Harlow

Project Management Institute (PMI) (2013) *A Guide to the Project Management Body of Knowledge*, PMI Inc., Newtown Square, PA

Sud Ouest (2014) Arcachon : '27 247 signatures contre le Pôle océanographique', 27 May, retrieved on 28 August 2014 from www.sudouest.fr/2014/05/27/arcachon-27-247-signatures-contre-le-pole-oceanographique-1567922-2733.php

The Washington Post (2014) Florida jury slams R.J. Reynolds with $23.6 billion in damages, 19 July, retrieved on 29 July 2014 from www.washingtonpost.com/business/economy/fla-jury-slams-rj-reynolds-with-236b-in-damages/2014/07/19/5457be3c-0f87-11e4-8c9a-923ecc0c7d23_story.html

Planning within projects

Introduction

If we have undertaken successful feasibility and business case work, or have confidence that this aspect has been fulfilled, we can start to move the project from a conceptual phase to one that is concerned with planning. As we discussed in the previous chapter, this may, of course, be a point at which we enter the world of projects. Depending upon the type, complexity and broader environmental context, this is normally the phase where the project is rehearsed in some detail, and it can be a particularly beneficial activity. In some cases, however, the well-meant planning might also generate content that is either superfluous or too rigid. While the argument could be that 'failing to plan is planning to fail', experience often informs us as to the optimal style and depth of planning required. Of course, the approach taken might be determined by the organizational setting (for example, where there is a pro-forma project planning template to use).

The area of project planning is well documented and many of the tools used are part of a commonly known vocabulary, such as the time-planning bar chart (Henry Gantt 1861–1919); the expressions 'critical path' and 'critical path analysis' are commonly used and there are a number of self-evident tools such as work break-down structure. We will discuss these later in the chapter. Taking a similar initial route to that adopted in the previous chapter, let us first consider the 'who' part and focus on stakeholders. This will help us to develop the planning and also provides further insights as to the 'project domain'.

Each of the following sections will build on themes from previous chapters and incorporate recurrent topics concerning risk and stakeholder, as these are crucial to the success of the project. This will be discussed within the section in terms of impact, consequence and, where relevant, associated additional topic(s). Within the stake-holder and stakeholder analysis section, one associated topic would be reputational risk. Although this will be covered in greater detail in later chapters, it is highlighted here since it has potentially significant strategic aspects.

Stakeholder aspects

We have discussed earlier that a challenge often faced by project managers relates to the role and position of stakeholders. For example, in multi-organizational projects, while many of the stakeholders might sit at the main table, the reporting structures can place the project manager in a relatively weak, or impotent, position. If the project is delivered within one organization, the need for coordination is likely to be high. In a scenario where delivery of a project requires the involvement of parties outside the organizational boundary (in whatever sense), the scale of the management challenge might provide an unwelcome surprise. Indeed, adopting good-practice approaches, such as introducing project-wide governance, might be almost impossible.

At the conceptual stage of a project we argued that it is important to be clear about stakeholders: who they are and what they want. In many respects the stake-holder element of planning the project is about building on the work outlined in Chapter 2. The key focus is on bringing to life the stakeholder strategy element and specifically being aware that the more we learn about the groups, their behaviour and the impact of this on the project, the better we will become at managing this important aspect of the process.

One approach to take would be to adopt the stakeholder focus shown in Table 3.1, adapted from Ackermann and Eden (2011:183).

TABLE 3.1 Stakeholder planning focus

Power/interest		Approach
Highest	'Players'	High power and interest; deserve sustained management attention
Moderate	'Context setters'	High power and low interest. Can influence future overall context; seek to raise awareness and develop
	'Subjects'	Low power and high interest. Keep informed; sustain interest
Lowest	'Crowd'	Low power and low interest; consider whether management effort worthwhile

SOURCE: adapted from Ackermann and Eden (2011: 183)

It is important also to recall the discussion regarding the possible change of stakeholder position (in terms of their power and interest) and therefore to factor into the planning actions that continuously monitor this aspect. Again, we need to bear in mind that this needs to be proportionate to the project, and of course one way we can assess this is to consider the impact of getting it wrong in terms of risk. For example, if the project is at risk from the deployment of an inappropriate stakeholder engagement strategy, clearly this justifies the effort involved in trying to get it right.

Specification – being clear about what is required

If the project has been defined well in the conceptual phase, the 'what' part may be clear. If this is not the case, there may be some work to do to establish the scope adequately. It is also worth mentioning that the main emphasis within some projects is to develop the understanding of the 'what' that is required. Bringing forward the two examples from Chapter 2, we consider the challenges faced in delivering (i) a piece of commercial work undertaken by a university researcher requested to undertake items A, B and C, and (ii) a construction project (comprising X and Y) that is part of a larger scope of works (X + Y + Z).

In example (i) the problem related to the delivery of A, B and C (expected by the client), when in fact C, D and E are provided (D and E are of interest but not requested by the client). This highlights the importance of recognizing the scope of the requirement and, in terms of planning, the experience provides an insight into how to approach the next piece of work. There needs to be a strong emphasis on the delivery-to-agreed-scope aspects.

In example (ii) the clarification of the scope position (to deliver X and Y only, Z to be part of the next set of activities) achieved in prior discussion with the lead member of staff provided sufficient clarification of thinking for more accurate and appropriate planning to be developed. This also helped the project manager avoid becoming accidentally accountable for actions beyond his or her sphere of control.

In both cases the individual is better able to plan the next project, but we have to be aware of instinctive character traits that cause us to choose a particular initial route. Recognizing that this aspect presents a risk is helpful during the planning phase. For each of these and any other examples, can we imagine the process? What needs to take place in order to deliver the final thing? For the first-timer this can be difficult, but with experience we will know what each might look like.

Breaking things down

In order to develop the planning further, it is normally helpful to break the 'what' down into smaller stages. The outcome of this is commonly known as a work break-down structure (WBS). Can it be broken down into smaller steps? If yes, do it. If no, why not? This may prompt some additional analysis or reflection in terms of the underlying activity and objectives.

There are a number of ways to break the work down into smaller stages – use a whiteboard, use some sticky notes, do it using an appropriate digital tool. It doesn't matter how we do it – the important thing is to do it. Also, we need to recognize that parts of it may be difficult (beyond our current understanding) and to acknowledge that we may get it wrong. This will help us to visualize aspects of timing, resourcing and other pertinent aspects such as logic.

When we are able to build a picture of the sequence of activities, at a higher or lower level, we can then develop a milestone/bar chart; from this we could start to identify the people capability required (this may not be known at this time); in turn, this can help us to create the project management organization (PMO). It is worth reminding ourselves that all people are different and they think differently. While this is a useful sequence to follow, we might approach this part of the planning in a slightly different sequence (or even leave out a stage). For example, some of us might instinctively start by trying to construct a time-planning bar chart; others might consider developing the people resourcing part at an earlier stage.

A key question that might get asked several times relates to estimating: How long will it take? How much will it cost? It might also be quite challenging to determine

FIGURE 3.1 Example of work breakdown structure

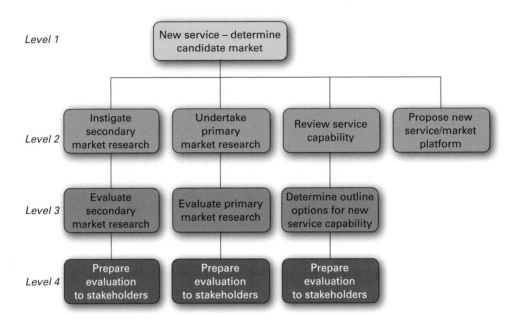

who will take on the various elements. Let's start with the WBS. When we have broken the project into a number of hypothetical building blocks, it could look like the example shown in Figure 3.1.

This might in fact represent the activities, events or milestones (a milestone could mean some significant event or specific goal during the project; definition and interpretation may vary depending upon the context or individual). Although this is helpful, it is just a starting point for a further analysis that should reveal the sequence of activities and the time associated, and it might also help to reveal any inconsistencies in our logic.

Time planning

With this analysis under way, perhaps our next task is to estimate how long the project will take. Of course, we may be presented with a deadline, in which case we would need to work 'backwards', that is, work back from the deadline. Instinctively we might take the WBS diagram, put the activities in a sequence and start to apply times to each activity. This process introduces a number of aspects that often present a challenge to many project managers, not least in terms of determining whether we have in fact got the logic right at the outset.

TABLE 3.2 Estimating times for activities with which we are familiar

Activity	Time estimate (wks)
New service – determine candidate market	2
Review service capability	1
Determine outline options for new service capability	4
Propose new service/market platform	2
Total for all selected activities	9

Time estimation

If this type of project has been done before, there may be some information that will help with the estimation of activity times. Using part of the example above, if the task is to undertake a subset of all the activities in Figure 3.1 and previous experience provides some insight so that an informed estimate can be used, the process can be pursued to provide a first estimate of total time required (Table 3.2).

Note, these are estimates; they are based on prior experience of similar or analogous scenarios, and are sometimes referred to as 'analogous estimates'. What problems might this present? Experience of a similar scenario is no guarantee that this new activity will follow exactly the same pattern and duration. It is an estimate, and it should be presented – and understood – as what it is. As the project moves forward we will find out more about the initial estimate. It might have been optimistic or pessimistic. We hope to see balance, with some of our activities in Table 3.2 taking place in less time than we estimated, to counter those that took longer, so that overall our estimate is 'close enough'.

If on the other hand the activity is completely new to us (a 'first-timer'), the process of estimating might be altogether more onerous. For an activity that is a first-timer to everyone, how do we estimate in such scenarios? What options do we have? We can guess. We can be scientific, using whatever analytical tools – and expertise – are available to us. Which approach does our instinct lead us to adopt? In part the answer lies with instinct, and this is sometimes problematic. Our approach may be influenced by our character style.

To provide context for both optimistic and pessimistic scenarios, I would like to draw upon two personal examples that demonstrate the upside and downside of taking on a task without prior direct knowledge of the work required. Although these could be regarded as somewhat trivial, they are perhaps not untypical of the challenges we often face in project environments.

Optimistic scenario: the first example relates to the replacement of a small piece of car-body trim (the plastic moulding that enhances the appearance of a car). Some over-zealous cleaning had loosened the piece of trim, and this subsequently fell off while the vehicle was parked at a client's premises, leaving an untidy gap requiring a replacement part. In order to reduce the cost of repair, I sourced what I believed to be an identical replacement part from a similar vehicle in a salvage yard (at a particularly good price). Fitting the part was not expected to present any challenges, and my estimate to undertake this was 10 minutes. How long did it take me? At least 50 minutes. Why was this? I discovered that a number of factors contrived to make this an unusually difficult job; apart from the main reason that the part was not identical (the fitting holes had a slightly wider separation), my attempts to overcome this required the locating of a number of additional parts (improvisation using initially oversize wall-plugs), the location of tools I didn't expect to use, and the progressive adjustment (cutting down) of the part until I achieved an exact matching fit, at which point the moulding popped into place and never moved again. Although I was ultimately delighted with the accomplishment of the task, it had taken five times longer than I expected.

Pessimistic scenario: the second example concerns minor damage to a guitar, sustained when my son accidently hit it against a wall; he was trying to play it and answer a telephone call at the same time. As he had spent most of his savings on this item, he was understandably upset and annoyed by the event. An interesting stakeholder dimension to this – he blamed the caller for causing the incident. Viewing the damage, initially I concluded that it was superficial and reassured him that it could be fixed easily. This was foolish, as a closer inspection revealed that the repair process would require soldering, something that I had never previously mastered. Recalling the car-trim experience, I concluded that this task would take me 'a while' (this reveals that I wasn't sure I was capable of doing it). In fact, the soldering task went particularly well and the guitar was fixed very quickly (under five minutes). My pessimism was unwarranted.

In both cases I could have been distracted or trying to do other things at the same time, the sorts of things that people in business frequently experience when asked to provide an estimate for the time to undertake something. They make an estimate; some will be too high, some too low, but they hope the highs will be balanced by the lows in the presented plan. It can be a very difficult thing to do and it can have a significantly detrimental effect on the performance of a project.

Returning to our example from Figure 3.1, if this includes all of the activities, of which several are new to us, how could we estimate the times required for these? We could (i) ask a colleague, (ii) research it, (iii) look for comparators or (iv) rehearse

TABLE 3.3   Estimating based on pessimistic and optimistic times

| | Time estimate (wks) | | |
Activity	Optimistic	Pessimistic	**Average**
New service – determine candidate market	2	2	**2**
Instigate secondary market research	1	3	**2**
Undertake primary market research	5	7	**6**
Review service capability	6	8	**7**
Evaluate secondary market research	2	2	**2**
Evaluate primary market research	1	1	**1**
Determine outline options for new service capability	4	4	**4**
Propose new service/market platform	1	3	**2**

it in an analytical manner. Following that, we might choose to generate pessimistic and optimistic scenarios, and calculate an unweighted average for these estimates.

Whichever scenario we are faced with (ie completely new or one with which we are more familiar), the information supplied is only as good as it is estimated. Unfortunately, the receiver of the information (which could be a busy executive, a pressure group, the media etc) will often not be interested in the associated narrative and disclaimers. Once the information is heard, it becomes their reality stick, a stick which may be used to beat the project.

Returning to our example, we can incorporate our estimates into the diagram (Table 3.3). We could also add all the optimistic times together to get a total time X; we could then separately add together the pessimistic times to get Y, and this would then give us a range of [X,Y] for the project duration. In our heads we may well do this quite regularly without formally working through the computations. For example, if we need to provide an estimate for how long it will take us to go through our e-mail or electronic correspondence, we could say 'between 30 minutes and 45 minutes', but some might immediately say '45 minutes'; the problem is that it might take us much longer.

Pursuing an analytical approach for a little longer, we may have some realistic (or acceptable) estimates for the duration of activities, and we calculate that the project will take 26 weeks. However, there is a problem that needs to be revealed: at the moment, our analysis regards all the activities as taking place in sequence, when in fact some of them can take place concurrently. This example can be analysed further.

The following section includes a generic network diagram. This is a simplified representation of a broader set of techniques, discussed in depth by Morris (1994: 31–34), that includes PERT (program evaluation review technique), CPM (critical path analysis) and related concepts, developed in parallel in the late 1950s within the US defence and commercial sectors.[1] We will explore this briefly so that we can reflect on the value of this type of analysis and also recognize some inherited vocabulary.

Diagrammatic representation

Figure 3.2 shows an activity box that would be part of a simplified network diagram – each box includes the earliest and latest start times and a label or code.

Normally we would expect to start the project as soon as possible in order to meet the end time. We could start at time '0' (putting a '0' into the EST part of the box), and we would add the expected duration of each activity from our previous table (these are the numbers above each arrow) (Figure 3.3). Adding these gives us our total time. Notice that the times are different depending on the branch sequence calculated, as an activity cannot start until the previous one has completed (in activity 60 it starts at 13 days). We then need to work from right to left to complete the latest start times, and the latest we would want activity 20 to start is after 2 days.

This reveals a path where there is no 'slack', and this is known as the 'critical path'... the one that needs the greatest attention because other activity paths will depend on it. Could we have revealed this without introducing and analysing a network diagram? Possibly yes. In fact, our brains have to do this type of analysis quite frequently, as this is not an uncommon scenario. For example, if we have organized a coach to take the team to the sports fixture, we prefer not to leave without all of the team as this would be problematic when we arrive at the contest. Ideally, we need to wait until all the team has assembled before the coach departs!

FIGURE 3.2   Activity box (simplified)

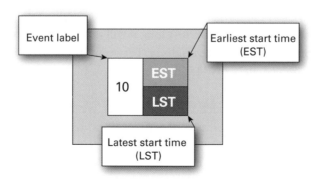

FIGURE 3.3 The example shown in a network diagram

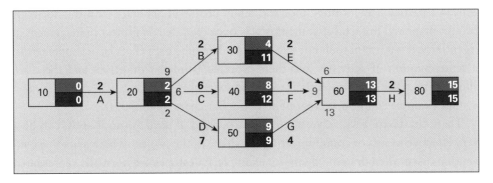

Moving from left to right there are three lines which look like this:

A	0 + 2 = 2	B	2 + 2 = 4	E	4 + 2 = 6	H	6 + 2 = 8
A	0 + 2 = 2	C	2 + 6 = 8	F	8 + 1 = 9	H	9 + 2 = 11
A	0 + 2 = 2	D	2 + 7 = 9	G	9 + 4 = 13	H	13 + 2 = 15

A problem often emerges, though, when we are faced with multiple activities, and then the critical path might remain hidden until a problem reveals it. For some, this might provide a justification for committing time to such an analytical approach.

Learning point

This section has introduced a number of techniques that can be interpreted in different ways, and they are open to criticism. For example, the network diagram and critical path analysis relied on knowing in advance the activities, the dependencies, sequence and 'duration'.

While it is often possible to anticipate the initial sequence of activities at a high level, duration, for one, provides a wholly different challenge. If these are based on estimates, they are likely to be wrong. If they are wrong, the outcome of the analysis will probably be invalid. If we use such tools to build our estimates and the analysis is ultimately presented to the board, this can be a difficult position to argue our way out of, should the analysis be incorrect. We need to be aware of the limitations of this type of approach and when to use it.

The fundamental principle is that we need to exercise our judgement for when we deploy such tools. We can take from this section some useful vocabulary, however – we can discuss earliest and latest start times, slack and critical path from a more informed perspective. The last of these, critical path, also provides a useful point to consider the most popular time-planning tool, the Gantt chart.

Time-planning bar chart

This is a particularly intuitive tool and many people might start with this for their project planning. In fact, for some this was once regarded as project management in its entirety. It is a useful tool, but one of many. The time plan chart is, in simple terms, a representation of activities and their expected/estimated duration, and these are shown within the diagram in their expected sequence.

Our example can now be represented as a bar chart (Figure 3.4).

These charts are relatively easy to construct and, if used appropriately, can be a very effective means of communicating the shape of the project. There are some conventions used when drawing them; for example, milestones are normally represented as a diamond. They work well when the number of activities is not too lengthy, and when the duration intervals (be they weeks or months, for example) yield a chart that is a neat A4 landscape shape. Unless we are using dedicated project-planning software, the drawing and redrawing of the chart can be a nuisance. This last statement reveals a further consideration – the chart is likely to be wrong the moment it is drawn and presented, as things change. The critical path may not be apparent, nor does it reveal resource requirements. Nevertheless, in the hands of a skilful project manager, the time-planning bar chart can be a useful component of the planning toolkit.

The following example reveals the value of deploying a time-planning bar chart. During a process of building a case for the commercialization of an academic project, a time-planning chart was used to explain the forthcoming activities to the team, many of whom had not been involved in the strategic development of the concept. While this approach is not the best means of gaining key support from a project team, in this case the explanation of activities, sequence and anticipated sequence enabled a number of the project team activities to take place from a more informed perspective.

Learning point

As we have worked through the time-planning topics, at several points many of us could have turned to a software tool to perform some of the analysis. Opening Microsoft Project™ immediately gives us a familiar Windows™ table ready for our activities, sequence and duration; input these and a time-planning chart will appear. Glance at the menu bar and you will see a number of familiar-sounding expressions or phraseology. It is as if this tool might do all our project management for us. If we know how to use it, the Gantt chart, scheduling, resourcing, costing are all there for us to develop. The appeal of using this type of software tool is very powerful; it can be used to model the project, but it is not an end in itself. It is a tool, and in the wrong hands the use of it can be counterproductive. In the right hands, it will be incorporated with a host of other integrating activities to influence the positive outcome of the project.

FIGURE 3.4 New service development project in bar-chart format

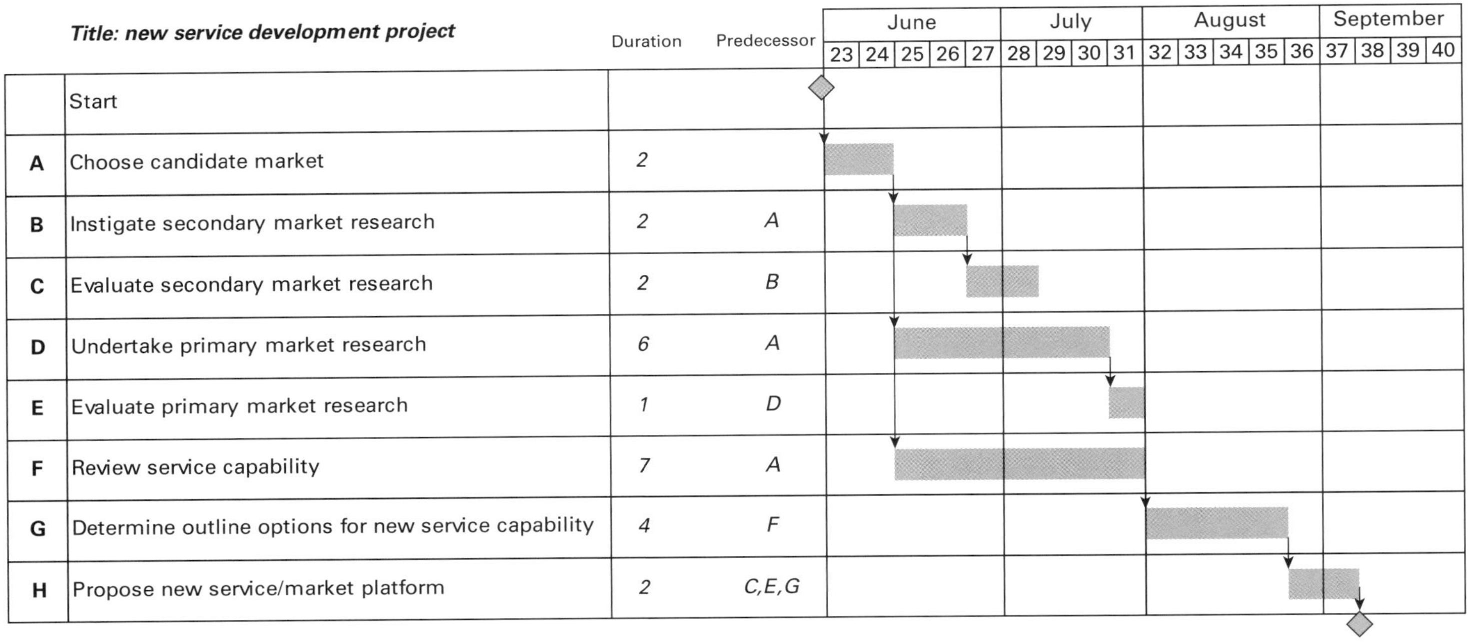

	Title: new service development project	Duration	Predecessor	June				July				August				September			
				23	24	25	26	27	28	29	30	31	32	33	34	35	36	37	38	39	40
	Start																				
A	Choose candidate market	2																			
B	Instigate secondary market research	2	A																		
C	Evaluate secondary market research	2	B																		
D	Undertake primary market research	6	A																		
E	Evaluate primary market research	1	D																		
F	Review service capability	7	A																		
G	Determine outline options for new service capability	4	F																		
H	Propose new service/market platform	2	C,E,G																		

Resource planning

Unless we are using project-planning software, one of the criticisms of the time-planning bar chart related to resourcing. How should we deal with this aspect, since it clearly is very important? What do we mean by the term 'resource'? This is something we need to enable the delivery of a component or the whole of the project. It could be a person, an item of equipment or expertise, among other things. Sometimes it will have a clearly defined cost, but often it will be something that we might want to 'borrow'.

In order to move the project forward, we may need to utilize a number of people, some of whom may be recruited directly, but often the team will comprise staff from within (and sometimes outside) the organization. These are resources. They may be difficult to control. They have a cost.

We may need to have access to equipment; this could range from specialist machinery to gaining access to more general, centrally managed resources, such as that associated with printing. These are resources. They have a cost.

In order to deliver the project we may need to draw on specialist knowledge or expertise from outside the organization, such as the initial legal support needed by early-start entrepreneurs. These are resources. They have a cost.

It is likely that we will need to continue this analysis in order to identify as many of the resources as possible, so that we can estimate the overall requirement and therefore the associated cost; this is covered in the next topic. Often we find that, despite what seems to be great analysis and considerable forethought, some key resources have not been planned in. While this might be expected in a first-timer project, it is also not uncommon within scenarios that involve the deployment of new technologies. Again, this has a cost. The cost could be significant and often this provides a risk to the project.

Let us consider some examples, firstly, the market research project that was featured in Figures 3.1 to 3.4. This type of work often tends to be undertaken by specialists who understand the nature of research processes and have particular knowledge that enables them to develop effective questionnaires (of whatever type), locate suitable respondent samples, and have the resources (and expertise) for data management, analysis and reporting. If we need to undertake this type of project, we might therefore regard the market research organization as the type of resource that we would wish to 'buy in', for which there would, of course, be an associated cost.

If we consider the same example but where we are in fact the market research organization, we will be deploying our staff and/or recruiting external resources, so our resourcing plan will look different. The associated costs will reflect associated staff and those for the hire of external resources.

In a third scenario, we may decide to take on the market research work ourselves; in this case, we might expect the resourcing to be entirely from within the organization and it may look as if we will be able to save some cost. It is worth considering that, without enough prior knowledge and with a lack of specialist systems, we will find that the research project is in fact difficult to undertake, and we end up in scenario 1.

Often, resourcing means people. We can do the analysis and determine the need for people, incorporating this into the plan. Where do these people come from – within our department or from a different department? There are some associated risks here, such as the degree to which people are actually 'devoted' to the project. At this stage it is sufficient to raise this as a risk; we will explore it further in later sections.

It may be possible to identify 'who' will do certain things, but this may not be known or be incomplete. Perhaps the most important aspect is to understand the outline content of activities that will need to be undertaken in order for the stage to be completed. This may require specialist input with knowledge or capability that resides outside the organizational setting or currently beyond the project domain.

CASE STUDY   Hosting the Olympic Games

Planning for the best; now where's the business case for that?[2]

Hosting the Olympic Games provides great opportunities to demonstrate ambition and capability and to celebrate achievements. All of these can help to build or promote a world-city brand, but what is left when the party is over? A legacy of stadia, memories and the accounting... a great Games at a great cost. Mega-events such as these provoke very different reactions from the nation's public and provide good examples of the difficulties with building business cases.

The winning by Sydney of the bid in 1993 to host the 2000 Games was greeted with celebration, but as the costs rose against the original budget, with slow initial ticket sales and gaps in sponsor funding emerging, additional support was requested from the New South Wales Government (Haynes, 2001).

A report from the Australian Bureau of Statistics (2000) after the Games reported that the awarding of the Games had a significant impact on Australia, and that this would continue after the event. It also discussed the 'promotional' effect of the Games, highlighting the likelihood of increased future visitors and that most – but not all – impacts would be positive; they noted that the event may have prevented certain economic activities taking place, either due to the event itself or associated with the concomitant disruption. A subsequent assessment in 2007 concluded that the Sydney Olympics had a negative effect on both New South Wales and Australia as a whole in terms of measuring economic variables, with a present value loss of $2.1bn (Giesecke and Madden, 2007).

Four years later, it was the turn of Athens to play host. Taking place in a quite different cultural environment, *The Sunday Times* (2004) reported the possibility that the Greek capital would not be ready to host this event, reporting on the concerns of the International Olympic Committee after a review took place within six months of the opening events. This also highlighted a number of unusually timed events that contributed to delays, including the nation's general election, freak weather conditions (snowfall in Athens) and the bankruptcy of a firm involved in a key renovation project. The event took place largely as planned.

A stark analysis of the Athens Games by *The Economist* (2004) highlighted that Greek and other European Union taxpayers contributed substantially helping to run the Games, preparing the facilities, and that overall the cost represented 5 per cent of 2003 Greek gross domestic product (GDP), which was roughly $800 per inhabitant. In contrast, more optimistic grounds for the impact of mega-events was maintained in an article subsequently published in the *Municipal Engineer* (Malfas, Theodoraki and Houlihan, 2004) that balanced the competing socioeconomic, socio-cultural, physical and political impacts.

Equally wary of the benefits to the UK of the successful London bid for the 2012 Games, *The Economist* (2008) reported 'the passing of the baton' from Beijing to London and the 'dire bottom line' where the initial £3.4bn budget had risen to £9.3bn by 2007. At $20bn equivalent, the Beijing Games were the most expensive hosted, but Bloomberg (2008) highlighted that, as the Chinese authorities seemed to recognize, the event was not an end in itself, as hosting 'could lead to an improvement in the city government's credit-worthiness'. It is unlikely that the typical fan of sport or casual observer would have considered this dimension.

Further scepticism associated with the hosting of the London Games continued through 2010, with *The Economist* (2010) highlighting that three criteria would determine the success of the event:

- money;
- time;
- making use of the legacy.

The BBC (2011) reported on the warnings of further budget overspend from the UK National Audit Office. Nevertheless, constructive economic impact reviews (Lloyds Banking and Oxford Economics, 2012) estimated that the London Games would support a £16bn contribution to GDP, but this would be spread over 12 years, and of the GDP supported by the event 70 per cent was prior and during, with 30 per cent expected to occur subsequently (as legacy).

The London Games took place and the nation seemed to be surprised that it was successful: 'Britain has shown the world – and its own sceptical population – that the country can stage a brilliant Olympic Games' (*The Economist*, 2012), with subsequent media reporting of substantial tourism spending, likely effective longer-term benefits and a boost to the economy by £9.9bn (BBC, 2013).

The voices of the sceptics remained. After the Sochi Winter Games cost £31bn (BBC, 2014), the Norwegian government refused to provide the financial guarantees required for the 2022 event and pulled out of the bidding process, leaving Almaty in Kazakhstan and Beijing as the two choices. A shift in economic power from west to east is reflected also in the hosting of sporting mega-events. Building business cases that adequately reflect all of these factors presents a challenge of a similar scale. The planning nevertheless needs to take place.

Case reflection

This scenario highlights the difficulty with establishing effective business cases for high-profile mega-event projects:

i   Does this matter? Consider the corresponding strategic case.

ii Evaluate the impact on planning for projects such as these.

iii Build the framework of a plan to host a mega-event; what issues are presented? To what extent can we have confidence in the planning? What factors contribute to this?

iv National reputations are put at risk; to what extent does the style of delivery contribute to this?

Cost planning

We have moved the analysis from resource planning to initial cost estimation; from there we would be able to aggregate these estimates into a budget for the project. This could be further aggregated for multiple projects. With this in place, we would probably want to use it as a basis for managing the cost aspects of the project (Figure 3.5).

FIGURE 3.5   Providing a basis for managing costs from resource planning

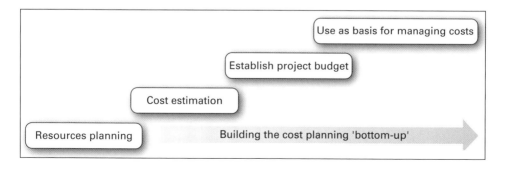

Use as basis for managing costs

Establish project budget

Cost estimation

Resources planning

Building the cost planning 'bottom-up'

In order to visualize these processes, let's bring forward the items of resource planning from the previous section for which we determined there would be an associated cost. There were four areas of cost identified; there could be more:

1 people;

2 equipment;

3 specialist knowledge or delivery expertise;

4 other item or other services;

5 unidentified or unknown items.

Cost estimation

In order to estimate the costs, we need to know a little more about each item. Starting with **item 1, people**, this can be, for the inexperienced, immediately ambiguous. For new staff specifically brought in, it is likely that we would want to record their cost against the project. There are a number of aspects to the costs associated with people, including their recruitment, salary and overhead costs. Some of these are often missed by an inexperienced project manager.

To provide some insight here, typical hiring costs for an employee recruited could include the following:

- salary;
- national insurance contribution (or regional equivalent);
- pension contribution (reflecting regional requirements or expectations);
- cost of vehicle or other transport (where applicable or agreed);
- accommodation allowance (if appropriate);
- other costs.

One positive aspect of this particular challenge is that the costs are associated directly with the project. Often a scenario emerges where the project requires human resources that are drawn from existing staffing, either inside or outside the department or function that is hosting the project. In order to estimate suitable costs for this situation, a different approach may be required. How much of their time will actually be spent on the project – one day a week, two days a week? Do we calculate this out of five or seven days in order to get a meaningful percentage? Tracking this sometimes creates its own project!

It is vital for the organization to account for its costs and deployment of staff, and other metrics such as 'staff utilization'. As well as presenting some practical difficulties, the problem is also often one of perception. In order to account for the staff within the project, a vital administrative function must be performed, one which is often unpopular with all of the staff affected.

At the planning stage, it is important to anticipate what is required in terms of cost management, which costs are 'direct' (this could mean directly associated with the project), and which are 'indirect'.

Before this may speed our thinking towards cost codes, allocations etc, let us consider **item 2, equipment**. While similar considerations might prevail, equipment tends to have less inherent unpredictability than people, often not moving, and normally following instructions. Items of equipment required by projects could fall into a wide range of categories, from everyday items for communication (this could include personal computing, voice and data communications technology) to significant items of shipping or construction engineering:

- personal kit;
- transport;
- specialist kit – small/large.

This area is of a highly practical nature, where an effective WBS can be particularly beneficial. For organizations used to delivering engineering paint-by-numbers projects, the WBS items might become the basis of the itemization of project costs and ultimately the cost control system. We might find an example of this in a large-scale energy (paint-by-numbers) project. The underlying project planning associated with the installation of wind turbines, onshore or offshore, can provide a basis for procurement activities. A WBS approach helps to inform procurement. This is an area where procurement staff need to understand the project at a sufficiently early stage.

Now let us consider **item 3, specialist knowledge or delivery expertise**. We have identified a requirement for a resource that is more difficult to specify, probably because it is highlighted as 'specialist'. The specialist might provide knowledge, and might also provide the delivery expertise. Some organizations have a modus operandi that incorporates a high volume of 'contracted-out' projects, or project activities. Concerned with attracting foreign direct investment (FDI) to one geographic area of the UK, the Welsh Development Agency (WDA) was an example of this type of organization. Before it was wound up in 2006, the WDA was a prolific buyer of third-party support, be it in the form of consultants, subcontractors or other type of external resources. In constructing project strategy, developing marketing campaigns and delivering services, a host of specialist knowledge and delivery expertise was procured. Often a programme would comprise project strategy, project(s) delivery and review phase. Sometimes this would even include the related operational activities.

Item 4, other item or other services, could include insurance, premises costs, particular logistics or subcontractor costs. These are listed as 'other' here, since the type of project will determine the significance of each, and this will determine how the categories are formed. In certain scenarios this could include items such as the cost of capital depreciation – this is one of many examples where a project manager needs to find out what something means or find someone who can explain the concept.

Establish project budget

One area that this example also usefully reveals is the challenge of budgeting for the overall cost of a programme of activities. Until the project strategy is developed, anticipating the project delivery structure and costs will be very difficult. This is a useful point to consider in terms of top-down budgeting; so far we have been examining the bottom-up form.

The need to buy in services leads us into a key area of knowledge with which the project manager needs some familiarity, namely procurement processes. This is covered in more detail in the following section.

Item 5, unidentified or unknown items. What can we say about this? We might prefer this category not to exist, but likely it will. Expect such a scenario, and if we have experienced a previous situation where unidentified items caused a major difficulty within a project, we are better prepared in terms of justifying extra analysis effort in order to ensure that we understand the situation better. One way of provisioning for this type of situation is to incorporate a contingency or resource within the project budgeting itself.

Although the prompt to introduce a contingency might be primarily related to concerns about project slippage, such additional resource could be required for a variety of reasons. For example, on the day after London was announced as the successful bid to host the 2012 Olympic Games, devices exploded in the city's transport network, causing severe loss of life and widespread trauma. Aside from significant personal impact experienced as a result of these incidents, in response to the perceived increased likelihood of a future event causing disruption to the Olympic Games, *The Guardian* (2012) subsequently reported that 'estimates of the Games' immediate security costs have doubled from £282m to £553m'.

Could this have been anticipated at an earlier stage and such costs reflected in the original budget? Perhaps, but we have to be realistic in acknowledging that our forecasting and analysis has limitations. We have to expect that the unexpected is likely to emerge. With this accepted, we can focus our collective minds on the facilitating, or enabling, of suitable contingency funds or, although often unpopular, in an extreme case recognizing that a project may need to be stopped.

At this stage, it is worthwhile highlighting that some project budgets will be established in a top-down style. At a strategic level within the organization, the budget to pursue a particular activity might have been agreed. This is the budget within which the project will need to take place, and this can tend to create projects that have a high emphasis on the cost constraint. Government-funded academic research projects are examples of these. The resource funding, or budget, is established at the outset (through whatever process), and that is the limit of expenditure – the project has to be delivered within that limit.

If we work top-down, many of the processes covered in this section will still be valid. We still need to understand the WBS, identify the activities, resource requirements and apply estimates, but the process is more constrained. We may therefore need to compromise something (or several things) in order to stay within the fixed budget. If a project starts with a high cost constraint emphasis, but seeks to deliver something which has a high quality or scope emphasis, such as an emergency response system, this may be a recipe for significant problems – there is a conflict of objectives to manage. A scenario that has some dimensions of this is the A400M project, the featured case in Chapter 4.

In practice, while we might seek to provide accurate cost estimates by working bottom-up, there is often a budget limit, so the work at these earlier stages often requires skills of negotiation. Negotiation is vital in ensuring that the project budget is adequate to enable the achievement of the goals of the project. Equally, the project has to have a limit.

Procurement and contracts: some basics

Once the purpose of the project is clarified and the objectives defined, the procurement approach can be fully developed. This will be informed by feasibility and business case evaluation work. Some will involve the use of industry-specific contract frameworks; there are useful information sources for this and elements are discussed in relation to construction and engineering roles highlighted in Chapter 11.

Above all, it is important to recognize that when specific items or services are required for the project, this is likely to involve dedicated procurement processes. When this includes some form of contractual arrangement, the client (or customer) pays for services sourced from suppliers or contractors, and an associated purchasing process will take place.

It is important to be clear about what is required and the associated processes needed to fulfil this. Mulcahy (2001) provided a useful introduction to procurement, highlighting the need for the following six stages:

1 procurement planning;
2 solicitation planning;
3 solicitation;

4 source selection;

5 contract administration;

6 contract close-out.

Stage 1 (procurement planning) reflects the rationale and preparatory work consistent with the content we have already discussed in the previous topics. Stage 2 (solicitation planning) includes the development of a scope of work, the evaluation criteria and the specific terms and conditions that will apply; depending how well this is articulated, it will take the form of an invitation to tender (ITT), request for tender (RFT) or quotation (RFQ). Other terminology is also used. The document is circulated to prospective suppliers.

Clarification of requirement is likely to take place during stage 3 (solicitation). Tenders or bids will be submitted. Although the process varies from case to case, it is likely that stage 4 (source selection) will involve the submission of bid documents, interviews and appropriate negotiation. Work begins at stage 5 (contract administration), normally after signing the contract. If the project is taking place in an environment where contracting is the norm, project management activities will take place on a relatively more formalized basis. This contrasts with those where contracts are less common. By relating to the objectives, the contract will also necessarily reflect the scope of work. In this respect, it is vital that the contract is robust, both in terms of defining sufficiently what is required while also being interpreted appropriately.

At stage 6 (contract close-out) the work is completed and approved final payments are made. All of these steps present a challenge for the project manager in quite different ways, such as the need to:

- have sufficient knowledge of the process;
- understand the time required to get this aspect right;
- ensure appropriate buy-in from relevant parties;
- recognize the importance of scope within the process;
- deploy effective facilitation skills and build good relationships with parties involved;
- understand and anticipate schedule issues;
- promote good practice and enhance the value of appropriate formality.

These also reflect the idealistic nature of project management; project managers will often find that they are under simultaneous pressures of needing to do things right but also to do things quickly enough when the contract activity becomes the key item on the critical path.

Quality planning

To continue the establishment of some of the core areas of planning the project, we must also consider the appropriate aspects of 'quality'. What do we mean by quality planning in the context of project management? In contrast with time and cost planning, quality can be a more difficult concept to elaborate. Of course, it depends on the type and context of the project. If the project is to construct a new flood defence, there will be a host of specific engineering parameters to meet. In contrast, the organizing of a new conference event has a different set of requirements, largely concerned with the provision of a service. Thirdly, the construction of a new visitor centre may have an altogether different set of quality requirements, straddling both engineering and service dimensions.

This reveals two distinct aspects of project quality planning – 'conformance', whereby there is a specific set of stated requirements to which the project delivery must conform, and 'performance', where the onus is to deliver to stakeholder expectations; unfortunately, performance requirements are often not clearly defined, and the clarification of these may become a key activity for the project manager to undertake. One could argue that all projects have a combination of conformance and performance characteristics.

Two important publications informed much of the thinking concerning the core parameters for quality planning. Garvin (1987) proposed eight distinct dimensions of quality. While this was framed largely from a product perspective, Berry, Parasuraman and Zeithaml (1990) explored this from a service quality perspective. These are summarized in Table 3.4.

Berry *et al* (1990) further drew attention to service quality being the gap between service expectation and service perception. Having utilized this framework in the

TABLE 3.4   Comparison of the quality attributes developed by Garvin (1987) and Berry *et al* (1990)

Product-based (Garvin)	Expectation and perception-based (Berry *et al*)
Performance, conformance	Tangibles, reliability, responsiveness
Features, reliability, durability	Competence, courtesy, credibility
Serviceability, aesthetics	Security, access, communication
Perceived quality	Understanding the customer

formulation of customer satisfaction evaluation processes, these can be a powerful ingredient in furthering insights as to how well a product or service performs. This can (and should) be applied in project environments. In fact, a key mantra of the customer satisfaction evaluation work was to understand the client ranking of importance of each aspect. Within a project environment it is vital to pursue a similar course of investigation with stakeholders; if we misjudge either the position or power of a stakeholder and also their ranking of a key quality attribute, this could put the project at risk. A better understanding of the likely client requirement for a service to be launched will improve the likelihood of success: for example, a system that is designed to operate within a specific technical environment but where the target client group cannot operate the system owing to local technical constraints.

To some extent, advances in technology may have distorted customer expectations and the specific criteria developed, but this still provides a useful differentiated basis, although the perspective we develop may be too narrow – for example, while the engineering associated with the installation of a hydro-electric power scheme has changed to an extent, stakeholder expectations with these types of project have changed perhaps disproportionately more. Do we need to defer to stakeholders in all cases? This is one key aspect of project management. Projects are delivered in a non-ideal world. Often expectations are initially unclear and sometimes unrealistic.

In order to deliver successful projects we have to ensure that we have understood stakeholder expectations and translated these into the project specification. Furthermore, this is something that we may need to revisit at regular stages throughout the lifecycle of the project. Sometimes the discussions will be awkward and frustrating, with the project manager spending a significant part of his or her time doing something that seems either unnecessary or perhaps even superfluous. Alternatively, the project manager could find himself or herself involved in a dialogue concerning things that should have been already established. This is the broader project management role that the following chapters will seek to reveal and provide a basis on which to reflect.

At this stage we need to recognize that there will be a need to plan the quality aspects of the project. The vocabulary we have just introduced has resonance within our projects, and we see areas of differentiation between projects in a service environment compared with those in a manufacturing or 'constructing' environment. Some of these will be specific and equivocal, such as the engineering specification or safety characteristics, and others will be more difficult to formalize, such as the emotive experience associated with the delivery of a performance event.

Project management organization

During the initial planning, it is important to consider how the project management will be organized, in terms of roles, expertise and structure. In reality, this aspect will develop over the life of the project. Like many other aspects of the project management, at early stages we may not be aware of the best arrangement, but we need to put something in place that is sufficiently robust and pragmatic. Without prior experience, it can be challenging to visualize the structure and composition of the project management organization.

Roles and responsibilities

The resource planning that developed from the WBS may have revealed the need for a number of roles directly associated with the delivery. To accompany this, there will be roles needed to support the organization, administration and management of project activities, and these may manifest themselves differently, depending upon the organization or project setting.

There are some models that can help us with the initial shaping. For example, Larson and Larson (2007) discuss the value of adopting a 'RACI' (responsibility, accountability, consult, inform) chart in relation to the challenges associated with multicultural projects. This is shown in adapted and extended form in Figure 3.6, including the identification of those associated with stakeholder relationships, leadership, and dependencies. These headings can be modified to suit the circumstances or requirements of the project.

We need to ask some more questions, such as how the project is best managed. We may assume that a project manager role is required. Is it a whole role (as opposed

FIGURE 3.6 Extended role and responsibility planning chart

Who...			Project phase (as appropriate)					
			1	2	3	4	5	6
R Has responsibility	for doing the work	R1						
		R2						
A Is accountable	for decisions	A1						
		A2						
C Is consulted	regarding the work	C1						
		C2						
I Is informed that	the work is taking place	I1						
	the work stages are completed	I2						
S Manages relationships	internally	S						
	externally	S						
L Provides leadership	to inspire and motivate	L1						
	to protect and help unblock	L2						
D Are the dependencies	internally	D1						
	externally	D2						

SOURCE: adapted from Larson and Larson (2007)

to a fractional form), is it two people, more? How will the administration take place – is this a function of the project manager role, or do we see it as a separate activity? When we are planning the project management organization, it may be helpful to consider looking to an expert source for initial guidance, perhaps one of the Body of Knowledge organizations such as the Project Management Institute (PMI) or Association for Project Management (APM).

The emphasis here is on role, responsibility and structure. It may be premature to start by picking the team. One immediate challenge could arise when one of the staff team leads a new activity; as this becomes the project, the same staff member becomes the manager of the activity. This staff member thus becomes identified as the project manager, by accident.

By contrast, in a different organizational setting, an activity starts, initiated from a strategic requirement, characterized and understood as a project, and managed as a project; a project manager is assigned to the activity. For this person, the initial setting-up period could be quite different from the one experienced by the accidental type in the first example.

Generally there will be a need to lead and manage the project. Support and development roles will be required, such as those concerned with the administration, and one or more specialist or technical roles. We need to have the right roles in the team, but the team shouldn't be unnecessarily big. This aspect may require some thought. Conversely, within a small organization with one or two people, the challenge may be the opposite of this: how to ensure that the team covers all the roles but with fewer people. In both scenarios it may be appropriate for one person to fulfil more than one role.

Project management structures

There are two main types of project management organization structure. Firstly, a dedicated project structure; this is established to enable the delivery of a project. It is project focused and likely to be seen in organizations for which projects is their business. Members of the team have a high level of project focus and priority, reflecting the strategic importance of the project. Figure 3.7 shows an example of a scenario where project services are 'bought in' as required.

Alternatively, the project takes place without a dedicated project structure. In a matrix management style, staff have line responsibilities and also undertake a project (or multiple project) responsibilities. With conflicting objectives, their commitment to the project may vary; as a lightweight matrix, this has an impact on the project management challenge and also on the likelihood of project success. Where staff are 'seconded' (ie they are dedicated to the project until returning to their ordinary role), the resulting heavyweight matrix structure has characteristics similar to the dedicated project form, largely arising out of the redirecting and congruence of individual

FIGURE 3.7   Organization adoption of a project-based structure

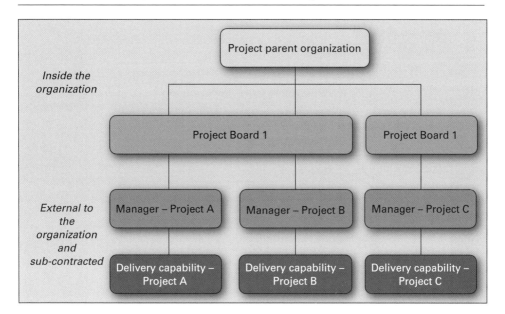

objectives. Both forms are applied contingently; in practice, we often seek to achieve balance between the two.

Figure 3.8 is a generic representation of the clustering of roles, comprising a project board, project management team and also reflecting the importance of incorporating major stakeholder groups more formally as part of the structure. The project board has a strategic role; the project management team has a delivery focus. These could be combined into one team but are shown separately, since this may be required in certain types of projects – for example, where different organizations are involved in the same project, it may be necessary to incorporate senior representatives from the stakeholder ('partner') organizations when the commitment of staff within the project delivery process is waning.

To the small organization, this diagram may seem superfluous. It is nevertheless important that the roles and linkages are established. Where this has been achieved, the diagram can be taken away, since it may not add any further value to the project management organization.

In summary, although this diagram looks quite 'busy', in essence it is relatively simple. Firstly, it reflects the notion that there likely will be a number of stakeholders (or stakeholder groups) who are part of the project. Here a stakeholder could represent an organization or a department within an organization.

Secondly, there are two key parts to the structure, a project board (concerned with the more strategic aspects of the project) and a project team. These could be constituted

FIGURE 3.8 Generic project management organization structure

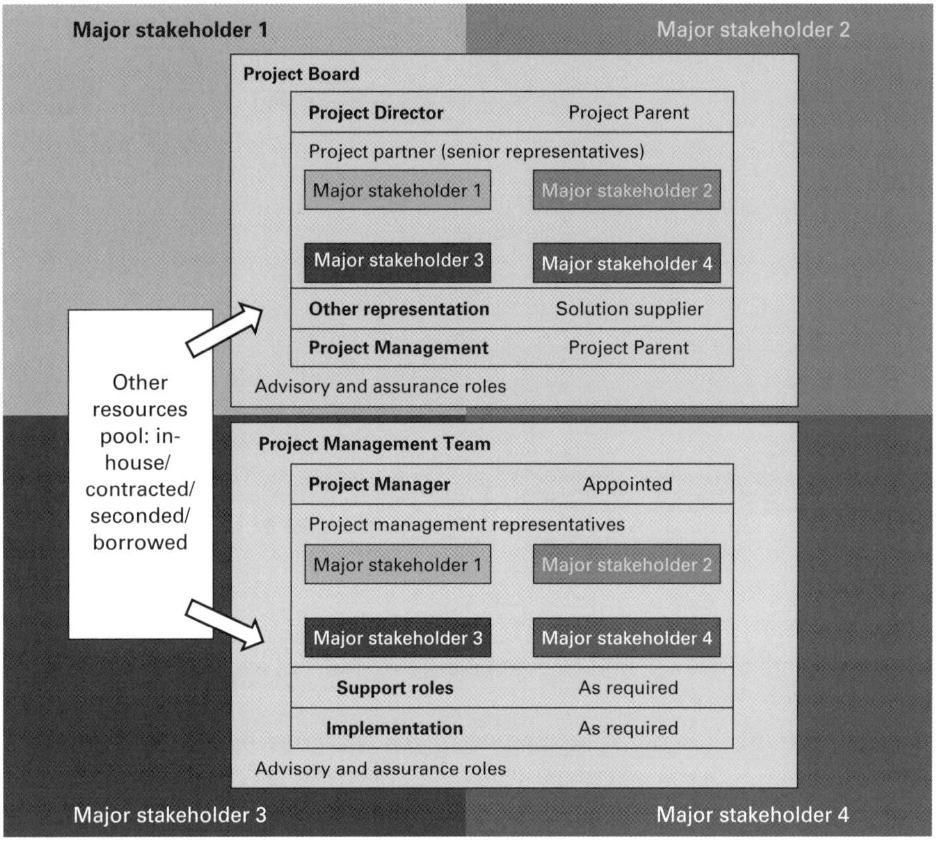

as one group, but have been represented as two, in part to emphasize the need to be clear about the role of the individual and also of the group.

Thirdly, it is very helpful if appropriate representatives from all stakeholder groups are reflected in the respective organizational grouping (both in the project board and in the project team). Fourthly, it is important that the relationship between the two groups is right, and that all individuals incorporated or active take full responsibility for their actions. A final point for the moment: this representation of the project management organization can be reduced considerably, but is shown in a fuller form here.

We also need to consider the broader context of this team – how will it receive strategic direction (beyond that which established the project activity at the outset)? What happens when there are problems requiring changes to budget, time or other parameters? This extended structure can ensure that these types of concern are considered.

It is also important to consider that a technical advisory group could provide the specialist support discussed earlier, and the value of a dedicated quality assurance (QA) role. This once again raises the issue of scalability; within a very small organization or project that takes place between small collaborating organizations, acknowledging the value of the roles may be straightforward, but the satisfactory enacting of them more difficult.

A further consideration may be associated with the nature of our activity and organizational basis; many project teams will not be co-located. With every change in the enhancement of communication technologies, and during any period of globalization, projects will be delivered across multiple geographies and cultures, and by disparate teams that could be located internationally. While this aspect will be developed further in later chapters, it is important to reflect these aspects within the preliminary project management organization.

Planning: some general aspects

The previous sections have discussed a number of approaches to planning aspects of time, cost and quality within projects. We have argued that while the first two of these are easier to formulate and visualize, they may also be difficult to estimate and present with confidence. They are subject to the problem of being relatively unknown at the start of (or before) the project, and they become known as the process takes place.

There are two key problems: one relates to the challenge of estimation, the other is in part psychological. It is worth summarizing the main methods used for estimation (APM, 2012: 126):

- comparative or analogous;
- parametric, using measurable attributes;
- bottom-up; analytical, based on the approach introduced in the previous topics.

A brief discussion of the second of these – parametric techniques – is useful. Where we have access to data from similar work, this approach can be particularly valuable. For example, if we need to work out how many bricks will be required for the building of 30 new houses of mixed design, this can be informed by using comparators to inform the analysis. Again, these provide estimates, but the technique has limitations in practice. In a contrasting example, the use of timber lengths required for an overhanging veranda on the outside of a circular building provides a challenge, since the timber is not cut at 90°, but rather at 45° or other angle reflecting the degree of curvature of the building. This caused a problem on a site where stocks of sustainably supplied timber were depleted rapidly (and in short supply). This is a further challenge for the project manager to address.

Summary

In this chapter we have explored some typical approaches often used during the planning phase of a project. We have considered the important aspect of stakeholders from a planning perspective and highlighted the benefits of being rigorous; although the breaking down of activities can be challenging, developing this as far as time, resource, cost and quality planning are concerned can be particularly valuable in helping to understand things such as the underlying logic, issues and achievability. As this is the last chapter which has a focus on projects from an ideal perspective, we have also incorporated the project management organization as a key area of planning. This will be followed by the chapters in Part Two, which introduce a range of challenges faced within the implementation of real-world projects.

We are now ready to deliver the project.

Notes

1 Morris (1994) highlights the evolution of CPM by DuPont engineers (led by Walker, M) with assistance from Remington Rand Univac (led by Kelley, J) and PERT within the Polaris programme (and subsequent adoption within NASA).

2 This case study draws upon information from the following sources:

Australian Bureau of Statistics (2000) Special article – the Sydney Olympic Games, 1 August, retrieved on 17 August 2014 from www.abs.gov.au/ausstats/abs@.nsf/featurearticlesbytitle/C1838DDB0786243CCA2569DE0029B848?OpenDocument#

BBC (2011) London 2012 at risk of exceeding budget, watchdog warns, 6 December, retrieved on 17 August 2014 from www.bbc.com/news/uk-16036435

BBC (2013) London 2012 Olympics 'have boosted UK economy by £9.9bn', 19 July, retrieved on 17 August 2014 from www.bbc.co.uk/news/uk-23370270

BBC (2014) Winter Olympics: What now for 2022 after Norway pulls out?, 2 October, retrieved on 1 November 2014 from www.bbc.co.uk/sport/0/winter-olympics/29455789

Bloomberg Businessweek (2008) Beijing Olympics—too large, too costly? Maybe not, 18 June, retrieved on 1 November 2014 from www.businessweek.com/printer/articles/305376-beijing-olympics-too-large-too-costly-maybe-not?type=old_article

The Economist (2004) A matter of priorities: those Olympic Games, 2 September

The Economist (2008) The other Olympics: passing the baton, 9 August

The Economist (2010) Field of dreams: London's Olympics, 24 July

The Economist (2012) The joy of the nudge Olympics: The London Games, 11 August

Giesecke, J and Madden, J (2007) The Sydney Olympics, seven years on: an ex-post dynamic CGE assessment, Centre of Policy Studies, Monash University

Haynes, J (2001) Socio-economic impact of the Sydney 2000 Olympic Games [online], Barcelona: Centre d'Estudis Olímpics UAB, retrieved 17 August 2014 from http://olympicstudies.uab.es/pdf/wp094_eng.pdf

Lloyds Banking and Oxford Economics (2012) The economic impact of the London 2012 Olympic and Paralympic Games, 1 July, retrieved on 17 August 2014 from www.lloydsbankinggroup.com/globalassets/documents/media/press-releases/lloyds-banking-group/2012/eco_impact_report.pdf

Malfas, M, Theodoraki, E and Houlihan, B (2004) Impacts of the Olympic Games as mega-events, *Municipal Engineer*, **157**, pp 209–20

The Sunday Times (2004) Athens losing the race to be ready on time, 29 February

References

Ackermann, F and Eden, C (2011) Strategic management of stakeholders: theory and practice, *Long Range Planning*, **44**, pp 179–96

Association for Project Management (APM) (2012) *APM Body of Knowledge*, APM, Princes Risborough, Bucks

Berry, L, Parasuraman, A and Zeithaml, V (1990) *Delivering Quality Service: Balancing customer perceptions and expectations*, The Free Press, New York

Garvin, D (1987) Competing on the eight dimensions of quality, *Harvard Business Review*, **65** (6), pp 101–08

The Guardian (2012) Olympics 2012 security: welcome to lockdown London, 12 March, retrieved on 1 November 2014 from www.theguardian.com/sport/2012/mar/12/london-olympics-security-lockdown-london

Larson, E and Larson, R (2007) Projects without borders: gathering requirements on a multicultural project can be a challenge. The right tools can make it easier, *CMA Management*, February, pp 38–39

Morris, P (1994) *The Management of Projects*, Thomas Telford Books, Newcastle-upon-Tyne

Mulcahy, R (2001) Contracts and procurement management: why should you care?, in *Project Management for Business Professionals; A comprehensive guide*, ed J Knutson, Blackwell, Oxford

PART TWO
Projects in a real world

After
the planning:
delivering projects

Introduction

Moving from the conceptual and planning phases into the process of delivery, some of the notions of the ideal project can evaporate quickly. This is often the point in the project journey where the efficacy of the prior planning is tested thoroughly; sometimes we will find that the delivery is very much as we expected, often it is different in some respects, challenging in many others.

This is to be expected, since our planning will inevitably have included elements about which we had a low level of certainty. If our project is a 'first-timer', the level of uncertainty is likely to be highest and therefore we may need to revise and re-plan activities throughout the delivery phase. If the project is similar to one we undertook previously, it is likely that areas of our planning will have been more informed, and the delivery of this type of project will be more predictable than the first-timer.

If indeed the project is a paint-by-numbers type, we will have better insight into more aspects of the activity, and therefore the delivery of this type of project might feel more like the action of converting the planning into a reality. This discussion is important; a point made to me strongly on several occasions by different Asia-Pacific students is that in some cultures the emphasis on planning is high because there is an associated expectation that if this part is done well, the project will run smoothly. We have to recognize that the type of project will inevitably have an impact on the degree to which the delivery process diverts from the prior planning.

Some aspects of the project cannot be rehearsed until we are in the delivery phase. The functioning of the project team, resource deployment, control and the emergence of problems are just some of the things that we need to manage during this phase of the project. This chapter therefore incorporates the topics developed in the conceptual and planning phases with the delivery topics we have just mentioned and any others that are specific to the dynamics of this phase. We will use examples to reflect further upon the challenge of turning our planning into successful deployment. Of course, for some of us this is our entry point into the project, which brings a host of other challenges; some will be considered in this chapter, other aspects will be developed in depth as part of later themes within the book.

Delivering: more than plan conversion

Delivering to the plan

In many respects, delivering a project is a process concerned with the conversion of planning into a completed outcome. If we have planned well, we would expect to be successful in delivery. Is this true? Well, yes and no; to an extent the answer may depend on both the quality (and flexibility) of the planning, and also on the context (and type) of the project. For a project that has strong similarity with one previously delivered (paint-by-numbers), we would expect to have more confidence. If we are delivering an as-but type of project, with some similarity (but also differences), our planning effort may need to be higher to enable us to deliver well.

A first-timer presents the highest level of uncertainty in most respects of the project, and this will provide a high challenge to the planners. Where a project has a significant stakeholder element, in terms of either the delivery or the outcome (for example, the implementation of a new pay and benefits system), the behaviour of a group affected by the development could be quite unpredictable and difficult to model in the planning. Some projects have this characteristic, perhaps akin to playing a game of chess… since we can assess the options, we can plan for the next move or two, but to plan further head for the next 10 or 15 will depend upon the reaction of the other player.

Nevertheless, we should seek to have planned sufficiently well to avoid surprises; in some scenarios, good planning followed by strong command and control will yield the project as expected. We can find extreme examples of this where a house is built in record-breaking time, or a hotel, in China, is completed in 48 hours.[1] There are many other examples of these types of activity around the world, but they have several elements in common: the activity has to be well rehearsed (or planned), it has to be well understood, everyone has to know their part in the process and, perhaps most importantly, they have to do it. Watching an accelerated-speed video of these types of activity prompts some reflection as to what is actually happening in these scenarios. Of course, we could argue that these start to fall outside our core definitions for a project.

Zhang, Zuo and Zillante (2013: 750) highlighted that construction project managers generally have a strong focus on the more traditional or hard skills, and also discuss the emphasis on planning and controlling, organizing and coordinating, predicting and managing potential problems, evaluated by Chen and Partington in 2006. In this respect, then, we could argue that in certain sectors the planning is a substantial basis for the delivery of the project.

Using the plan as a basis

A second approach to delivering the project is to use the planning as a basis for the delivery, and to acknowledge that there may be an unknown amount of development work required during the delivery phase. We need to accept that, for a variety of reasons, the delivery phase will incorporate a number of activities that require on-going development. This does not mean that particular objectives will change, rather that the project is delivered in a more iterative style and changes to the specification might be quite normal during this period. Of course, there are associated consequences; we will consider some of these later. What we are acknowledging here is a dimension of the aforementioned scope; there is a difference in the scope of the planning and the scope associated with the delivery of the project. This presents some challenges to the project manager.

Delivering a project without conspicuous planning techniques

A further and somewhat extreme variation of the delivery process is to undertake this without conspicuous prior planning. We would immediately argue that this would lead to the failure of the project, yet we may see forms of this approach in certain organizational settings or sectors – or at least that may be how it appears to the untrained eye. The lack of observable and more formalized project management is sometimes mistaken for a lack of planning, when in fact considerable informal forethought and analysis have been undertaken.

We should distinguish good planning from inappropriate planning, which can be superfluous and unnecessary. Indeed, the recent increasing prominence of project management seems to have provoked a reaction in some market sectors where having a dedicated project manager had been previously eschewed are now embracing the notion. The legal sector has provided an example of this; these organizations are based on the successful delivery of projects, where good underlying project management has to be business-as-normal. The form of this may be changing, as a feature published by *The Lawyer* in 2014 carried the headline 'Are project managers the way forward?' This article examined 'the growing trend for firms to hire specialist project managers on a firm-wide or departmental basis...' This may reveal a trend in thinking within a range of similar sectors.

Working with stakeholders

Through the early part of this book we introduced stakeholders as an important part of the project. After spending some time establishing what we meant by the term, the conceptual chapter focused on the importance of adopting a strategic approach. When considering planning, this was developed further; throughout all of these we have been promoting thoughtful yet pragmatic approaches.

At the delivery stage, this is still a particularly important aspect of the project management process, yet the way that we work with stakeholders will depend on the type of project, the position of particular groups, and the practical activities that are set in train during the delivery. Can we still regard this as a risk to the project? On which stakeholder groups do we depend? In many respects, by this time we should be regarding stakeholders as a business-as-normal element of the project management challenge. This should be an integral part of the whole process. We could summarize these activities as follows:

- Review the preparatory work with stakeholders as a basis for the ongoing management.
- Work with the different stakeholder groups in the most appropriate and effective way.
- Acknowledge that the stakeholder may own the project.
- Management processes associated with the stakeholder should be incorporated within all other appropriate project management areas.

Delivering to specification

We discussed in Chapter 2 the importance of understanding the *what* in terms of the project requirement, as the ambiguity regarding scope and specification might be either costly or contribute to difficulties with meeting delivery times. The analysis also recognized that in a project scenario where the project is a first-timer, uncertainty over the specification and scope will present challenges in the management process.

Inevitably, for almost every project scenario, the delivery phase will fully explicate the specification, through the realization of the idea and planning; the degree to which this departs from the originally defined scope will determine the time spent dealing with changes. These aspects are developed in the following sections.

Dealing with what? Specification, scope and quality

As we are now focused upon the delivery aspects of the project, the specification becomes clearer, unknowns become knowns and, in turn, this might put pressure on the scope; for example, in a systems development project the realization of the requirement into an application provides a strong basis for a need for adequate visualization. Of course, we would not want to wait until the final delivery before the potential customer uses the product, so we would wish to incorporate earlier-than-delivery sight of the system wherever possible (unless we knew exactly what they wanted!). This area provides a good basis on which to consider this aspect.

One of the challenges may then be concerned with managing the scope; users stimulated by what they can now see might be prompted to suggest additional requirements. While this immediately has an impact on the scope, we could argue that it is natural behaviour. We need to manage expectations (and therefore scope) or accept the need to meet the user requirement. Why would we choose this latter position? Projects have been set in the planning phase with some core components, including time, cost and quality management. If we are concerned to deliver the project at the right level of quality, we may need to accept a revision to the scope.

The problem that has emerged concerns the impact on these other core components. A change in the quality objective because of a change in expectation is likely to change the time and cost objectives (either or both). The word 'change' was deliberately used three times in the previous sentence to provide emphasis. The challenge presented here is how to manage different elements of the process at a point in the project where the pressure is building. This is just one area of pressure-build, but may be the first moment when the project manager needs to learn how to juggle.

Surely this should not arise, since we worked so hard on the development of a clear concept and made a substantial investment in planning the project. Taking this point, we can consider an alternative example, a paint-by-numbers or as-but project, the delivery of a conference. This type of project has been undertaken by the organization before; the person managing it is clear about the concept, and the planning is undertaken on a similar basis to previous events. The risk profile is also similar, and a number of items have been identified that might have an impact on the transportation of speakers and delegates, but contingencies have been made for these. During the early part of the delivery stage, the organization of venue, speakers, delegates, accommodation, catering and other services is going well. So is there a problem?

Around the date of arrival for speakers and delegates, an airport opens a new passenger terminal, experiencing unexpected but significant problems and causing particular issues for passengers. The scale of disruption is much greater than might have been expected; some of the speakers and delegates due to be at the conference are affected, and this has an impact on the event specification. The conference programme has to be changed. This change to specification affects the quality of the delivered project. In this second example, some might argue that the risk planning should have been better. The problem facing us is associated with dealing with the unknown. We do not have perfect knowledge, but after the delivery of the project we understand it well, but retrospectively. The project manager will have learnt from this situation and will be better equipped for the next time.

Learning point

Before moving to the next topic, concerned with the management of change within projects, it is useful to reflect on the balance between planning and action. Some of us will wish to undertake extensive and rigorous planning before delivering projects; others will instinctively want to start the delivery. We will explore these traits in Chapter 11.

Change management is project management

We have argued that some degree of change is almost inevitable; for some projects, change is central to the delivery of a product or process that has never been delivered before. Project management is change management. For some of us, accepting change management might feel like a euphemism for accepting that the planning was wrong. This is not the case, as we need to embrace change as a likely central aspect of delivering projects.

The term 'change' might also be extended in terms of our thinking. In the previous section we discussed changes to the specification; dealing with this will require appropriate project management responses. Change might apply to all aspects of the project process and, perhaps as importantly, the term will also characterize the impact of the project. For the project manager this requires skills and awareness of how to deal with internal and external change. It is worth reminding ourselves that stakeholders, as parties or individuals affecting or being affected by the project, are also key to change aspects.

During the delivery phase, some of the dimensions of change will be acute. What are the sources of change and how will we deal with this?

Sources of change

There are a number of ways that this can be framed: we can consider that change could come from the project team, client or external sources. Building on this, let us put stakeholders at the centre of our framing and use this as the basis for subsequent responses.

TABLE 4.1   Change control process: summary of approach proposed by APM

Request	The requesting stakeholder is asked to provide information; data are recorded
Review	Change is reviewed to determine high-level impact; clarification may be sought but change may be rejected
Assessment	Options captured and evaluated; impacts estimated; recommendation
Decision	Communicated to team and stakeholders
Implementation	Change is implemented after updates to plans (if change approved)

SOURCE: adapted from APM (2012: 128–29)

How will we deal with these requests for changes?

The PMI and APM both include change management planning or change control as an essential part of the knowledge associated with the execution (or delivery) of the project. The APM (2012: 128–29) propose a five-stage process, summarized in Table 4.1.

Gardiner (2005: 287–98) neatly summarized a change management plan in the following five elements:

- Identify the change.
- Analyse the effects of change.
- Develop a response strategy.
- Communicate the strategy and gain acceptance for the change.
- Revise the project plan and monitor the effects of change.

The reader is encouraged to reflect on these two similar approaches, in terms of the language adopted. The first is relatively more systematic in approach; the latter is relatively more holistic. We can embrace and adopt either of these. We have focused on this area here in order to prompt some critical thinking: a project is driven by stakeholders and it is likely to be riven with change. Attempts to maintain control of the project process may be helped by implementing the approach proposed by the APM. Further strengthening would be achieved by delivering the project within an appropriate contractual framework, as we discussed in Chapter 3.

> ### Learning point
>
> During the delivery phase, a project manager will have to deal with change. Depending upon the type of project, change will be either welcomed or feared, contributing to issues of scope or profitability, or providing opportunities to deliver solutions with high stakeholder satisfaction. This discussion opens up some more difficult areas: we took care with our planning, it was thought through, and we supported it with analysis. This could be described as taking an analytical – or scientific – approach. During the current delivery phase we are faced with change, and this challenges our planning. We respond constructively to the issues that are raised but start to realize that there is a gap between planning and delivery that is wider than we expected.

Time and schedule management

Moving from planning into delivery

Time was introduced in Chapter 1 as a core component of projects, primarily regarded as a constraint. Posing the question 'When do they want it?' in Chapter 2 helped us to develop the dimension of time as a distinct but dependent aspect of project management: distinct, in that a project might be presented as a sequence of timed stages, dependent in that each stage has a number of associated activities incorporating dimensions of the specification, costs and other relevant factors.

By breaking things down (using a 'work breakdown structure', or WBS), in Chapter 3 we developed the time aspects into time-planning bar charts and network diagrams and introduced some important vocabulary such as 'milestone' and 'critical path'. We will now explore the time component during the delivery phase; moving from planning into delivery often presents the project management team with one of several dilemmas: whether to seek to control the project in order to deliver to the time plan, or to start to address the issues that immediately arise since, in almost every case, the time plan was wrong the moment it was completed.

Emphasis, approach and style

The emphasis on time within the project management delivery process will depend, to an extent, on the importance of time relative to other key constraints. For example, if the project has a sequence of must-do milestones or a hard end-date that cannot be missed (such as those in an event project), the emphasis on time clearly is high. This type of scenario can be contrasted with other projects where meeting the specification is paramount or where the budget is the main anchor point.

There may be other reasons why time has high emphasis; for example, where it is used as a perceptual constraint in order to:

- demonstrate project management control over the project;
- generate urgency among the delivery team;
- help measure the performance of a project management team.

The approach to managing the time component will vary in the light of the emphasis and also the particular personal importance attached by the project manager. Figure 4.1 highlights scenarios that emerge, ranging from time being the highest-order constraint to scenarios where it is subordinate to others.

For example, at the highest level this could be represented by a project concerned with the delivery of a major event (or item of infrastructure) with expectations from

FIGURE 4.1 Emphasis of time within the project

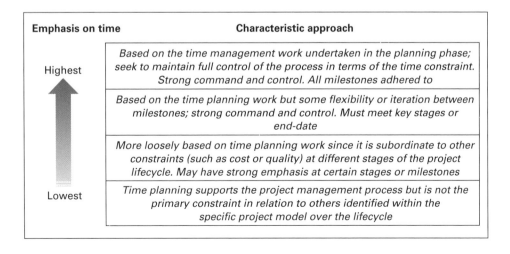

Emphasis on time	Characteristic approach
Highest	Based on the time management work undertaken in the planning phase; seek to maintain full control of the process in terms of the time constraint. Strong command and control. All milestones adhered to
	Based on the time planning work but some flexibility or iteration between milestones; strong command and control. Must meet key stages or end-date
	More loosely based on time planning work since it is subordinate to other constraints (such as cost or quality) at different stages of the project lifecycle. May have strong emphasis at certain stages or milestones
Lowest	Time planning supports the project management process but is not the primary constraint in relation to others identified within the specific project model over the lifecycle

a significant number of stakeholders (or on which many others depend immediately). At the lowest level, the group could include the outcome from projects that are concerned with ensuring the safe operation of equipment or systems (such as the supply of hydrogen as a fuel for vehicles). The middle two could include examples where time flexibility is a necessity owing to the requirement of technological breakthrough (but thereafter a firm delivery schedule can be put in place) and, in multi-organization projects, where limited flexibility is important owing to constraints inherent within the overall structure.

The emphasis can also oscillate over the life of a project, and our management during the delivery phase must reflect this. In terms of the style adopted, communicating and managing aspects of the schedule, milestone or detailed time planning will be determined by the collective experience and personality of the team, and also by the expectations of stakeholders. For example, we may wish to provide this as a strong visual in the project management environment, as a 'dashboard' or on mounted display-boards (sometimes intended to generate urgency or stimulate competition). The availability of an ever-increasing range of platforms and suppliers providing project management information systems gives us plenty of options – and difficult choices to make. There is no one way to do this; style will vary from environment to environment.

Managing using schedules and milestones

As a means of demonstrating the sequence of milestones and associated activities, a schedule is a valuable management tool for the project manager. A time-planning bar chart is a common example of a scheduling technique, which can be developed at a high or low level (ie summary or detail). The management of the time constraint is a multifarious activity. At the summary level, it is important to be managing in a more strategic manner. At the same time, it is vital to be aware of the important details that might make the difference to success or failure of a stage or the project overall.

The schedule will contain milestones, and these can provide a particularly effective means of monitoring progress. Andersen (2008: 132) sets out the use of milestones as building blocks; Gardiner (2005: 289) highlights the value of milestone monitoring, arguing that it is a simple method ('needing only a modest amount of management effort to set up and maintain') and that it 'can be used when the project plans or schedules are not particularly detailed'. The project activity either meets the milestone (100 per cent), or it doesn't. Milestone monitoring brings project activities into sharp focus.

Time realities: forecast and actual

So far we have highlighted that much of the managing of time within projects is based upon uncertainty and therefore required estimating. As such, it is always likely that some aspects of our statements, charts or plans will be wrong. At the end of delivering the project, this may not present any problem, since we took a flexible approach to planning, responded with corrective actions when needed, presented this to the project management team and stakeholders in an appropriate way, and managed to deliver what was required when it was required.

Throughout the project there may be a difference between the forecast and actual. While these terms might look more familiar in an accounting context, they have currency here too – a forecast time for an activity, an actual time. The forecast contained assumptions, the actual reflects the reality, with accompanying explanations where necessary. Do we monitor these in the same way as forecast and actual numbers in a budget? In some ways, yes we do; if we continue to see a target time missed, increasingly we will doubt the effectiveness of the estimating or the ability of the project resource. There is a psychological effect here. In order to maintain effective management of the delivery process, we might start to change our style, for example by bringing forward deadlines or creating artificial ones.

Analysis, variance, response

Increasingly, our opportunity to analyse is significant. We routinely store large amounts of data and information, and have access to tools that help us build databases without thinking that we are doing it. We create digital resources of messages and calendars and almost unwittingly benefit from the opportunity presented by easy-to-use search facilities that enable the associated analysis. It is also difficult to lose information, since it exists in many places even if we try to lose it. What does this give us? Well, during the management of the project we could spend considerable effort analysing our time planning. We can evaluate the milestone summary, the time-planning bar chart or the network diagram: Where is the slack? How can we bring things forward?

There are three core areas that we should be concerned with: firstly, the value of analysis. Whether we start with a review of the achievement of milestones, from an assessment of a time-planning bar chart, or because of something that crops up within a project stage review activity, we will often need to analyse the situation. We will inevitably look at the progress made, framed by where we believe it should be, and this will reveal the variance – the difference between these. The level of this difference will determine the appropriate response.

It is always important to keep a sense of perspective and also to recognize that we will often need to be pragmatic. Acknowledging we got something wrong is a good route to solving a problem. Using an appropriate analysis process will help to reveal slippage. How do we deal with this? What is causing the problem? What do we do about it? The quality of our response to slippage, where time is a key constraint in our project, will make a big difference to the achievement, stages, objectives and the project overall. We have explored a number of tools introduced during the planning phase and considered how useful they are during delivery.

This latter aspect will develop as inherent elements of later chapters, but at this stage it is useful to recognize that the achievement of milestones is not solely a mechanistic process; there is normally a significant human dimension. To end this part of the discussion, let us reconsider briefly an example from earlier, the major sporting event. The final deadline has to be met. Although people will work at different speeds over the life of the project, a strong component of this activity is concerned with urgency and motivation.

Resource management

Planning, management, planning, management

In Chapter 1, we introduced the project model and the mechanisms that enable the delivery of projects. This set included people, tools, techniques and equipment, and could also be described as the set of resources required to convert the idea or concept into the outcome. As we developed our initial thinking within the conceptual phase of the project, the focus was on things such as the establishment of what would be required, or how it might be delivered. In each of these, we sought as much clarity as is possible at early stages.

In Chapter 3 we argued that breaking down the proposed project using a WBS would help to inform the project planning; this would include the articulation of required resources, thereby leading to resource planning. In this chapter we will explore the area of resource management. Although it is subsequent in topic sequence, it is worth highlighting that both topics could be enacted many times during the delivery sequences, as new information becomes available.

Resource management is general management

This topic provides a good example of the project manager utilizing skills and knowledge that are normally associated with general management. Hitt, Black and Porter (2009: 9) regard managing resources as 'a major part of a manager's job', adding that the manager needs 'to ensure the efficient use of resources' and also to 'use resources in ways that maximize the achievement of the organization's goal'. They also discuss the building and managing of 'a portfolio of resources' and the need for managers 'to allocate and coordinate' these.

We can translate these into a project manager role and this helps provide a focus for the type of challenges typically faced during the delivery phase. One further point to make is that we need the skill-set and experience associated with resource management to be focused in the domain of projects. Often the project with a tight timeframe will have resource requirements that do not fit well with the management processes established within a parent organization.

For example, funds have been successfully secured for a project that will take place in a relatively more bureaucratic and unenlightened government organization operating in the educational sector. Resources required by the project include a number of specialist skills not available within the organization, and these require procurement for the delivery phase. The parent organization insists that standard recruitment procedures must be followed, leading to a minimum three-month lead-time until appointment. If the project delivery phase is expected to last a maximum 12 months, this dynamic could have a significant bearing on the success or failure of the project.

There are four important areas relating to resource management: efficiency, maximization, resource portfolios and the allocation and coordination of these. It is difficult to propose generalized principles to achieve efficiency since the use of resources will depend on the specific context of the project and resources. However, we can say that resources need to be managed efficiently in project environments, as they have a cost when they are – and when they are not – being used. Project managers are likely to understand this well, since they may have put together the original cost plan and budget, and therefore recognize the value of the resources to the project.

With regard to maximizing the achievement of resources, we can make a consideration here similar to that in the previous point: if the project has been instigated to maximize the organization's goals, resource management should be focused on these goals through the project. The project manager should be fully aware of this. If this is not the case, this is clearly an area requiring personal development and enhancement. There may be an argument for the project parent to ensure that staff tasked with delivering projects should be adequately trained, made aware of any resource-maximizing processes or provided with direct support. Related to these last points, staff associated with procurement should be involved in, or at least made aware of, the early stages of a project.

In terms of building and managing the resource portfolio, during the life of a project a host of knowledge and physical assets are brought together or created. This portfolio of resources is therefore established for the project and it needs to be managed. Although this is a key area of responsibility for the project manager, the ownership of specific resources (owned by or borrowed for the project) can make some aspects of this ambiguous.

Scenarios that emerge could include the need for service level agreements (SLAs)[2] or short-term contracts, as well as those with more informal arrangements. For example, if a project requires a data centre and significant computing power, options to provide this cost-effectively could include third-party hosting. This is part of the resource portfolio but access to it is achieved via a contract and SLA.

The final aspect, allocating and coordinating, builds on the discussion developed in the previous points: the power to allocate and coordinate resources within the project will, to some degree, depend on the autonomy of the project. Higher project autonomy will enable the management of project resources to be undertaken with greater focus and speed; lower project autonomy may well require considerably higher effort to allocate and coordinate, if the project manager does not have ownership of the resources.

CASE STUDY   JLR Evoque[3]

International project – Indian investment; British brand; timely global customers

Introduction

As a 'downsized, tarted-up reengineering of the SUV for the 21st century' (*Financial Times*, 2012), the Range Rover Evoque has certainly transformed the fortunes of the Jaguar Land Rover group, a formerly ailing British car manufacturer which has seen its fortunes turn around since being purchased by Tata in 2008. By 2012, a headline 'Made in Britain. Saved in India. Craved in China: How the Jaguar Land Rover Group was saved… by Indian cash and Chinese drivers' (*Daily Mail*, 2012) captured the essence of the transformation at the JLR group: Indian investment in a historical British brand popular in markets that were strong due to growth in the economies in China, Russia and Brazil. The Evoque model was a big contributor to this situation.

Tata bought the car maker just prior to a crisis in the industry that took hold from 2008; the crisis led to the contraction of sales to the United States and the halving of some international markets. These were difficult times for JLR and the wisdom of the purchase was questioned. The enthusiasm of Mr Tata for the brand did not seem to affect his managerial approach or strategy. The running of his business was left to Ralf Speth, the CEO from early 2010, and the autonomy afforded the British management was variously attributed to the subsequent success of the business. An ambitious plan to build new cars succeeded in part because of the compromise and cooperation that maintained good industrial relations; the five-year plan to invest £1.75bn over five years saw a flexibility in working arrangements and remuneration which was quite an achievement given the history of this industry in the UK.

The project

The JLR Evoque project was complex (MagBook, 2013): here was the development of a completely new car that would be based upon an original concept; it was to be futuristic, needed to have strong road-handling characteristics but also needed to be more capable than its competitors when being used off-road. The engineering of the off-road capability provided a significant challenge: in developing the Evoque, JLR wanted to reduce the weight of the vehicle as much as possible. Achieving good off-road capabilities puts a vehicle under a higher-than-normal level of stress, so it needs to be stronger than an equivalent vehicle that doesn't do this. This prompted the use of lightweight materials wherever possible, with clever design innovations to overcome the futuristic design, such as the integration of aerial and telematics equipment within the rear spoiler. The use of aluminium in different areas of the vehicle helped to limit the mass of the Evoque.

An interesting aspect of this particular development was the choice made to develop a vehicle based on one design; this helps with the speed of the process. The testing process involved running the vehicle in hot deserts, on race tracks, under high-load towing and with high stress placed on the braking system. At peak, 500 people worked on the development project; it is noticeable that articles featuring the activity use the terms 'programme' in relation to the engineering and 'portfolio' in relation to the parent organization. This was clearly a complex and energetic development project that required substantial innovation and effective management.

Market

The success of the Evoque in international markets saw the Halewood plant in the North West of the UK operating 24-hour production in late 2012 and a trebling of staff from 2010. Given the impact of the sub-prime and Eurozone crises, this scenario reflects the successful delivery of the right product at the right time; the purchasing ability of brand-conscious consumers was helped by other factors such as favourable exchange rates. It seems that some customers regarded the JLR vehicles as a novelty, with one Chinese buyer dismissing comparable models from other high-end marques, saying that 'anybody in China can have a Mercedes-Benz' (*New York Times*, 2012).

This final point is perhaps part of a combination of factors behind the success of this project. Wise investment, effective management arrangements, good design, favourable market conditions and some more unusual factors have contributed to the success of both the Evoque and JLR overall. As the *Daily Telegraph* reported in 2013, 'the Indian industrialist has proved the sceptics wrong in a spectacular fashion. A relaxed but adventurous business style, a product range that holds more appeal and a little luck has turned JLR into the business "steal" of the decade.'

Although there will be difficult strategic issues to overcome in the future development of the business, the Evoque model has helped put JLR on a strong footing; in 2014 *The Guardian* reported that while the purchase by Tata of both Land Rover and Jaguar had been described as 'reverse colonialism' almost six years earlier, 'manufacturing at its West Midlands bases has thrived since'. They also remarked that the takeover that reflected an east to west power shift also highlighted the complementarity of the firm's historical roots, traditional employment rights and the principles of the 'most enlightened British industrialists'.

In February 2014, the BBC reported that 'Jaguar Land Rover quarterly profits double to £842m', and that during 2013 as a whole, JLR sold a record 426,006 saloons and SUVs, with sales particularly strong in Brazil, China, India and the United States. The cyclical nature of markets will provide a source of future challenge; currently the JLR group is enjoying success. New projects will need to provide the bridge to the next ideas to maintain production at record high levels.

Case reflection

i Evaluate the project delivery aspects of the case scenario in relation to the strategic brand impact on the business; what were the risks, significant change aspects and opportunities?

ii Determine the key challenges associated with delivering the aspiration, meeting stakeholder expectations and the inherent resourcing, budget and management aspects.

iii Discuss the project from the perspective of the people involved: in directing, managing, delivering, negotiating and inspiring.

Cost and budget management

This is an important element of the project manager's responsibilities. Although it may take different forms depending upon the scale, sector and geography, there is a common need to have effective financial management processes. This presents a number of challenges. Firstly, this may involve the use of skills of which we lack experience or are not confident (conversely, we may need to ensure balance of project management style if we have strong financial management skills). Secondly, the project manager needs to also be aware that the parent organization is likely to have rules and regulations that seek to ensure that funds are disbursed effectively and appropriately; thirdly, we may be trying to maintain control of a budget which was poorly estimated prior to our involvement or is inappropriate for the expectations associated with the activity. This is not an exhaustive list; other issues will emerge.

Although much of this aspect of the project management role is associated with the appropriate committing of funds, evaluation acuities and ensuring that adequate records are maintained, there are linkages of financing with almost all other aspects of the project management process. For example, if a scenario facing a multinational business arises due to the change in labour costs across territories or geographies, good cost management suggests that a production facility should be relocated to take advantage of this. The financial argument and management of the budget may be relatively straightforward compared with the stakeholder issues that need to be managed.

Keeping cost under control

The notion of cost was introduced in the first chapter as one of a number of constraints within a generalized project model. In Chapter 2, by asking the questions 'What is required?' and 'How much will it cost?' we started to explore the cost aspect within projects, acknowledging that this may have a pre-start upper limit or be something completely unknown at the start.

Within Chapter 3 we argued that the resources required to deliver the project would provide a basis to estimate costs, leading in turn to the establishment of a project budget. Or, following elements of the approach above, the overall budget limit might already have been set for the project; nevertheless, the resource planning would inform the setting out of the budget, clearly with a goal of maintaining expenditure within the limits stated.

In this chapter we will consider the cost component in a project scenario where the challenge presented is often one of maintaining the spend in accordance with the forecasted budget levels. We should also bear in mind that the management of a budget involves a second component: income. A financing process will underpin the delivery of the project. Whether the project takes place in the public or private sector, the financing mechanism is very important, as it will inform a further set of processes for the management of the project. In the following sections we will discuss budget and cost management in a more generalized form.

The style and format

The style and format of cost and budget management will vary depending upon the project type, context and the organizational setting in which it is delivered. For example, although it might have had some difficulties securing the financing for a new project, a small business may have higher autonomy with the financial aspects of its activity when compared with a public-sector organization involved in an externally funded multi-party project. An autonomous private-sector business will often notice that its processes for any associated procurement seem less bureaucratic than those in environments where it is deemed very important to have appropriate checks and balances.

However, whatever the circumstances and setting for an individual project, money is still money, and ultimately the management of this aspect will always retain similarities. For project activities there will be budgets; there will always be expenditure and, for some, income; through the life of the project, 'forecasts' will become 'actuals'; during this period there will be analysis, variances, issues and responses; individual and aggregate activities will need to be accounted for. This is another example where project management meets general management; these are management processes vital in the running of any organization.

Furthermore, there will be organizational processes and rules which need to be followed, some very carefully, certainly where audits are a likely component of wider governance processes. The accounting aspects of projects are important, but the perceived nature of some of the associated activities perhaps reinforces the notion that cost is a project constraint, as we introduced in Chapter 1.

Activities and budgets

It is likely that much of the work for this particular topic will have been done in the planning phase of the project. If it hasn't, we will need to address this in order to perform the cost and budget management. In Table 3.3 we considered how the building up of project budgets from resource planning would provide a basis for managing costs. At the delivery phase of the project, we would expect to use this foundation work as the basis. It may need to be revised in terms of structure and content, but this will now provide one aspect of the monitoring, control and reporting that we discussed in the section above on 'Managing using schedules and milestones'.

Expenditure and income

We often see these words together in a different sequence as income and expenditure. There is an intended subtle psychological effect of seeing the word expenditure (or cost) first here. In projects there will always be an expenditure (in one form or another), but the income will have different connotations depending on whether the project is income generating (typified by a new market project undertaken by a private-sector business), or whether income to the project is provided through some form of internal or external funding. Projects associated with external funding could be concerned with delivering a public-sector asset (such as a public building or infrastructure works); internally funded projects might include those concerned with enacting some form of change within an organization, such as the introduction of a new management structure.

By expenditure we mean costs, and in projects these are often the aspect that is monitored and reported most frequently. Given the need to account also for sources of funding, it is likely that the project manager will need to manage some form of cash-flow statement, as this is a particularly effective mechanism to bring the two together. Cash-flow statements often provide one basis of the overall reporting.

Forecast and actual

The uncertainty at the early stages of a project will therefore have required estimates. Aggregated estimates provide the basis for forecasts, and forecasting expenditure is an essential element of the ongoing planning process; updating these through the delivery phase, estimates become actuals and greater clarity is achieved in terms of the actual cost of the project. Depending on the effectiveness of the original estimating process, this can provide a source of concern.

Analysis and variance

It is important to undertake sufficient analysis in order to determine whether the level of expenditure is as expected, acceptable or of concern. For example, if the delivery phase of a project takes place over six months and the expected expenditure is highly consistent at £3,000 per month, we would expect to see £9,000 spent by the end of month 3, as per Table 4.2.

If the actual at the end of month 3 is in fact £8,000 (a variance of −£1,000), is this a problem? Similarly, if the actual had been £10,000 (a variance of +£1,000), would this also present a problem? The answer to both questions is possibly 'yes', possibly 'no'. Without further information we do not know the answer, so we would need to ask some questions.

The example serves to raise a couple of points to consider:

- Rarely will forecasted values become exactly the actual values.
- The shape of the spend may not be linear (increasing in a graph as a straight line).

TABLE 4.2 Monthly and cumulative expenditure

Month	1	2	3	4	5	6
Expenditure (monthly)	3,000	3,000	3,000	3,000	3,000	3,000
Expenditure (cumulative)	3,000	6,000	9,000	12,000	15,000	18,000

- An under-spend may be good for one group of stakeholders (those managing cash during a period of cash-flow pressure) but not for another, as it might reflect a delay to works that should have taken place.

- We might make false conclusions from the information provided.

Extended versions of Table 4.2 are routinely used to monitor and control the budget aspects of projects. The example in Figure 4.2 shows the movement of the spend as stated at project review meetings; you can see the movement of the estimate at each review stage and the final outturn, which is lower than the 'contract sum'. Specific responses to concerns raised will need to be managed appropriately. This could include problems related to over- or under-spend. Although the former is more likely, both are possible, and our response approach will need to address the particular issue. This could involve negotiation for further funding or taking uncomfortable decisions regarding spend. Similar approaches might be required to ensure there is a carry-over when funds are not spent, or an appropriate response when this is not possible.

Management responsibilities in this area could include a number of other aspects, for example where a project has time conditions attached; in some, the invoicing process has to be completed in a specific timeframe, and this provides a further sub-contractor management function for the project manager.

The people part: delivering through the structure and team

What we envisaged and what emerged

During the conceptual phase the project team may not have existed. We argued that a key aspect of planning would be to establish the structure, roles and responsibilities that comprise the project management organization. The delivery phase tests the robustness of the intended structure; the structure, in turn, reflects the arrangement of people who provide management and/or resources to the project. The adequacy of this important project-enabler is tested. If this part does not function well, we add it to a growing list of things that will undermine the work undertaken during the early phases of the project. We can also reflect on these as risks.

What are the key challenging elements within the project management structure? Aside from the more obvious aspects of structure, role and responsibility which we have already highlighted above, this area could potentially be very wide, since it is about managing people, relationships and teams. We could also reason that it is about aspects of culture, language, ethics and gender. In fact, we could argue that it

FIGURE 4.2　Example showing progressive budget tracking

Budget management

The chart in this example shows two key measures, the 'contract sum' and 'estimated outturn'. The budget is reviewed at each project meeting and the outturn is estimated for each one (as best known at the time); this is informed by known variations (which is determined by comparing the omissions and additions). In this example, at the time of the final review meeting the spend was running lower than the contract sum.

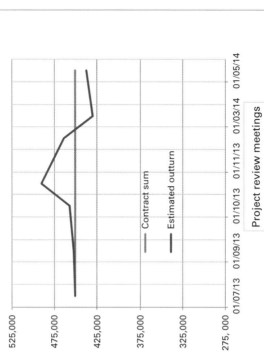

Currency	04/07/13	29/09/13	06/11/13	10/12/13	28/02/14	28/03/14	31/05/14
Contract sum	450,000	450,000	450,000	450,000	450,000	450,000	450,000
Estimated outturn	450,000	452,000	457,025	490,005	462,950	430,145	437,125

Variations						
Omissions	-4,000	-8,000	-10,000	-35,000	-40,000	-27,875
Additions	6,000	15,025	50,005	47,950	20,145	15,000
Over/under spend	2,000	7,025	40,005	12,950	-19,855	-12,875

is absolutely central to the success or otherwise of the project. This chapter opened with a delivery-phase consideration of stakeholders; this last section will start to explore the fundamental project-people part, opening a number of core topics that will provide a platform for further development in the second half of the book.

In order to provide a basis for this preliminary discussion, let us use a figure from Chapter 3, the project management organization scenario. We can use it to explore the core topics of structure, roles and responsibilities, and teams during the delivery phase. For each heading we will explore a commonly encountered problem in order to prime our thinking.

A first view of the impact of structure during the delivery phase

When we introduced a potential structure such as that in Figure 4.3, we recognized that this would be appropriate as a general model, helping to establish the underlying

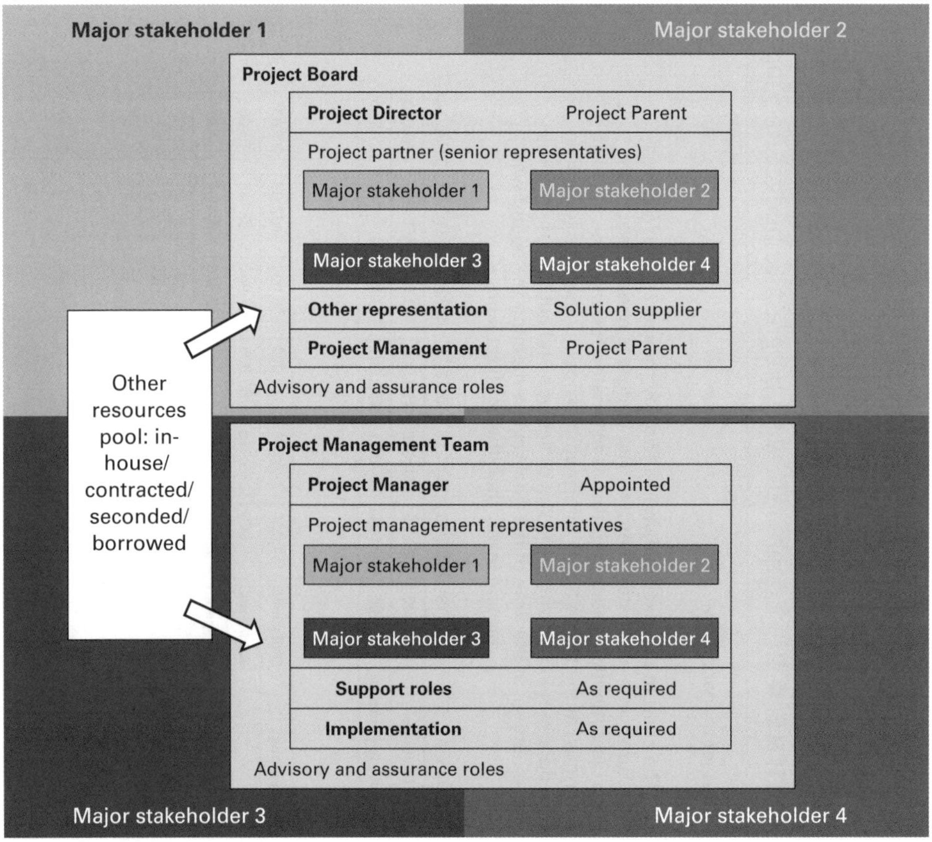

FIGURE 4.3   Generic project management organization structure

anatomy of the way the management of the project management is organized. We also highlighted that this approach should be tailored to a particular project scenario; in a more extreme form, with a very small project in terms of participating organization and people, the project board and the project team could merge into a single entity. We argued correspondingly that the important aspect is to reflect adequately the roles and responsibilities.

One aspect that was not discussed relates to the impact of the project organizational structure in relation to the underlying or background structure prevalent in the parent, stakeholder or other project delivery (or participant) organization. This is often a source of difficulty and takes up, in aggregate form, considerable management time. A common issue arises in situations where we find that we have two (or more) bosses, shown in Figure 4.4.

Arising from the use of matrix approaches, the situation is quite commonly encountered but the impact is often not understood. Either through the explicit appointment of a project manager or the emergence of a new activity, an individual in the existing organizational hierarchy gets involved in one or more projects, leading to a situation of having multiple bosses (see Figure 4.4). This is quite a simple concept, but raises a number of issues centred on conflicting priorities, and who is in the best position to resolve it. Running projects within a matrix style can be shown in two extremes. Firstly, in a heavyweight form, the team members are involved through secondment (or equivalent mechanism). Secondly, in a lightweight form, members participate but their objectives and performance management still take place at the functional level. Motivation and participation level can vary between these two scenarios, creating significant challenges for the respective project manager.

FIGURE 4.4   The emergence of two (or more) bosses

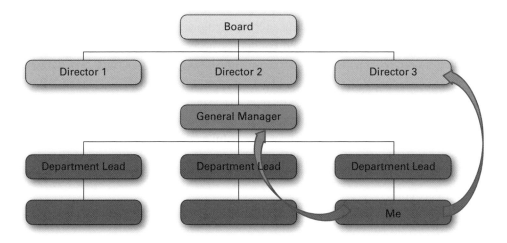

There are ways of resolving these issues, largely through being aware of the problem. Diagrams reveal things quite quickly, yet it is often not obvious when a management team is stretched, struggling to deal with the symptoms of the problem. Busy people in busy environments sometimes need to take a step back to reveal the source of a particular problem, and this could be an example of something we might need to address under the heading 'problem solving and decision making'.

Roles and responsibilities

The definition of roles and responsibilities during the planning phase is very helpful but not an end in itself. We can anticipate how these might look, but we have a greater understanding of the situation in the delivery phase. With some similarity to other topics in this chapter (such as those relating to cost and time), there will be a difference between forecast and actual.

Here we are moving into the areas of human resource management and organizational behaviour, and project managers may realize that the hats they need to wear are getting more numerous at every stage of the project. This is to be expected. Roles and responsibilities were defined; there are difficulties with this, associated with the aforementioned change from forecast to actual, with recruitment, personality, and pressures from the structure such as the two-bosses problem. Having been challenged by the need to understand a number of salient financial management concepts, project managers have to draw on a range of soft skills as they find a need to understand what is meant by 'emotional intelligence', recognizing that every member of the team has unique DNA with completely different personalities, preferences, motivation and abilities.

It's a team game

The project is delivered by a team. We can use a sporting metaphor immediately. A great idea (or aspiration) is followed by meticulous planning; a heavy investment in commitment and financing often counts for little if the team does not perform. Building on the comments made in the previous two topics, this third area presents a further challenge. If the team has come together during the delivery phase, this is the period when it will experience its own lifecycle, especially if the team ceases to exist once the project ends. This is a significant branch of knowledge that we need to build in order to ensure that we deliver successful projects. We may have planned the project as if it were to be assembled of toy blocks, but individual and collective human factors should not be underestimated. We will develop this very important area in Part Four.

Summary

In this chapter we have examined some of the challenges associated with moving from a conceptual and planning mode into one concerned with delivery. We have considered the contrast between the processes of preparation and those more often associated with a relatively dynamic role; from working with stakeholders, dealing with change and other parameters, the project manager role is often at its most active during the delivery of a project.

This has impacts in terms of meeting expectations within timeframes and the need to manage budgets; this could also mean negotiating for more of each of these. We concluded by developing some initial perspectives regarding the project management organization. This chapter has also revealed the extent to which project managers, whoever and wherever they are, need to have a wide skill-set and an insight into the character of themselves, the team and the project. We have moved into the delivery phase and will continue to explore some linked themes in the next chapter.

Notes

1 Examples such as a 'world record for house speed building' retrieved on 4 November 2014 from https://www.youtube.com/watch?v=O0ph0rA-A9U and the construction of a hotel in China completed in 48 hours retrieved on 4 November 2014 from http://www.youtube.com/watch?v=FynWETakS9U

2 Used commonly in many industries, service level agreements (SLAs) are intended to provide a basis for the agreement of a specified level of service between two parties. For an example see http://www.slatemplate.com/

3 This case study draws upon information from the following sources:
BBC (2014) 'Jaguar Land Rover quarterly profits double to £842m', 10 February, retrieved on 22 August 2014 from http://www.bbc.co.uk/news/business-26120593
Financial Times (2012) The car that saved JLR, 28 September, retrieved on 22 August 2014 from http://www.ft.com/cms/s/2/93481c40-0831-11e2-a2d8-00144feabdc0.html#slide0
Daily Mail (2012) Made in Britain. Saved in India. Craved in China: How the Jaguar Land Rover group was saved… by Indian cash and Chinese drivers, 25 August, retrieved on 27 September 2014 from http://www.dailymail.co.uk/home/moslive/article-2192468/Jaguar-Land-Rover-Made-Britain-Saved-India-Craved-China-How-group-saved–Indian-cash-Chinese-drivers.html.
The Guardian (2014) Tata: the Indian powerhouse behind Jaguar Land Rover success, 12 January, retrieved on 22 August 2014 from http://www.theguardian.com/business/2014/jan/12/tata-indian-powerhouse-behind-jaguar-success/print
MagBook (2013) *Land Rover: Past, present and future*, Dennis Publishing, London

New York Times (2012) Tata Motors finds success in Jaguar Land Rover, 30 August, retrieved on 22 August 2014 from http://www.nytimes.com/2012/08/31/business/global/tata-motors-finds-success-in-jaguar-land-rover.html?pagewanted=all&_r=0

Daily Telegraph (2013) Jaguar Land Rover: £1.3bn Tata gamble pays off as big cat purrs at last, 15 September, retrieved on 22 August 2014 from http://www.telegraph.co.uk/finance/newsbysector/transport/10310725/Jaguar-Land-Rover-1.3bn-Tata-gamble-pays-off-as-big-cat-purrs-at-last.html

References

Andersen, E (2008) *Project Management: An organisational perspective*, Pearson Education, Harlow

Association for Project Management (APM) (2012) *APM Body of Knowledge*, APM, Princes Risborough, Bucks

Chen, P and Partington, D (2006) Three conceptual levels of construction project management work, *International Journal of Project Management*, **24** (5), 412–21

Gardiner, P (2005) *Project Management: A strategic planning approach*, Palgrave McMillan, Basingstoke

Hitt, M, Stewart Black, J and Porter, L (2009) *Management*, Pearson Education, Harlow

The Lawyer (2014) Are project managers the way forward?, 28 February, retrieved on 20 July 2014 from http://www.thelawyer.com/analysis/the-lawyer-management/editors-note/are-project-managers-the-way-forward/3007478.article

Zhang, F, Zuo, J and Zillante, G (2013) Identification and evaluation of the key social competencies for Chinese construction project managers, *International Journal of Project Management*, **31**, pp 748–59

Managing to completion

05

LEARNING OUTCOMES

By applying the topics within this chapter you should be able to:

- recognize the need to manage actively throughout the delivery phase;

- reflect upon the value of managing risk and the challenge of maintaining control;

- determine generic approaches to deal with questions, problems and decision making;

- explore approaches to achieve salience in project reporting and communicating;

- understand the emphasis in completing and closing projects;

- explain the need for effective handover and resource management during this phase.

Introduction

In this chapter we will further consider activities that are necessarily part of managing the project delivery process. Complementing those introduced in Chapter 4, this group includes proactively managing risk and undertaking appropriate activities to maintain control of the process. These important activities help to move the project towards completion.

We will focus on the dynamic challenges faced by project managers presented by questions, problems, and the need to make the right decisions. The chapter will also highlight the value of analysis to inform decision making and will explore the area of reporting in project environments, in terms of perceived requirement and the difficulty of avoiding information overload.

The chapter will conclude by exploring the activities that take place towards or at completion, including handover actions. We will consider a number of scenarios that would have different means of determining whether they are complete, and reflect on some aspects of the resource management challenges that emerge at this stage of a project.

Managing actively

In order to steer the project through the delivery phase to completion, it is important to actively manage a number of areas that might have been developed more passively during the planning phase; this could be likened to the difference between activities taking place offline and online. Although we could argue otherwise, in some project settings the conceptual and planning phases include a number of activities that could be deemed relatively more passive, in that there is limited active response or resistance to them. By this we mean that it is possible to build a grand plan because it will not be tested fully until the delivery phase. The counter-argument to this is that undertaking feasibility analyses will have mitigated this aspect, but in reality it is at the delivery stage that project management is often most active.

For example, a project manager could spend hours, weeks or even months undertaking substantial analysis, building time-planning bar charts and risk profiles, in order to ensure that the planning is sufficient as the basis for a major engineering refurbishment project. Much of this time is largely focused upon rehearsing the project. This does not mean that all of the early-stage activities are passive – in contrast, the development of a new public building might have provided a traumatic experience for some, especially if they presented this to a stakeholder group who reacted emotionally against the concept or the project. This counter-example is the type of scenario that the project manager has to deal with and is quite normal during the delivery phase; this is about the conversion of planning into action, the change from unknowns into knowns. We will therefore focus on this aspect in this section, and split it into four areas:

- managing risk in the delivery phase;
- effective monitoring and control; reviewing;
- the emergence of problems and the need for decisions;
- reporting; communicating.

Managing risk in the delivery phase

In Chapter 1 we explored the core aspects of uncertainty and risk, and argued that these are core components of project management. Further, we reasoned that there is a strong relationship between project management and risk management. It is with this in mind that risk is the first topic in this section. What does risk management look like during the delivery phase of a project?

First of all, as an ever-present and endemic consideration, it should be continuously reviewed though the conceptual, planning and delivery phases as a business-as-normal activity, but the context of the organization and the project might frame the actual approach taken. Bringing forward our example from Chapter 1, we saw an organization setting out the risk profile in five areas; the associated risk register included risks in these categories. These provide the basis for risk aspects to be managed in the delivery phase. This, of course, does not mean that it defines the entire set of risks that might affect the project; doubtless, actions under way in the delivery phase will raise additional ones.

The important point here is to ensure that the set of risks, which may be presented in the form of a register, is reviewed and updated, and that appropriate actions are taken as a result of this. With experience, the project manager will develop an approach that will ensure that this happens efficiently and effectively (and ideally, therefore, optimally), where the introduction and evaluation can then take place without the audience or participants feeling that it has been overdone. This is about achieving salience.

Monitoring and control

We mentioned earlier that, for some, time-planning bar charts once epitomized project management; now, we could argue that monitoring and control is another of those areas that many regard as a key mechanism to ensure success in the project. While this is largely true, it is important to recognize a limiting aspect of these management mechanisms that we will need to deploy during the delivery phase: if we have got something wrong in our planning, it doesn't matter how well we monitor and control it… it will still be wrong. This is nevertheless a very important aspect of the project management role. After all, if we do not measure, we cannot monitor, and we cannot analyse to understand what we need to do to make adjustments in order to keep the process in control.

While we have already explored the need to maintain control of scope, time and schedule management, resource, cost and budget management, it is also worth highlighting that we need to ensure that this is applied to all the parameters that were used as the basis for the planning of our project. For example, if there are a set of milestones leading to the final deadline for the delivery of the new conference event, we will be measuring and monitoring against these; this will then form the basis of any analysis and inform any adjustments, or corrective actions, that need to be made. We are seeking to keep this part of the project process in control, to meet the deadline.

The same principles should be applied to the other parameters (such as cost); this will generate a different set of management parameters and potentially quite different challenges. With experience, the project manager will determine the balance required between a justified urge to keep the project in control and the need for the team to feel that they are not being over-managed or overly scrutinized. Beware of the risk of exerting control in an inappropriate style, for example within the context of stakeholder groups or choosing the wrong approach while seeking to control the people part; we need to ensure that we adopt the appropriate approach.

Some analytical methods used in particular types of project may not be used at all in other project scenarios. The APM suggest (2012: 97) that, for small projects, control can be achieved through the deployment of charts to monitor actual progress against that in the baseline version. They also argue that, for larger or more complex projects with a relatively well-defined scope, it may be appropriate to utilize earned value management (EVM) methods. These are analytical techniques that are suitable for certain project environments, such as construction, where the delivery path for the project is relatively clear.

A simplified example of this technique is given in Table 5.1; the top half of the table shows a 10-month project intending to deliver activities (at 10 per month) with associated planned cost (of $200 per item). The situation is reviewed at month 3 and by this time the **p**lanned **v**alue (PV) is $6,000 (the total planned activities at planned cost).

Actual values, shown in the lower part of the table, reveal that the **a**ctual **c**ost (AC) was $5,800. The 'earned value' (EV) is calculated as the actual activities delivered at the budgeted cost. In this example, the delivery of activities is behind schedule, but while the spend is under budget by $200, the EV is in fact $5,200, reflecting the lower-than-forecasted delivery of activities that were valued at the original budget values.

Learning point: the value of analytical tools in appropriate project settings

The insights gained by reviewing EV methods provide a basis for broader reflection. Firstly, these are powerful analytical tools that have greatest value when used in an appropriate setting or project context; while they may not be appropriate universally, the general principle is valuable. Secondly, their useful application relies on analytical skills and knowledge; this may or may not be a core skill of the project manager, and specialist input may be required.

TABLE 5.1 Earned value example

	Month	1	2	3	4	5	6	7	8	9	10
PLAN/ BUDGET	**Activities** Monthly	10	10	10	10	10	10	10	10	10	10
	Cumulative	10	20	30	40	50	60	70	80	90	100
	Cost per item	$200	$200	$200	$200	$200	$200	$200	$200	$200	$200
	Total	$2,000	$2,000	$2,000	$2,000	$2,000	$2,000	$2,000	$2,000	$2,000	$2,000
	Cumulative	$2,000	$4,000	$6,000	$8,000	$10,000	$12,000	$14,000	$16,000	$18,000	$20,000
	Planned Value (PV) at month 3 = $6,000										
ACTUAL	**Activities** Monthly	8	8	10							
	Cumulative	8	16	26	26	26	26	26	26	26	26
	Cost per item	$250	$225	$200	$200	$200	$200	$200	$200	$200	$200
	Total	$2,000	$1,800	$2,000	$0	$0	$0	$0	$0	$0	$0
	Cumulative	$2,000	$3,800	$5,800	$5,800	$5,800	$5,800	$5,800	$5,800	$5,800	$5,800
	Actual Cost (AC) at month 3 = $5,800										
	Earned Value (EV) at month 3 = $5,200 = (actual activities x original budgeted cost)										
	Cost variance (= EV – AC) = –$600										
	Schedule variance (= EV – PV) = –$800										

Questions, problems, decisions and answers

Previously, we encouraged the practice of asking questions. In Chapter 2 a set was suggested to prompt discussions seeking clarification of important conceptual things such as expectations, specification, costs and timings. The change of the project phase often means that the person managing it now is asked most of the questions. During the delivery phase, the project manager will have to deal with a large number of queries; these will arise from a wide source and range in type and topic.

On several occasions so far we have highlighted that a particular aspect or activity will take up a lot of the project manager's time. This area is no different. Questions, problems, decisions and providing answers will be a significant component of the project management process. These are often highly interrelated; questions will be raised in association with problems; some will be seeking clarification; problems will emerge; decisions will be required; answers will be provided.

Although much of this activity can be regarded as problem solving and decision making, this labelling is too narrow. A project manager needs to understand which ones are actually problems that require solving and respond with the most appropriate analysis and decision-making style. This is an area where our character style and experience can help or hinder us. This section will focus on generic scenarios and introduce some examples to promote critical thinking. Later chapters will develop some of these further in relation to the development of individual capability.

Let us start by checking our understanding of these topics. Problems and decisions are closely related, and decisions cannot follow problems without some form of analysis or evaluation. If, as the dictionary says, a problem is 'an unfavourable matter or situation to be resolved', a decision is likely to be concerned with the resolution of the problem. A decision could also be a response to a question that is not associated with something unfavourable (and therefore not a problem). 'Which type of shoes shall I get?' 'Shall I have tea or coffee?' These questions are not normally deemed to be indicating a problem. We make a decision; some of us will make it quickly, others will need more time.

Deciding which automobile to purchase will take longer than the one associated with the shoes. Although these are not problems, these examples start to reveal the challenge of making the right decision. What is the cost? What is the impact of making the wrong decision? For one of us, making the right decision about the shoes could be just as important as another of us purchasing the right automobile, especially if the shoes are worn every day in an area where there are few roads and yet fewer automobiles. The point here is that every decision has an impact and it is important that the impact is understood.

These impacts are frequently part of the project management challenge. Expectations from one stakeholder group might seem quite trivial; delivering the

TABLE 5.2   Speed of decision making and characteristics

Time to respond	Example	Some characteristics
Seconds	Sporting scenario	Reflex reaction
Minutes	Urgent phone call; information needed at immigration	Immediate
Hours	Requires clarification or action; decisions required	High focus
Days	Loss of key resource	Effective management of time and prioritization
Weeks	Project planning	Can be planned or evaluated; scope to defer
Years	Longer-term strategic decision	Needs wide consensus; may lack urgency

product to meet those expectations might be difficult. Something that doesn't start as a problem in fact becomes one.

There are a number of ways to categorize problems based on the perceived time required to problem-resolution. Table 5.2 shows a range of different scenarios and is intended to encourage us to reflect on the response in relation to perceived urgency. In other words, some situations require a rapid response. The urgency provides a strong incentive to respond quickly, especially if life is at risk or the correct decision affects the outcome of a competitive scenario.

In a game of tennis doubles, the exchange of volley shots when all four players are close in to the net means that each tennis player has to make much quicker decisions than when waiting for a ball to fall back into the court from a high lobbed shot. The instinctive or reflex action of the volley also provides less time for the player to think about how they might miss the shot.

In a project scenario we may have parallels, in that some situations will require an immediate response, others will provide more time to consider what to do. If we are forced to make a quick decision, we will rely on our instinct and experience to help make the right one. If we have longer, there will be more time to evaluate before making a commitment. We try to avoid mixing up the two scenarios; on several occasions when pressed for a key decision I have often heard the reasoning: 'Do you want a quick decision or the right decision?' It is not difficult to recall situations where the quick decision was the right one and several where it was not. There are always consequences to be managed.

A final point to reflect on is that the tennis player, who has in fact been coached and trained how to play, sees the ball well, has quick reflexes and has practised for many years, makes the volley shot look instinctive. Instinct is based on a number of things, including the development of skills and accumulation of experience.

Approaching decision making

It is important to frame decisions, since it often feels as if some are far harder to make than others. Furthermore, a project manager will be faced with a difficult situation and cannot make a decision quickly. He or she is criticized for making the decision too slowly. It is helpful to bring in the terms introduced by Simon (1960: 5–6) of 'programmed' and 'non-programmed' decisions – 'programmed to the extent that they are repetitive and routine to the extent that a definite procedure has been worked out…'; 'non-programmed to the extent that they are novel, unstructured and consequential'.

This sets out two extremes for types of decision. The language could also be applied directly to categories of project that could be described as 'novel', 'unstructured' and 'consequential'. We could argue that the first-timer project, or first-timer aspects of a new project, would create just the right conditions to encounter non-programmed decision making. Indeed, this also reflects the associated level of uncertainty, as shown in Figure 5.1. Whether we are faced with making the right decision or solving a problem, the challenge may be in many respects similar; if we don't know the correct answer or decision, we have to perform some analysis. This is the secret to getting things right. What type of analysis?

Problem-solving insights

Simon (1960: 27) provides a further insight that we could embrace; he discussed a scenario where 'we are camping in the woods and decide we need a table'. He promoted

FIGURE 5.1 Type of decision and certainty

| Type of decisions | Programmed | Non-programmed |
| Certainty | Highest | Lowest |

the articulation of the problem as 'we need a flat horizontal surface', and the consideration of a route to the solution – 'we have all sorts of trees around us and some tools'. This is drawn together by encouraging us to consider the difference between what we have and what we need, and then to realize that the tools we have might help us to reduce the difference: use an axe to cut down a tree. We could argue that this example needs to be subjected to a further analysis, one of potential environmental constraints, but it is nevertheless a useful example to highlight an approach to problem solving based on the following steps:

1 Identify the goal.

2 Determine the difference between the present situation and the goal.

3 Find a tool or approach that reduces the difference.

4 Apply this.

5 Do it again until the problem is solved.

If we add 'consequences', we can generalize and adapt this where we need to, as it can be applied to the example scenarios included. There are a number of decision-making and problem-solving frameworks that are routinely cited in the project management world and sometimes used in practice. For example, decision trees in terms of the former, and cause–effect–cause analysis is a useful application for the latter. It is valuable for the project manager to be aware of these and to recognize that he or she may well be deploying them without realizing that this is the case. The previous example reveals this.

The value of taking the time to undertake appropriate analysis cannot be understated. Critical information that will help inform the decision or provide the answer to a problem may be buried in data that we already have, but we need to investigate it. For example, within a service organization scenario, the cost discrepancy across locations of providing user IT support was investigated using the site call-out visit records. In what seemed at first to be a laborious exercise, once the call-outs had been grouped and evaluated across locations, the cause became much clearer and a second not-asked question was answered – almost 30 per cent of the call-outs were associated with activities that could have been resolved through the deployment of localized diagnostic support. This informed the building of a cost–benefit business case and a proposal was made to deploy an additional resource.

The previous example is a form of intuitive analysis. We have the data; we have a spreadsheet; sometimes we need to set time aside to analyse the situation. In several sectors, such as those including systems development or with significant financial emphasis, the role of analyst has long been a dedicated part of the overall skill-set. Periodically, the project manager needs to take on this role – or acquire it from somewhere – at necessary points within the project lifecycle. It is likely that a cause–effect–cause analysis would have revealed the same conclusion, shown in Table 5.3.

TABLE 5.3 Applying cause–effect–cause analysis

Problem: a support contract seems to be unusually costly due to high call-outs at location X	
What is the cause of the problem?	High levels of call-outs are occurring at a specific time.
What is the effect?	The problem is resolved but only temporarily.
What is the cause of the problem?	It seems to be the same group of technical problems.
What is the effect?	Technical support is providing similar fixes.
What is the cause of the problem?	These are associated with system administration.
What is the effect?	The support contract is being used to provide a system administration role.

Reporting

'Reporting' or providing reports is a key activity concerned with providing information. Although this is just one mechanism for disseminating information (and therefore communicating), historically it has been an important element of the process of managing projects, largely through the notion that it will help to maintain control. Also, while the core information comprising a typical report is similar today to that a decade earlier (for example, an area of a report concerned with progress against a specific milestone), technology keeps adding new opportunities to deliver this in a different way.

Reporting incorporates the synthesis and structuring of information, and it is perhaps this aspect that sets apart the person involved in the project from the information; the incorporation of a project management system (PMIS) provides opportunities for the provision of automatically generated reports, based on data built up from a variety of sources. The integrity of the data in turn yields efficacy in the reports, but the positive aspects of greater transparency might need to be moderated in particular contextual scenarios or when political factors are prevalent.

So what does reporting comprise? The answer could be to say 'anything of relevance to the management of the project – progress, issues,…'; if we consider the audience first and respond to their expectations, we might find the provision onerous, and although technology can help us, this in turn can help to widen already-wide expectations.

Let us instead start by considering the topics within this section – risk, monitoring and control, problem solving and decision making. These are potentially core headings for the reporting. By looking at these first, it also reminds us that reporting is not an activity exclusively for the delivery phase; we argued earlier that risk is ever-present through the lifecycle of a project, and we must therefore have been reporting on this at earlier stages. The complementary activities of monitoring and control can be visualized as pertinent to the delivery phase; these are also likely to provide the basis for much of the reporting, especially when combined with the other topics of problem solving and decision making.

These are all important components of the story that needs to be told in the reporting. By 'story', we don't mean fiction. Tell the story factually but keep the audience interested and on side. For some project managers, this area of reporting takes up a considerable proportion of their time, but it is a very important activity since it provides a means of maintaining control over the communication process.

For example, the building of a new nuclear power facility[1] will provoke a wide variety of reactions from an equally wide stakeholder group. This is one area where there is significant work to be done to ensure that the rationale for the project is communicated effectively. This aspect of the project management process could take place over a period of years. This is also seen in projects concerned with the siting of wind turbines, railways lines… any project where stakeholders can be pivotal in the outcome.

We can extend the discussion of reporting to include additional previous topics, for example those relating to the specification and scope. If the project delivery phase includes arguments about scope and change management, this is another key aspect of reporting for the sponsor, funders, whoever needs to know. It is probably quite apparent by now that the scope of the reporting itself could be quite wide. The subsequent topics in this chapter also provide potential headings: time, resource, cost management and, perhaps as importantly, relevant aspects of the project management organization can also be usefully be reported, especially if there are gaps in capability or particular issues associated with the dynamics or location of people and facilities.

Lastly, we also need to consider the overall aspect of project stakeholders; this group might in fact set the agenda for the reporting in the first place and we could have considered this aspect first. Discussing it last has allowed us to build up some perspectives of the likely detailed information that may be required. With all of this in mind, it is difficult to propose specific guidance for reporting, but Table 5.4 is offered to provide some more general insights. Although the areas for reporting and target audience will be informed by the particular context of the project, it is likely to be based upon the framework introduced earlier.

TABLE 5.4   Some likely aspects of reporting

Audience	Internal and external parties, relevant other stakeholder groups, project management and wider organizational parties
Content	Progress of project against key performance parameters, specific issues related to areas such as resourcing, budget, team, technical challenge, contract, ad-hoc issues
Timing	At key stages, scheduled or on ad-hoc basis
Style/format	May be defined by project parent, informed by adoption of external standard, agreed with project management organization or ad-hoc
Medium	Depends on the project, expectations and preferences; informed by personality and location of team; must be appropriate, efficient and effective

This reinforces the notion that the scope of reporting might be difficult to manage. An alternative strategy would be to propose, from the outset, undertaking the reporting within a management by exception approach, wherein the emphasis is on reporting and managing events or incidents that vary from 'normal'. This would streamline information provision and provide better efficiency. We will say more about this towards the end of the topic.

For projects managed using a project board structure, Table 5.5 is provided to inform the thinking. This is a sample agenda that could be used at a meeting of a project board. Although it might appear somewhat bureaucratic, other than the item called 'management review', it sets out the minimum required for constructive discussion and resolution of management issues associated with the project. We can use this to explain further some aspects of reporting and also to introduce some scenarios that might emerge during the delivery of a project. Most of the agenda points are self-evident. A brief explanation of each follows.

Reviewing minutes is a process that seeks to ensure that the record of the previous meeting is accurate. This is often more important than we might realize, especially if there is an audit or occasion where blame is attributed, or when the route to resolving a problem is by analysing a sequence of previously taken decisions. This can be a lengthy process, though.

Standing items refers to the key areas of a project that need to be reviewed at each meeting by the project board. Defined by work breakdown structure (WBS), milestone or other appropriate means, it is worth emphasizing here that the level of discussion and reporting of this must retain salience. An appropriate level of detail and actions

TABLE 5.5   Example of an agenda used at meeting of a project board

Agenda points	Notes/explanation
Review of minutes	A record of the previous meeting of the board
Standing items	Defined as appropriate for the project, sometimes by the WBS or milestones
Management review	Optional inclusion; this or an equivalent may be used in particular circumstances
Ad-hoc reports	Optional inclusion; this or an equivalent may be used in particular circumstances
Any other business	This enables the controlled inclusion of additional items
Date of next meeting	Self-explanatory

required will be determined by the particular items and nuanced role of the project board. In a more extreme case where the number of people involved in directing and managing the project is small, project board and project management might become the same thing.

A **management review** report might be required if there is a need to summarize a very wide range of items to be covered or if the project has relatively lower autonomy and is dependent upon the activities of external parties (and the activities need to be documented). For example, in a public-sector project with stakeholder groups that can influence the adoption of technical aspects, procurement or other frameworks, these 'external dependencies' need to be understood fully for the project board to respond appropriately. A focused management review can help with this.

Furthermore, if in this example a member of the project board is also a source or associated with such a dependency, the route to resolution of associated issues might be through that member. A management review can be aligned with the standing items, to also serve to provide a status report of key activities, processes and frameworks, raising issues or alerting the board to the need for action.

Ad-hoc reports will be specific to the items that require coverage. Topics for these could include technical (such as anything relating to system architecture), procurement (for example if there are delays) or resourcing (especially when there is a shortage of skills or adequacy of personnel).

The above is provided as an example; although we can gain further guidance from expert sources, there is no universal prescription here. It will depend on the context, complexity and personality of the project.

One final aspect to develop is concerned with stakeholders. The area of reporting to stakeholders is potentially vast. If the project has a substantial stakeholder dimension, expect commensurate activities associated with communication and reporting. A project manager could be consumed by this responsibility. It is also worth considering the question: are we reporting or consulting? If we are informing, we can use bulletin-style communication and similar mechanisms. Discovering that our reporting provokes an adverse response from a key stakeholder group suggests that we may need to re-evaluate the stakeholder analysis and re-set the tactics.

To draw this section to a close, let us consider the role of reporting in the responsibilities of the project manager involved in the example above. The project manager realized that the reporting had been classified with two types of report recipient: (1) primary recipient, who must be aware of the content; and (2) secondary recipient, who may need to be aware of the content and information should be provided unless the project manager is advised not to do so.

An analysis of the distribution is shown in Figure 5.2. At peak, this involved the establishment of almost 40 different recipient report routes. Even allowing for improvements in distribution enabled by technology change, this situation became

FIGURE 5.2   Reporting distribution routes

Management control document: distribution list

Group	Abbreviation	Management reports				Minutes of meetings				Working documents				
		Management review	Strategy group report	Information bulletin	Ad-hoc	PB	RIWG	NIT	NIWG	Business rules & processes	Coding structures	System architecture	Pilot project	Establishment of hub
Project board	PB	●	●	●		●	●	●	●	○	○	●	●	●
Regional implementation working group	RIWG			●			●		●	●	●	●	●	●
Parent organization director	ParD	●	○	●			●	○				●	●	●
Parent organization information service director	ParISD	○	●				●	○				●	○	●
Regional organizational consortium	ROC		●											
Regional business centres	RBC		●											
National organizational consortium – project manager	NPM	●	●			●	●	●		●	●	●	○	○
National organizational consortium management board	NOC		●											
National IT strategy group	NIT	●	●					●	●					
National implementation working group	NIWG		●			○	○	●	●	●	●	●	○	○

Key		
	●	Primary recipient of document: must be aware of content
	○	Information provided unless requested not to do so: may need to be aware of content

unmanageable as it directly impacted the time spent by the project manager on other key activities. After an analysis was presented to the project board, the situation was critically discussed and resolved. This reinforces the case for adopting a management by exception approach, as this would render a substantial number of items within Figure 5.2 as unnecessary.

Learning point

> With regard to reporting, overloading ourselves or the project stakeholders with information may mean that the important parts are missed (and not responded to); this presents a risk to the project. Seek to keep the balance right.

Completion challenges

Completion of the project

Completion... what does this mean? In the various lifecycle models and bodies of knowledge we see terminology such as 'closure', 'termination' and 'handover'. For an information systems project, the final version of the product is delivered following acceptance testing, it is handed over to the client, the systems become operational and the project is terminated and reviewed. Although it doesn't always run in that exact order, the terminology seems appropriate.

If our project is the organizing and running of a tour of venues in China by a Russian ballet company, is the vocabulary still appropriate? The delivery of the project would likely be in phases (venue 1, venue 2, etc); at the end of the tour the project will have finished; a review of the individual performances/events and tour overall will have been undertaken. We could say that the project had been 'terminated', but for cultural and contextual reasons, although the principles hold, the language needs to be considered carefully.

If in a similar type of project an objective is to provide a dance experience and training to instructors, there could be a 'handover'. In this case, we would mean that the knowledge or insight had been handed over. While the vocabulary works well with more traditional types of projects such as those in systems development or construction, the core principles apply equally well with a more generalized set of projects.

Different types of project will have different types of ending, not always happy ones. Projects are terminated (but may not be complete) for a variety of reasons; we will explore some of these in the following section.

Let us consider projects from the perspective of their core components, such as specification, quality, time and cost. Each of these could be used to determine whether a project is complete. For example, if the project specification is to organize and deliver a world cup downhill race event, then, once the activity has been completed, that particular project is complete. The moment in time has passed.

Alternatively, if the final deliverable of a project is an emergency control system (where time and budget might necessarily have more flexibility), the moment that the product is accepted, as it meets the specification, might herald the completion of the project.

Thirdly, if a government department has been given a target to provide a service until a budget is expended, the moment when the money is completely spent might mark the completion of the project.

Of course, we could argue that in our first example there were activities associated with the next scheduled event that needed to be undertaken, that in the second example there would be a commissioning and acceptance period, and in the third that situations would not be as abrupt as the example described. Nevertheless, these examples serve to highlight that projects can become 'completed' for a variety of reasons. A framework such as that in Figure 5.3 helps visualize this phase.

The ordering (or prioritization) of the table should enable us to evaluate in turn the targets and constraints. If these are deemed to be sufficiently complete so that we also define the project to be complete, then this in turn suggests that the enabling mechanisms have also been 'completed'. The resources that were organized and the tools that were used (as per our resource plan in Chapter 3 and developed through the delivery phase) might all have become 'terminated'. Will they be back in a future project incarnation?

Getting to the completion point might prove to be challenging. Even if we have done our best monitoring, controlling, reporting and problem solving and made the correct decisions throughout the project, there might still be a need to push things hard as we move into the final lap. This athletics metaphor holds up well in project scenarios.

FIGURE 5.3   Perspectives of completion; against defined project parameters

Targets and constraints	Progress against each target					
	0%	25%	50%	75%	100%	>100%
Time objectives						
Cost objectives						
Quality objective						
Others						

Quite natural human behaviour traits can contribute to this; the project manager may need to create an atmosphere of urgency for those whose natural setting is laid back. Alternatively, we may need to provide incentives to speed up the finish, or threaten penalties to ensure that all the activities are completed to deadlines. Although some of these approaches can be effective when used in project environments where time is subordinate to other constraints, deploy with care – pushing activities to a premature finish increases the risk of causing associated problems through compromise or pressures to act.

Learning point

This discussion prompts us to look deeper into the dynamics of projects and recognize that the reality may have multiple dimensions of conceptualizing, planning, delivery and management.

At the completion point, what is incomplete? Putting this another way, at the point of delivery to the stakeholders, will *they* be satisfied with the outcome? If not, what are the consequences of this? If we meet the deadline but cannot deliver all of the specification, they will probably be unhappy. If we meet all the specification by delivering three months late, the stakeholders might be unhappy. Equally they might be happy, since we had managed their expectations well through the latter stages of the project (and the delay was acceptable).

Figure 5.4 extends this thinking by bringing forward the original questions posed in Chapter 2, during conceptualization, with the objectives defined at progressive stages of the project management process.

FIGURE 5.4 Perspectives of completion; against original request and defined project parameters

Request	Component of planning	Defined in project as...	Have we delivered to the plan?
Who is asking for it?	Stakeholders	Expectations	Expectations met?
What do they want? (What is it)?	Specification	Outcome	Outcome delivered?
Why do they want it?	Rationale	Business case	Meet the business case?
How much will it cost?	Budget	Agreed budget	Delivered within the agreed budget?
When do they want it?	Timing	Agreed timescale	Delivered within the agreed timescale?

If we do not meet all of the planned specification, deliver late and also exceed the budget, it may be very difficult to meet stakeholder expectations; but then we could argue that this only matters if the stakeholder is important to us. Given this last discussion, it might seem odd that this occurs frequently in government procurement activities, particularly in defence projects.

CASE STUDY   The A400M Project[2]

At what cost, and can it be delivered?

In April 2009, *The Economist* highlighted that the future of the A400M, the in-development military transport aeroplane, 'hangs in the balance'. By this time the project was in some difficulty. Already three years late and $2.7 billion over budget, the first flight of the aircraft was not expected until 2010.

Concerns about the project stemmed from a number of perspectives; without prior experience of big military programmes, Airbus had underestimated the complexity of building the A400M. *The Economist* highlighted the requirement for propulsion system management software that was highly sophisticated and needed for novel engine designs. The aircraft has some characteristics similar to the US-designed C-130 (Hercules transport) and larger jet C-17 (Globemaster). The specification was particularly challenging and this substantially contributed to doubts that the aircraft could meet all of its performance goals; whether indeed it would fly.

In fact, Bloomberg (2009) reported the congratulations from Hamilton Sundstrand, a supplier of power and other systems, to Airbus on the first successful flight at Seville, Spain, on Friday 11 December. In February 2010, Globalsecurity.org reported that this prototype MSN1 would be joined by up to three further aircraft by the end of the year, and a fleet of five aircraft would be used for test flying, with a planned first delivery of a production aircraft to the French Air Force (Armee de l'Air) by the end of 2012.

The front cover of the 16 June 2010 edition of *Jane's Defence Weekly* was dominated by a photograph of the A400M with the headline 'Premiere performance; A400M makes public debut in Berlin'. Their feature highlighted the first public demonstration of MSN001 at the Internationale Luft- und Raumfahrtausstellung Berlin (International Aerospace Exhibition) on 8 June 2010. This display 'included hard turns that saw it exceed 100 degrees of bank and a low-speed pass to simulate a precision lower level air-drop'. This was an upbeat and positive portrayal of the project that did not belie any of the associated concerns or doubts in other reporting.

On 26 September 2011, Defencetalk.com reported that the A400M had passed a series of key certification tests that included braking systems and emergency evacuation, and the feature concluded with a summary sentence asserting that A400M 'is the most cost-efficient and versatile airlifter ever conceived... absolutely unique in its capabilities'.

By 6 March 2013, Airbus.com proudly carried a headline 'The first production A400M soars on its maiden flight'. Again from Seville, Spain, aircraft MSN7 made a smooth 5-hour and 42-minute flight, deemed to be successful. The French Air Force was now anticipating receiving the initial A400M delivery in the second quarter of 2013.

On 2 August 2013, Aviationweek.com reported that the first A400M delivery had been made to the French Air Force, after certification by DGA (the French defence procurement agency), and aircraft MSN7 was expected initially to provide aircrew training. They also reported that Airbus was still undertaking development work on a number of critical capabilities (such as air-to-air refuelling) and that a number of development aircraft were involved in the work to establish operational capability standards.

By February 2014, two A400Ms had been delivered to the French Air Force; a further 11 aircraft were scheduled to enter service, in France, Turkey and the UK. *Aviation Week* (2014a) reported that ADS (Airbus Defence and Space; the company formerly known as Airbus Military) asserted a bright future for the A400M 'Atlas' product. They also highlighted that the chief executive of ADS acknowledged that a list price for the aircraft had not been determined and that '… with the aircraft in production this is an unusual situation… in a number of respects this confirms the difficulties with the extensively revised contract'. Set against this, the chief executive highlighted that in 2014 'an estimated 1850 military airlifters currently in service around the world are thirty years old'. Clearly these will require replacing and this situation therefore appears to present a strong market opportunity.

Shortly afterwards, *Aviation Week* carried a further feature titled 'A400M: The horror, the horror' (2014b). Quoting the Airbus CEO Tom Enders at a speech in Washington, 'I am determined, at least for my company, not to ever again walk into such a program, and rather to resist (that kind of) contracting and say "no, we're not going there"'. This article also highlighted concerns that the European defence industry has 'too many national interests', 'too much overlap' and 'certainly too much waste'.

Time will tell whether the A400M is ultimately a successful project; similarities can be made with other projects of this type. The Concorde, a project that overcame considerable technological challenges but never fulfilled its commercial objectives, always provokes a debate as to whether or not it was a success. Future events, such as the response to natural disasters, may underline the significant load-carrying capability of the A400M. That its breadth of talent is currently matched by nothing else could well make it a major success.

Case reflection

This scenario highlights challenges that are often associated with highly innovative projects or those with an ambitious specification:

i   Evaluate the case in terms of strengths and weakness of project management strategy. Consider also the project management process.

ii Should this type of project be stopped? Will this situation occur again in future projects?

iii If the A400M achieves all of its operational objectives and becomes an export success, will we ask these questions in 2020?

Handover

For a project that generates a physical product as the final outcome, there will be an associated acceptance/transfer/commissioning of this, a handover from project to post-project environment. The post-project environment may have a number of stages prior to the product becoming fully operational.

One way of defining the end of a project is based upon payments for work completed. Once the final payment is made, this may denote the termination of the project. It is important to raise the consideration of contract here, as this will actually provide clarification of the arrangement and terms. There may be conditions associated with the delivery of the final outcome.

For example, within construction projects, the client will often include in the budget an item called 'retention'. This amount is reflected in the contract but will normally be retained until the client is satisfied that all works are satisfactorily complete and any appropriate post-delivery problems resolved.

While these considerations may be substantial, once the project outcome is delivered as a physical product, it may be at the start of a long operational career. The handover between project and operation may require its own dedicated management process. Specific responsibilities will need to be assigned, and the process might involve awareness training. These might constitute mini-projects in their own right. Some might not be 'mini'; for example, consider for a moment the activities associated with the commissioning of a massive engineering project such as the Panama Canal.

We can see comparable examples in other fields; for example, the following list shows a selection of ongoing or required activities at the handover point of a systems implementation project:

- training programme;
- stakeholder communication;
- in-operational-mode system support frameworks;
- quality management processes;
- data management activities;
- activity management and organization;
- reporting and management systems.

Each of these activities could be broken down into a number of components, revealing that the handover process itself is quite a substantial management undertaking. Figure 5.5 shows the first of these, 'training programme'. The letters a, b, c and j denote people who have had pre-handover development responsibility. The '?' indicate that responsibilities post-handover need to be identified.

FIGURE 5.5   Handover; sample activities associated with 'training programme'

			Responsibility	
			Pre-handover	Post-handover
Training	Training plan	Development of plan for period	a	?
		Revisions to plan period	a	?
	Deployment	System introductory	b	?
		System administration	b	?
		Reporting modules	a	?
		Operating system aspects	c	?
	User need evaluation	Questionnaire	a	?
		Analysis and deployment	a	?
	Other activities	As defined	j	?
		As defined	j	?

Insights

As we move towards completion, our knowledge of the project has been increasing steadily. We have much better insights into the estimates, assumptions, risks and organization, among other major facets of the project; if we could start again we would be able to do it much better. One area that often gains in clarity is the resource portfolio. Decisions taken to hire experts, establish (or develop) the right skill-set and utilize particular space or infrastructure make sense. Was a particular decision the right one? Towards completion, at the latter stages of the project, the decisions are often associated with the intensity of activities and the subsequent management of a resource portfolio that is no longer needed (for this project).

Resource management at completion

It is again quite difficult to discuss a generic approach to the management of resources during the completion of a project, since the context will determine the specific management emphasis and activities. Consider the resource profile assembled to organize and deliver a UCI Mountain Bike World Cup event[3] at Fort William in Scotland. This will include organizational staff, external contracted resources (for specific equipment required on-site during the event), external non-contract resources and volunteers. Once the event has been delivered, what will happen to the resource portfolio? It is likely that core organizational staff will start to work on preparation for the next one; external contracted resources will be contracted by a different party at a different event; non-contract resources will probably undertake something similar elsewhere;

volunteers may or may not get involved in further events, as we would normally expect that they have a greater degree of choice. The resource portfolio effectively disbands at the end of the event (once it has been completed).

If the event has been successful, the resource group will probably look forward to the next project for several core reasons, including:

- satisfaction;
- reward;
- passion.

These are a number of characteristics associated with the people side of projects and are often especially strong when the resources are providing something that they enjoy doing; this is important to bear in mind and we should take into account reactions to unexpected scenarios and outcomes that are not as successful as expected.

The intensity of these characteristics may not be as strong in our other examples. It might take a period of time to elapse before the delivered emergency control system is used for stakeholders to be delighted with the value of it. Within the government department example, the service might not have been something that delighted its stakeholders anyway (such as the traffic congestion associated with infrastructure improvements), and the ending of this project owing to the limitation of budget might be greeted with a mixed response from stakeholder groups.

We can discuss reward and passion similarly. The essence here is that the resource portfolio has been developed over the life of the project, it reaches a peak in terms of usage and, once the project is completed, returns in many respects to a pre-project state – except for one key dimension: the resource has learnt and developed insights from the experience. This is naturally the point when we seek to review the project overall, understand it – and learn the lessons for next time. If only it were that simple.

Summary

In this chapter we have further examined some of the challenges associated with managing the project through to completion. We have considered the increasingly dynamic nature of some activities that were launched in either the conceptual or planning phases of the project. This highlights additional contrasts between the processes of preparation and those more often associated with dealing with a relatively dynamic role; from managing risk, trying to maintain control, making the right decisions, and reporting, the project manager role needs to maintain an active approach during the delivery of a project.

We also explored some specific aspects of the process as the project nears completion. The emphasis has changed, the team has a much greater retrospective awareness of the project, and there are a number of managing-to-completion activities that bring together much of the earlier preparatory work. Determining completion differs project by project. We have moved through the delivery phase. Next we will consider the question 'How did it go?'

Notes

1   For an example of extensive stakeholder consultation process see: Horizon Nuclear Power (2011–14) Wylfa – Public Documents and Materials, retrieved on 15 November 2014 from http://www.horizonnuclearpower.com/wylfa-public-documents

2   This case study draws upon information from the following sources:

Airbus (2013) The first production A400M soars on its maiden flight, 6 March, retrieved on 3 August 2014 from http://www.airbus.com/presscentre/pressreleases/press-release-detail/detail/the-first-production-a400m-soars-on-its-maiden-flight/

Aviation Week (2014a) ADS clings to belief of A400M's viability, 17 February, retrieved from http://aviationweek.com/awin/ads-clings-belief-a400m-s-viability

Aviation Week (2014b) A400M: The horror, the horror, 2 May, retrieved from http://aviationweek.com/blog/a400m-horror-horror

Bloomberg (2009) Hamilton Sundstrand Congratulates Airbus on A400M First Flight, 15 December, retrieved on 4 August 2014 from http://www.bloomberg.com/apps/news?pid=newsarchive&sid=aArlge01I2k0

The Economist (2009) European defence; heavy going, 9 April

Global Security (2013) A400M Loadmaster; Future Large Aircraft – FLA / Avion de Transport Futur – ATF, 30 September, retrieved on 3 August 2014 from http://www.globalsecurity.org/military/world/europe/fla.htm

Global Security (2013) Airbus Military celebrates first A400M delivery to French Air Force, 30 September, retrieved from http://www.globalsecurity.org/military/library/news/2013/09/mil-130930-eads01.htm

3   For an example of this type of event, see Fort William event UCI Mountain Bike World Cup, retrieved on 16 November 2014 from http://fortwilliamworldcup.co.uk/

References

Association for Project Management (APM) (2012) APM Body of Knowledge, APM, Princes Risborough, Bucks

Simon, H (1960) The New Science of Management Decision, Harper & Row, New York

Reviewing and learning in projects

06

LEARNING OUTCOMES

By applying the topics within this chapter you should be able to:

- consider the learning opportunities presented through informal and formal review processes;

- explore the differences between audits and reviews when deployed in the project environment;

- reflect on the gap that emerges between the ideals and realities of delivering projects;

- reflect on the terminology of project success and failure;

- understand how a concern to ensure success drives investments in project management knowledge development.

Introduction

In this chapter we will explore two distinct but connected areas. Firstly, by focusing on the need to learn from the delivery of the project, we will consider the different types of evaluation that take place during and after the project. Informal evaluation is inevitable; the formal review processes in place that can provide the often much-needed insights into project performance vary in approach and style, depending upon the context of the project and the organizational frameworks. They also reflect the motivation to improve long-term project performance.

Secondly, we witness the reporting of regular project failure, which seems to affect a significant proportion of activities in certain sectors. We will explore and understand some of the reasons for these.

The chapter concludes by looking at the gap that often emerges between the conceptual and planning framing of the ideal project with that of the completely delivered project that provides the actuality of all the effort. A variety of examples will provide the basis for reflection on what is frequently a challenging area for project management teams: the need to meet high stakeholder expectations. This encourages organizations and nations to invest in project management development schemes.

In turn, this will provide a platform for us to open up the subsequent chapters, by recognizing that projects provide a source of significant challenge to individuals and organizations, and that we need to extend our understanding of project management into areas not always expected.

What we have learnt about the project so far

Instinctive and informal perspectives of performance

The reviewing process has been taking place throughout the period of the project. At an individual and group level, actions are reviewed, sometimes formally, often informally. The team learn and apply their knowledge at the next opportunity; this is repeated. At a future point, a member of the team does something instinctively; they follow their instinct, based on experience.

Informal reviews take place at every level within the project management structure and include perspectives from functional and general management. Individuals reflect on a particular event during the project process and they discuss this with their colleagues within the team: meetings, discussions, messaging, many more opportunities using an ever-increasing digital platform. Project teams, management and stakeholders generate a lot of noise. This noise actually contains a lot of valuable insight and, if it is possible to process well, yields valuable information that can inform the better management of future projects. This might include:

- management perspectives;
- insights into team performance and development opportunities;
- resource portfolio perspectives;
- stakeholder participation, contribution and optimization.

Objective evaluations

In order to open this topic, let us start by considering a number of initial questions:

   i Why do we evaluate projects?

   ii When should we evaluate projects?

   iii How do we evaluate projects?

Although these seem to be quite straightforward to answer, it is not always immediately apparent how best to do this. Although we will answer these in later topic sections by looking at some approaches that are popular in both project and non-project activities, it is worthwhile considering why we review. Some reasons may be procedural; others out of necessity; a third group arises from a genuine desire to improve performance.

Learning point

Continuing professional development and business management degrees often provide constructive opportunities to undertake an in-depth review that has a dedicated and value-adding focus. These scenarios present the reviewer with the opportunity to deploy a dedicated approach that is informed by lateral learning within the scheme. These reviews are often of a reflective, value-adding type that can contribute to the development of business strategy.

Two widely used techniques provide objective evaluations: audits and reviews. While these are commonly in use within organizations, the value of deploying them can vary widely. Indeed, these can be challenging to undertake and the recommendations difficult to implement.

The term 'audit' is synonymous with inspections of an organization's accounts. This is often framed as an official action that will typically be undertaken by an independent body. By contrast, reviews tend to describe assessments that include an intention to make value-adding changes. While these are also regarded as formal evaluations, the semantic emphasis is on the recommendation of change in relation to increased value expectations. Applying these terms within the domain of projects, we might therefore expect a project review to provide insights as to what actions would be required to make changes where they add value. Both terms encompass the aspect of formality; the first (audit) suggests that the activity should be undertaken by an independent body.

Examining this further, the PMI (2013) combine the terms audit and review with quality and performance as 'quality audits' and 'performance reviews', respectively. 'A quality audit is a structured, independent process to determine if project activities comply with organizational and project policies' (2013: 556). Correspondingly, a performance review is 'a technique that is used to measure, compare and analyse actual performance of work in progress on the project against the baseline' (2013: 549).

By contrast, the APM (2012: 133) discuss the term 'audit' threefold within 'configuration management' as physical, functional or system audits. For example, 'a physical audit looks at the relevant elements of... confirms that the item meets specification... check the results of... confirm that...' All three areas discuss the need for checking performance against functional designs. Review is defined (APM, 2012: 196) as a 'critical evaluation of a deliverable, business case or P3 management process'. 'P3' is an expression representing projects, programmes and portfolios.

This provides us with some insights as to the use of the terminology within an organization or in environments where particular projects are managed in accordance with these standard frameworks. Interpreting this rationale, it suggests that audits are more likely to be conducted retrospectively (or in a more detached form) than reviews, which are planned to take place throughout the lifecycle of the project.

Maylor (2010: 372) compared a variety of project criteria in terms of how each might be evaluated within either an audit or a review. For example, for the time criterion, an audit would explore the degree of conformance to plan, whereas a review might reveal the associated levels of customer satisfaction. For both criteria of 'human resources' and 'environmental' he argued that where an audit would seek to examine the conformance to policy, a review could help us to learn about the extent to which team spirit and motivation had developed for the former, and such things as environmental impacts in the latter. This reasoning is compelling and a useful basis both to distinguish between the two forms of evaluation and also to argue that the review can be a strong value-adding exercise. If it is done well, this will help to make genuine improvements in future project performance.

Adopting the APM suggestion of reviewing throughout the project lifecycle, we could organize this activity so that the final review complements the accumulation of work that has already been undertaken. We need to ask whether this is sufficient or, in certain cases, overdone.

Project review processes

We have established the underlying basis for objective evaluations in project environments and introduced the two main mechanisms: audit and review. Further, we have argued that the latter of these, review, can provide significant value to enable the improvement of future project delivery. We have also seen that, through informal and formally planned activities, the review process takes place throughout the lifecycle of a project.

For reviews that are planned for the post-completion phase, the schedule and content will vary; some will follow an organizational template, others may be undertaken based on a set of headings that follow the project management process. For those that use an external party, the recipe may be agreed at the start of the process, and for reviews instigated by an external stakeholder, the precise scope and specification may have been developed through consultation with a third-party research organization.

There is a very wide range of possibilities here; the title 'review' could mean a lot of different things in terms of reporting, presentation and how it is used as a basis for action. Is there a common formula or recipe? Once again, this depends upon the context, scale and complexity of the project. In order to help develop our understanding, the following section is based on a number of examples of review processes, frameworks and guidance.

Post-implementation reviews

In order to provide some context for post-implementation reviews (PIRs), we will start by considering two scenarios from practice. In the first, an internally focused PIR was required following the delivery of a new sustainable-build construction project. This exercise revealed a number of key points that are common to this type of process:

- the importance of establishing common standards for measurement;
- the need to source pertinent documentation;
- emotional involvement of people directly involved in the project;
- the management of expectations;
- challenges associated with the availability of key people and impact of timing, participation and cooperation.

The approach taken was to evaluate the original or modified objectives, the associated deliverables and to review the project management process; the scope of this is shown in Figure 6.1.

Review questions were framed around how well objectives and deliverables were met, with further evaluation of other areas and the project management process itself. The review sought to reveal the extent to which it met the direct project measures of time, budget and quality. The project management process probing included 'how efficiently?', 'what have we learnt?' and 'what can be carried forward?' and these were examined in terms of leadership and management competence, appropriateness

FIGURE 6.1   Specimen scope for post-implementation review

Project objectives	Objective-related deliverables	Other areas evaluated
	Deliverable 1	Other areas of project and overall perceptions
Objective 1	Deliverable 2	
	Deliverable 3	
Objective 2	Deliverable 4	Evaluation of project management process
	Deliverable 5	
Objective 3	Deliverable 6	
	Deliverable 7	Measures evaluated across a range of criteria
Objective 4	Deliverable 8	

of project management organization (structure), project controls deployed and in terms of organizational interfaces.

The undertaking of this review presented some challenges but was revealing. Firstly, the core delivery staff resources were very busy with their 'next projects' and it was difficult to get their feedback. Secondly, when this was provided, it yielded some intriguing perspectives. The team seemed to be relatively self-critical, seemingly feeling that the project had not been delivered particularly well. A cost overrun of around 8.5 per cent appeared to contribute to this collective, somewhat negative, perspective.

In fact, the building had been designed for a sustainable-construction process; an article in *The Economist Technology Quarterly* (2008) regarding inconsistencies that can emerge during a design process of this type quoted Dr William Mitchell (Massachusetts Institute of Technology): 'inconsistencies can account for 2% of a construction budget, and clashes up to 5%'. Given that the building had been constructed using such processes, we could consider that it had been delivered reasonably well against the cost component. If this had accounted for 5 per cent, there is a further 3.5 per cent of cost overrun to explain. Other issues that were well understood seemed to explain this.

We could argue that this had in fact been delivered well, especially given the high level of satisfaction from clients in the post-delivery operational phase. In fact, very soon after opening, space and capacity for visitors were under pressure. On the one hand, this characterized success, and on the other, revealed that the original vision was, in some respects, not sufficiently ambitious! Hindsight helps us to carry forward our learning to the next project.

A further scenario is offered to help inform our thinking; this example is based on a PIR that was deployed in a multi-organizational project scenario. This is included

since the headings and the use of the approach can also usefully inform the development
of a review process. It is worthwhile explaining these with some further detail, as the
value of the sections may not be immediately apparent from their titles. We may also
find that there are some generic principles here. For example, in the first of these,
document control should be applied to other reporting scenarios where documents
have progressive revision and require good file management.

The PIR headings were as follows:

Document control – for quality control purposes, it is helpful to incorporate a
document control section (or page) that shows the development process and
circulation as shown in Table 6.1. For example, this might include version
number, status and date of version.

Introduction – this helps with the readability of the document.

Scope of PIR – this should be stated for clarification, in the same sense that we
agreed in an earlier chapter regarding the scope of work.

Achievement of objectives and deliverables – this incorporates the original
objectives, final scope, any changes and constraints that may have affected
this. It should also consider whether this affected the extent to which
objectives have been met. This section could also include a review of key
decisions made during the project process and relevant risk impacts.

Changes to scope and constraints – this highlights the agreed changes and
relevant constraints.

Costs and benefits – as a minimum, this should include projected costs and
benefits, as per the final working version of the business case (or appropriate
accepted equivalent as per the context of the project).

Alignment with strategies – the outcome of the project should be presented
within the strategic context or basis that the project took place. This should
also reflect any relevant external strategic frameworks that affected the progress
of the project. For example, within a public-sector scenario there may be national
(or international) frameworks within which the project has to be delivered, or
that affected the project during its lifecycle. It should also reflect any more
localized, regional or specific departmental strategies where relevant.

Client and stakeholder satisfaction – this should be structured to reflect the
framing of the client and stakeholders that would have taken place during the
project lifecycle (primary/secondary or whichever basis was used). This might,
of course, have presented a source of difficulty for the project, and this is one
of the opportunities where it can be documented. Within each area here it
may be appropriate to remark upon the specific areas of success or difficulty.
For example, analysis by distinct client and stakeholder group could be provided.

TABLE 6.1   Example of document version control

Version	Status	
0.1	Template sent through to client	Date
0.2	Early draft pre-issue/circulation	Date
1.0	First issue for internal review (by client)	Date
2.0	Second issue for review (by client)	Date
3.0	Third issue incorporating feedback (from client)	Date

Further revisions as required

Potential future developments – within information systems projects, this might include headings covering strategic alignment, business processes and possible extensions. The specific content of this section should be developed to reflect the particular project (although this could also apply to all sections).

Externally deployed reviews

For publicly financed projects, the funding stakeholders should have an interest in the outcomes of the project. How was the money spent? Was it well spent? We would normally expect funding stakeholders to insist on regular and final audits, as this will help to answer both questions and ensure the destination and purpose of the money spent. Reviews, however, can further help to determine effectiveness, and also inform future policy development and strategic planning.

Governments may provide guidance for the structure and content of reviews. For example, the Presidency of the Republic of South Africa (2011) provided a National Evaluation Framework stating that: 'If we are to improve our performance we have to reflect on what we are doing, what we are achieving against what we set out to achieve, and why unexpected results are occurring. We cannot advance without making mistakes on the way, but we must evaluate and learn from our successes and our mistakes. Without this we cannot improve.'

The framework includes sections that cover the rationale for, approach, the types and uses of evaluations. They also include information that explains the process of evaluation and how to ensure the quality and credibility of work undertaken. The document encourages the fostering of this as an integral aspect of government approach by institutionalizing it as a process; it also considers the management and coordination aspects.

In the UK, a guide to appraisal and evaluation issued by HM Treasury (2003, 2011) includes a statement of purposes 'to ensure that no policy, programme or project is adopted without having the answer to the following questions:

- Are there better ways to achieve this objective?
- Are there better uses for these resources?

Both are good examples of review frameworks, but these may just be fine words. The questions I can hear you thinking might include 'Will it get used?' and 'Do governments actually do what they say?' To help address these concerns or doubts, let us take a look at an example.

The European Regional Development Fund (ERDF) supported numerous projects across the UK (UK Government, 2013). One programme that was evaluated provided, for London, a total of €181m for investment, associated with the promotion of 'sustainable environmentally efficient growth... in areas where this is most needed' (Greater London Authority, 2013). This was intended to capitalize on the innovation and knowledge resources available in London, and the focus was on 'promoting social inclusion through extending economic opportunities to communities'.

The evaluation was undertaken in August 2012, reviewing the programme strategy and performance, the four associated priority areas, aspects of the programme with 'cross-cutting themes', and also including an evaluation of the implementation and management aspects. The scope for this review was extensive. A key point to consider is that this evaluation was undertaken by an independent organization; similar review projects have taken place for ERDF-supported projects across the European area, including the UK; in Wales, projects similar to the one in London were reviewed in the same geographic area of the Hafod Eryri case introduced in Chapter 1, again undertaken by an independent organization.

The reviews will have some similarities in terms of structure and common headings, but the type of evaluation will vary across projects and geographies; the style will reflect the reviewing organizations. The mechanisms are in place to address the two rhetorical points made earlier.

Were we successful?

In the first part of this chapter, we have explored both informal and formal aspects of reviewing projects and also considered a number of types of learning, both opportunistic and of the more directed form. This has followed the relatively more scientific and logical approach to the planning and delivery of projects that we set out in Chapters 2 and 3. The cases incorporated have demonstrated a mix of challenge, success and expectation. It is now appropriate to review the review element itself and consider, using a variety of new examples, whether a generic project has been successful.

The rationale for taking this approach is based upon the challenge of meeting expectations, not only those of the stakeholders but also, importantly, our own. In fact, our own expectations may have changed during the lifecycle of the project. The hindsight that is generated through the lifecycle may have enabled us to realize that the ambition was either too great, or not great enough. If the objectives that were set at the start of (or modified during) the project have been met, we can state that the project has succeeded... but this might not be the basis on which the project is judged by the stakeholders.

The converse is also often true. The original objectives had not been met; we state that the project therefore failed, but again this may not be the perspective that develops over the life of the outcome of the project. We can look at this in three ways:

i   Did we meet the performance objectives?

ii Did we deliver to stakeholder expectations?

iii How will it be judged?

We could ask a fourth question:

iv Did we deliver something of different value than expected (ie to a greater or lesser extent)?

This starts to help us understand whether the project has been genuinely successful or not. It is also important to reflect that, since they are often difficult to quantify, the perspectives developed are often subjective. Let us pursue this further as a basis to develop broader perspectives that will help inform and shape our thinking in terms of the development of project management capability. Indeed, we may reflect that our capacity to deliver successful projects is often constrained.

Project failure appears to be a constant

Wherever we look, it seems there are reports of projects 'failing'. Across the globe, projects are routinely reported as a 'failure', a 'catastrophe' or a 'disaster'. Is this true? If it is, what are the reasons? We could also ask whether the opportunity to provide a good story is greater than the opportunity to reflect in a more sober manner. The news market seems to like the former.

To develop our discussion here, let us look across the world and pick two examples described as a failure, a disaster or a catastrophe. The first example we will use is the Sydney Opera House; from a project perspective this icon of Australia presented many opportunities for news stories. An interesting aspect to this scenario is that the 'bad project' headlines are still associated with the Opera House decades after it was constructed and even when it continues to provide a significant input to the Australian economy.

From the architect competition in 1957 to the inauguration of the building in 1973, and 40 years later in 2013 when headlines might have been highlighting the celebration of its 40th birthday, instead some still focus on this project as a form of disaster.[1]

It was late; it was over budget; it caused significant trauma among the project team and stakeholders – 'yet, by fluke, it has turned into one of our most valuable assets. According to modelling by Deloitte, the Opera House adds $775m to the Australian economy every year in direct ticket sales, retail and food shopping and by boost to tourism to Australia' (*Courier Mail*, 2013). This does not seem the language of failure.

In contrast, let us consider a second example, the 'lessons from Jindal's Bolivian failure' (Gateway House, 2013). In 2007, the Indian company Jindal Steel and Power Ltd secured a contract for an integrated mining and steel project in Bolivia. Intending to invest $2.1bn, the project was expected to create 12,000 jobs and $200m per year for the government of Bolivia.

The project had been on hold for five years when in July 2012 Jindal terminated the contract with the Bolivian government, citing issues over the supply of gas. As disputes between Jindal and the government escalated, 'Bolivia encashed $36m of bank guarantees given by Jindal' (*The Wall Street Journal*, 2012). By August 2014, Jindal had 'won a $22.5m arbitration judgement...' (Bloomberg, 2014).

Gateway House (2013) offered an analysis of this in two perspectives; they identified four areas that contributed to the failure as:

- complex political relationships;
- a misjudgement of political power;
- disproportionate size of investment raising unrealistic expectations;
- a failure to evaluate the scenario sufficiently.

Secondly, they suggested that key lessons had been learnt, remarking that 'a brilliant business plan is not enough' and emphasizing that a 'thorough political and risk analysis is necessary'. This example appears to exhibit the characteristics of a project that genuinely failed to realize the original objectives.

A sense of perspective

In 2003, in their instructive work exploring the incidence of cost overruns in transport infrastructure projects, Flyvbjerg, Holm and Buhl (2003) drew a number of conclusions that make clearer sense of public projects and uncomfortable reading for those who are involved in taking on the risk of projects such as these.

Referencing this research in 2011 in the article 'High-speed rail: tres grand vitesse, tres grand cost overrun', *The Economist* (2011) focused on the likelihood that the cost of the proposed high-speed rail project for California would escalate by three or four times. The article referred to the Flyvbjerg *et al* findings that with the mean cost escalation on rail projects at 45 per cent, by implication 'if we were going to cancel infrastructure projects when they start to run more than 25% over budget, we'd never build any infrastructure'. The last point is a particularly strong one.

It is worthwhile considering the Flyvbjerg *et al* research further, since the conclusions drawn provide quite a stark insight into the realities of cost estimation in public infrastructure projects; these point strongly to the continued bias of optimism in these areas. In their research on 258 projects that had been completed between 1927 and 1998, they found that 'nine out of ten transport infrastructure projects fall victim to cost escalation'; the average for rail projects was 45 per cent, fixed links (tunnels and bridges) 34 per cent and for roads 20 per cent. Almost as striking was the conclusion that 'cost escalation has not decreased over the past 70 years. No learning seems to have taken place'.

As the research covered a sufficiently long period, they argued that the stakeholder impact on delays causing cost overruns was accounted for, so having no effect on the conclusions. They offered a further consideration that 'cost escalation is a simple consequence of cost estimation and underestimation is used tactically to get projects approved and built'. These thoughts are certainly worth reflecting upon; if this is the case, then even with extremely well-developed techniques, a project manager would struggle to deliver projects on budget, therefore immediately offering a source of missed targets for the failure-hungry reporters of public projects. Clearly this will also have a direct effect on stakeholder groups, who will need to make up the shortfall in funding.

Therefore, projects do fail in terms of exceeding their original (target) performance parameters. But does this mean that we should regard this as a failure of the project or, more specifically, its project management? It is worthwhile examining the phraseology to help inform our thinking and, perhaps more importantly, our future approach or strategy. Failure is defined in three ways in the *Oxford English Dictionary* (2007) as:

0 Lack of success: an economic policy that is doomed to failure

1 The neglect or omission of expected or required action: their failure to comply with the basic rules; A lack or deficiency of a desirable quality: a failure of imagination

2 The action or state of not functioning: symptoms of heart failure, a chance of engine failure.

Reviewing the use of these words in the reporting of the example just mentioned, we could draw a number of conclusions here; bad news is often good news, and the coverage of the Sydney Opera House seems to confirm this – even more than 40 years after the venue opened, the main story often portrayed is of failure.

Does good news about a project make good news for readers? From time to time we see examples of a project that was originally deemed to be a 'bad' project becoming a 'good' one. One particular example of this is Eurotunnel, the connection of France and England under the channel known as La Manche or the English Channel. Often a companion in failure to the Sydney Opera House in case and text-book reading, Eurotunnel cost twice as much as budgeted to build, as described in *The Economist* (2014).

This feature described how, 20 years after opening, the tunnel was used by half as many customers as planned. *The Economist* added that the first shareholder dividend was paid in 2009 (14 years after it was promised), and that many of the original investors had seen their savings 'vanish in the restructuring of Eurotunnel's unpayable debt in 2007'. Yet, in 2014, there was room for optimism over the next 20-year period – passenger numbers had increased and rail freight was higher by 12 per cent (2013 over 2012). The reason for optimism was described as the likelihood of greater competition; the European Commission was enthusiastic about opening up the route to train operators from other member states, such as Deutsche Bahn (a German rail company). *The Economist* reported that this was expected to stimulate growth in services and hence revenues.

This is a project that was completed over budget, that did not provide the revenue expected (required) in the business case projections, which classified it as 'bad'. Market conditions may well change to enable the achievement of relatively more successful returns, therefore enabling us to describe it at a future point as 'good'.

Learning point

Our discussion has considered that some projects are described as failures despite succeeding in a number of respects. The terminology is often misapplied and sticks to the project for a long time. We have also seen examples of projects that are more characteristically failures, as they are stopped for a variety of reasons, often leaving at least one stakeholder group with a hole in their investment, a gap in their expected capability, or a project situation which is completely unfinished.

Reasons why projects might be deemed failures

We should also spend some time considering other reasons why projects do not perform as expected. In 1994, the Standish Group provided its first public report, documenting significant amounts of budget seemingly wasted on IT application developments. As the publications were timely, they were also quite provocative, usefully providing a focus for examination and reflection by organizations that were experiencing difficulties with the very same things.

In an interview with Deborah Hartmann Preuss for InfoQ in 2006, Jim Johnson of the Standish Group explained the background and use of vocabulary, as their survey results in 2004 used the terminology 'failed', 'succeeded' and 'challenged'. This group established a number of core reasons determining the success of projects. This included user involvement, support from executive management, and the need for clear business objectives (also referred to as having a 'clear statement of requirements').

Periodic evaluations are published, revealing further insights. In 'A study on project failure', the British Computer Society (2008) reported that 'only one in eight information technology projects can be considered truly successful'. They described failure as those projects that 'do not meet the original time, cost and (quality) requirements criteria'. This reinforces the categorization of projects as failures when there may be legitimate reasons why these criteria are exceeded (or not met).

In New Zealand, KPMG published the 'Project Management Survey Report' (2013) reporting an average spend per project of NZ$15m. As well as reporting that they had seen an increase in project failure rates over the previous period, they also found a number of factors strongly correlated with 'high-performing projects' to be those that:

1 are commissioned with robust business case and are aligned with corporate strategy;

2 have an effective sponsor who provides clear direction;

3 have project managers that use methodology consistently and who have a high level of project management capability;

4 manage risks actively, report variations and implement early recovery actions;

5 are run within a programme of work or portfolio;

6 are coordinated by a project management office.

This report usefully draws our attention to some key points, and provides emphasis and an opportunity for linkage with topics throughout the book.

It is worthwhile referencing one further insight from industry: McKinsey & Company (2012) reported that on average, large IT projects (defined as having an initial price tag exceeding $15m) run 45 per cent over budget and 7 per cent over time, while delivering 56 per cent less value than predicted. They argue that the research, undertaken with the University of Oxford, provides findings 'consistent across industries', and that their 'surveys of IT executives indicate that the key to success lies in four broad dimensions'. These include 'focusing on managing strategy and stakeholders instead of exclusively concentrating on budget and scheduling', the need to secure 'critical internal and external talent', the value of 'building effective teams…', and also the need to excel at the 'core project management practices…'.

These statements reinforce the extent to which the project management focus needs to be at a high (strategic) as well as at a detailed level (core project management practices). While the focus of the reports mentioned latterly here is predominantly in the area of information technology projects, we will see that the advice is applicable more broadly. It also provides a useful entry point to the next topic, which is concerned with one of the points made earlier, 'methodology'. A project management industry has been born in the form of generally applicable methods and guidance that complements the already-existing delivery industries, which include engineering, construction and professional services.

Incentives to succeed

In order to set out some context for the final set of topics in this chapter, we can draw on a specific example that highlights the response of an organization to public criticism. The following case considers the two large projects that were completed at Heathrow Airport in 2008 and 2014. The first, the opening of Terminal 5 (in 2008), attracted considerable public criticism. The second, the opening of Terminal 2 (in 2014), attracted comparatively little. While the case will explore both projects from a general public perspective, it will start by setting out the market conditions facing BAA, Heathrow Airport's operator, in the period prior to 2008. The reader is encouraged to reflect on the wider perspectives and challenges facing any organization whose brand image may be seriously damaged by a 'bad project'.

CASE STUDY   Heathrow Airport Terminal projects[2]

… from five to two, over six years

On 27 March 2008, the much-vaunted operational opening of Heathrow Terminal 5 turned into a fiasco. The cancellation of flights, thousands of lost bags and initial chaos announced the project to the world. For the media it provided lots of news; for stranded travellers it presented lots of problems; for the operator of the airport (British Airport Authority, BAA) and the airline (British Airways, BA), damage to reputations. Yet, in June 2014, six years later, the opening of Terminal 2 was greeted with little brouhaha. Fewer opportunities for media stories, few passenger problems and reputations enhanced.

This two-scenario case provides some insights into the critical learning that can take place when an organization has a second opportunity to put right things that didn't go well the first time. Concentrating first on the Terminal 5 project, it is worth recalling some background context: prior to this project, Heathrow Airport was regularly criticized – on 9 August 2007 *The Economist* featured an article titled 'Britain's Awful Airports; Another summer of delayed flights, lost bags and moaning about Heathrow'. They highlighted the criticism levelled at Heathrow, at the time the busiest airport in Europe, processing 67m passengers through facilities designed for 45m (almost 50 per cent more). A combination of industrial disputes, poor weather and security scares had contrived to keep the airport a focus for frustration and anger. *The Economist* also highlighted that the airport had been bought, in a deal financed by borrowing, by the Spanish firm Grupo Ferrovial.

Furthermore, during this period, the Competition Commission (a now-defunct UK non-departmental public body) was investigating whether BAA's ownership of all of London's three airports was inhibiting competition in the market. The inquiry was instigated during 2007 and pundits suspected at the time that this would result in the break-up of BAA. In hindsight, 2007 looks like it was a troubling year for the owner of Heathrow Airport.

BAA made other headlines, too. In January 2008, *The Sunday Times* reported that investment bank J P Morgan warned that 'BAA may run out of cash', with a large capital expenditure programme and a high interest bill. While there were mechanisms associated with the sale of assets that could ease this, it seems that there were a number of sources of pressure for BAA. Then *The Sunday Times* reported on 16 March 2008 that airlines were pushing for a break-up of BAA. This highlighted an 'unusual' meeting between four of Britain's top airlines and the government's transport secretary. It was against this backdrop that T5 might provide a welcome distraction.

On Thursday 7 March, the terminal opened; unfortunately, progressively through the day, many parts of the world were hearing about Heathrow's fiasco. On 31 March 2008, the BBC summarized the problem areas as shown in Figure 6.2.

As the reporting took place shortly after the events transpired, details were accumulated quickly but the picture was not particularly clear. On the same day, the *New York Times* reported that 'British Airways had cancelled 54 more short-haul flights at Heathrow Airport's problem-plagued new Terminal 5 on Monday'. This feature highlighted that almost 300 flights had been cancelled and some 50,000 bags separated from their owners since the terminal had opened four days earlier. In discussing the chaos, the article focused our minds on the reputational damage suffered by both BA and BAA.

FIGURE 6.2   Timeline showing key opening-day issues

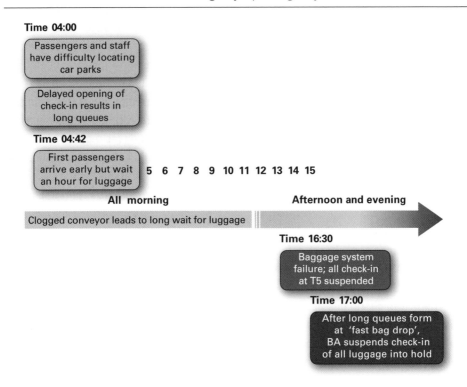

It also highlighted some of the background issues faced by the airport, the consequences of the problems, but reassuringly reflected that Heathrow was not in a unique position – they mentioned the 'deadly roof collapse at Charles de Gaulle Airport (Paris, 2004)' and the 'losing of baggage nine months after the opening of Madrid's terminal four in 2006'. These somewhat more reflective thoughts may not have provided comfort to the stakeholders affected at Terminal 5.

The high-profile nature of this project launch provided scope for analysts, experts and writers to revel. *Computer Weekly* (14 May 2008) reported that 'British Airways has revealed the full extent of the IT problems that marred T5's opening'. Based on written evidence that had been submitted to the subsequent UK government enquiry, it revealed both the emergence of various problems and also that staff had been unable to deal with these.

Time passes. Problems are resolved. A new facility moves to a 'normal' operational state. Client satisfaction increases. Reputations recover, but as damage has been done, clients need to be reassured that everything is fine. In September 2008, BA was buying full-page advertisements in newspapers such as *The Times* with a headline 'Yesterday at T5 average time through security was 5.2 mins…'. The feature asserted that this was the average time based on research with 818 T5 customers who passed through security on

10 September 2008 between 6 am and 2 pm. The narrative finished with 'Terminal 5 is working. Try it for yourself'.

And so it passes into history, providing an example to ask the question whether or not this was a failure or expected 'teething problems'. A paper published in the *International Journal of Project Management* in 2010 provided a more considered evaluation of the project launch. The authors analysed the problems reported by the media, those experienced by customers and staff, and drew upon the subsequent UK government transport committee enquiry, to highlight the key problem areas for the T5 building that 'was nineteen years in the planning and construction'.

They discussed the notion that 'whilst T5 opening has been called a disaster, this is mainly in terms of public relations. No-one was put at risk of death or serious injury because the system broke down on opening day'. This provides a sense of perspective. Already having articulated that the opening-day chaos was the result of several separate problems (in isolation these may not have had such a catastrophic effect), they also highlighted that BAA had tried to develop some foresight for this project by examining previous major projects – 'BAA carried out a two-year in-depth study of every major UK construction project of over £1bn conducted over the previous 10 years'. This included a review of international airports that had opened over the previous 15 years. Following this evaluation, BAA approached the T5 project based on two underlying principles: firstly, the client bears the risk, and secondly, deploying integrated project teams. They argue that applying these principles contributed to the construction project being achieved on time and within budget.

Their analysis also revealed that the 'togetherness' (of BAA and BA) deteriorated around, or just prior to, the opening. 'The failure of BAA and BA to function as an integrated team' was a contribution to the chaos of opening T5. They argued that, had this been still in operation prior to the T5 opening, the catastrophic combination of smaller problems might not have occurred. They also quoted the BAA CEO: 'it was unfortunate that we created an expectation of perfection in what was an extremely complicated programme'.

Fast-forward to Terminal 2, the new facility opened in June 2014. The same organizations were involved, BAA and BA. BAA is now different in terms of operating fewer airports as an outcome of the Competition Commission investigation in 2008. Both organizations would have vivid recollections of the T5 opening. In setting realistic expectations 12 weeks ahead of the launch, *The Guardian* reported that 'Heathrow bosses admit Terminal 2 is likely to face opening-day problems'. This article highlighted the testing through 'a series of 180 trials with 14,000 volunteers' and quoted John Holland-Kaye, Heathrow's development director, who had 'a copy of the transport select committee report into the T5 debacle in my bag... to make sure that we learn from the lessons'.

On 4 June 2014, the *Financial Times* reported that 'Heathrow's Terminal 2 avoids a repeat of T5 launch chaos' and a *Daily Telegraph* headline stated that 'first passengers praise Heathrow's new Terminal 2'. The time is different; the challenges were similar; the outcome is satisfactory. The launch of T2 was not a good item for the media, perhaps proving that it was a much more successful launch than the previous operational opening, that of Terminal 5.

Case reflection

Evaluate this scenario in terms of:

i   The prevailing conditions at the time of the T5 opening project.

ii Stakeholder perspectives and brand image.

iii Balance: how serious were the problems during the first opening?

iv Lessons learnt and project reviews: what was carried forward so that T2 created few bad headlines?

The need to improve

While the delivery of things as projects is clearly not new in any society, the emergence of formal methods used by practitioners has grown. This has developed from a domain with a vocabulary such as critical path methods (CPM) and work breakdown structure (WBS) to such recent abbreviations as Prince 2® (a method) and APMP® (a qualification). We can add to this mix PMO (project management office), PMI, APM and IPMA; there are now a large number of terms. Alongside the growth in the bodies of knowledge (initially championed by the PMI), the area of practitioner methods and certification has grown and is now endemic within the world of project management.

These methods and approaches have grown in a manner not always complementary to the already-existing project management techniques enshrined in areas such as construction. For example, the presentation of a part-drafted project initiation document (PID) at a meeting concerned with a novel construction project can provoke a negative reaction from an architect who is used to dealing with all aspects of the project management.

Why have we seen the growth of these tools and techniques and significant investment by some nations in associated training courses and accreditations? Aside from a rational belief that this will help manage projects better, a key reason is associated with the fear of failure. A move towards providing tools, techniques and qualifications is a way of providing a form of capability that should help to overcome the possibility that the next project will 'fail'. If we can subject the new activity to exhaustive scientific methods and rigour, the outcomes will be more predictable.

We have discussed the somewhat emotional way that projects can be reported by the media reported (a bad project is often good news), and often this is of a public nature. Many public-sector (or government) projects are of a public nature or, as we may seek to argue, since these are funded by some form of taxation, the tax-paying stakeholders have a right to know how their money was spent. Also, it is therefore our desire to understand the nature of the progress and outcomes. Aside from the problems of interpretation we discussed, there are a number of considerations here.

If a government is accused of (or punished for, in certain political systems) failing to deliver its projects, what can it do to improve the likelihood of success in these? One option would be to invest in methods which it believes will improve this likelihood. What will this look like? The UK scenario provides a good example of this. It is important to bear in mind that the perception of failure in projects is not something reserved to the public sector. Many organizations, concerned by the value lost through delayed projects, will probably also seek to improve this likelihood factor (and ideally they would see 100 per cent of projects successful), hence a reason to invest in methods-based training and development.

Practitioner-based approaches

In addition to some key project management inventions, the UK has seen moves to professionalize project management though institutional recognition and accreditation, the emergence of support networks and the spawning of training and development courses associated with these. Further, the letting of some contracts has been detailed with a requirement for budding bidders to demonstrate their project management competence. While this seems laudable, it has not been welcomed universally; often the requirement had been for an organization to be accredited, certified, or populated by staff who are all qualified within a framework such as Prince 2®. This has sometimes provoked a question: 'As a design and build consultancy, our organization has been successfully delivering projects over the past thirty years; what difference will this additional investment make to our delivery capability?'

This is a fair point, made constructively. There is certainly a cost associated with this, but in a tendering situation all bidders should be subject to the same criteria (and hence opportunity costs). But it could also be a point made that reflects a reluctance to change. The organization nevertheless takes the decision to invest in this accreditation as it has little choice; it is a condition of bidding for the contract. The additional costs are absorbed into the business and it becomes business-as-normal. With a keen eye on profitability, they will evaluate their costs and benefits. They may go back to their first view of this when they see the emergence of a different form of central guidance, one that seems to be the antithesis of Prince 2®. Some might say 'this is what we have been doing all the time'. Therein lies another of the many challenges faced by businesses in terms of project management. Despite the wide array of tools and techniques at their disposal, many organizations find that there is a gap.

There is a gap between the delivery level achievable using acknowledged, more scientific tools when compared with the wider and ever-changing expectations of stakeholders. It is also worth highlighting that some of this gap is associated with things that are not new; they are sometimes about politics, culture, strategy, organization, people, people, and people. Knowing about the formal methods is not enough. It is also about a deeper understanding of project management, the science and art.

Summary

A review of the preceding sections in this chapter provides an opportunity to reflect upon the various things we have learnt; despite our investment in conceptualizing and planning, there are a host of things that we didn't, or couldn't, have known about early in the project lifecycle. There is a gap that has emerged between the somewhat idealistic early conceptualizing/planning phases and the outcomes of the delivering/reviewing activities.

This is entirely expected and provides us with a platform to open up the next chapters of the book. We have introduced a number of general principles and applied them to a number of project scenarios. Each of these principles is like an iceberg... for what we can see above the water, there is considerably more that we cannot see. There is more depth to many of the topics, and there are more principles that we need to introduce. The discussion associated with evaluation here helps us to understand this better.

We can also include in this discussion an argument that evaluation is one of the most important parts of a project. This is often the point at which people enter a project, at the point where it is finished. Passengers on the new metro line, aeroplane or ship; a purchaser of perfume; a customer on a heritage steam railway; a spectator at a sporting event; a user of a new IT system, operating system or device – we enter the project as a user or customer of the outcome of the project. We are often not interested in the project until we benefit from it.

Yet, surely this is the point at which the project will become judged as a failure or success. This also marks an important point for us: up to this point we have considered the somewhat idealistic translation of concepts into plans, and through the often more challenging delivery period into a completed and evaluated project. We have really just begun our project management learning journey. The following chapters will build upon the concepts introduced so far and consider a different angle where projects are not only business-as-normal, they are essential to the dynamics of global economies, and where stakeholder communities are interconnected to a degree never seen before. The project manager role is about to get more challenging.

Notes

1   The Sydney Opera House construction: A case of project management failure, retrieved on 23 August 2014 from http://www.eoi.es/blogs/cristinagarcia-ochoa/2012/01/14/the-sidney-opera-house-construction-a-case-of-project-management-failure/

2   This case study draws upon information from the following sources:

BBC (2008) 'What went wrong at Heathrow's T5?', 31 March, retrieved on 4 August 2014 from http://news.bbc.co.uk/1/hi/uk/7322453.stm

Brady, T and Davies, A (2010) From hero to hubris – reconsidering the project management of Heathrow's Terminal 5, *International Journal of Project Management*, 28, pp 151–15

Competition Commission (2007) Market investigation into supply of airport services by BAA, 9 August

Computer Weekly (2008) British Airways reveals what went wrong with Terminal 5, 14 May, retrieved on 4 August 2014 from http://www.computerweekly.com/news/2240086013/British-Airways-reveals-what-went-wrong-with-Terminal-5

Daily Telegraph (2014) First passengers praise Heathrow's new Terminal 2, 4 June, retrieved on 04 August 2014 from http://www.telegraph.co.uk/finance/newsbysector/transport/10874166/First-passengers-praise-Heathrows-new-Terminal-2.html

The Economist (2007) Britain's awful airports, 9 August

Financial Times (2014) Heathrow's Terminal 2 avoids repeat of T5 launch chaos, 4 June, retrieved on 4 August 2014 from http://www.ft.com/cms/s/0/806a4d1e-ebd3-11e3-ab1b-00144feabdc0.html#axzz39Pp2rJcv

The Guardian (2014) Heathrow bosses admit Terminal 2 likely to face opening-day problems, 12 March, retrieved on 4 August 2014 from http://www.theguardian.com/world/2014/mar/12/heathrow-terminal-2-opening-problems-airport/print

The New York Times (2008) Problems continue at Heathrow's Terminal 5, 31 March, retrieved on 14 August 2014 from http://www.nytimes.com/2008/03/31/world/europe/31iht-heathrow.1.11548289.html?_r=0

The Sunday Times (2008) BAA may run out of cash, warns bank, 27 January

The Sunday Times (2008) Airlines unite to push for BAA break-up, 16 March

The Times (2008) Yesterday at T5 average time through security was 5.2 mins, 11 September

References

Association for Project Management (APM) (2012) *APM Body of Knowledge*, APM, Princes Risborough, Bucks

Bloomberg (2014) Jindal Steel wins $22.5 million verdict against Bolivia, 23 August, retrieved on 1 October 2014 from http://www.bloomberg.com/news/2014-08-23/jindal-steel-wins-22-5-million-verdict-against-bolivia.html

British Computer Society (2008) A study in project failure, retrieved on 19 August 2014
    from http://www.bcs.org/content/conwebdoc/19584

Courier Mail (2013) Why Sydney's Opera House was the world's biggest planning disaster,
    22 October, retrieved on 23 August 2014 from http://www.couriermail.com.au/news/
    why-sydneys-opera-house-was-the-worlds-biggest-planning-disaster/story-e6freon6-
    1226744769556?nk=f2626620e5bf37271f78e86552fc2c7c

The Economist Technology Quarterly (2008) Computing: from blueprint to database, 7 June

The Economist (2011) High speed rail: tres grand vitesse, tres grand cost overrun, 15 August

The Economist (2014) Eurotunnel: The next 20 years: a bad project comes good – with
    better yet in store, 10 May

Flyvbjerg, B, Holm, M and Buhl, S (2003) How common and how large are cost overruns in
    transport infrastructure projects, *Transport Reviews*, **23** (1), pp 71–88

Gateway House (2013) 'Lessons from Jindal's Bolivian failure', 19 July, retrieved on
    23 August 2014 from http://www.gatewayhouse.in/lessons-from-jindals-bolivian-failure/

Greater London Authority (2013) London ERDF 2007-13 Programme: Interim evaluation,
    retrieved on 16 November 2014 from https://www.london.gov.uk/sites/default/files/
    Executive%20Summary.pdf

Hartmann Preuss, D, InfoQ (2006) Interview: Jim Johnson of the Standish Group, 25 June

HM Treasury (2003, 2011) *The Green Book: Appraisal and evaluation in central government*,
    TSO, London

KPMG (2013) Project management survey, New Zealand, retrieved on 19 August 2014
    from http://www.kpmg.com/nz/en/issuesandinsights/articlespublications/pages/project-
    management-survey-2013.aspx

Maylor, H (2010) *Project Management*, Pearson Education, Harlow

McKinsey & Company (2012) Delivering large-scale IT projects on time, on budget, and on
    value, retrieved on 19 August 2014 from http://www.mckinsey.com/insights/business_
    technology/delivering_large-scale_it_projects_on_time_on_budget_and_on_value

Project Management Institute (PMI) (2013) *A Guide to the Project Management Body of
    Knowledge*, PMI Inc., Newtown Square, PA

Republic of South Africa (2011) South African National Evaluation Policy Framework,
    retrieved on 17 July 2014 from http://www.thepresidency.gov.za/MediaLib/Downloads/
    Home/Ministries/National_Evaluation_Policy_Framework.pdf

UK Government (2013) 2007 to 2013 ERDF programmes: progress and achievements,
    retrieved on 18 September 2014 from https://www.gov.uk/erdf-programmes-progress-
    and-achievements

The Wall Street Journal (2012) Jindal Steel exits Bolivia project, 17 July, retrieved on
    1 October 2014 from http://online.wsj.com/news/articles/
    SB10001424052702303754904577532592283910030

PART THREE
Projects in a challenging world

Projects: a way of thinking

Introduction

This chapter will explore two project worlds: firstly, one where projects are articulated specifically since we believe them to be different from business-as-normal, and secondly, the world where projects in fact constitute the business or organizational activity. Such organizations may not promote their businesses as 'projects'. In fact, in many respects this may not be conspicuous.

We will consider scenarios where projects are understand as a distinct unusual activity and explore further the emergence of practitioner expertise and its impact on the organization project theatre. How can this type of development contribute to the future scenario where project management is the standard for delivering the organization's objectives? Our evaluation will look at a representative example from one region.

The chapter will also examine the organization where projects are the building blocks of their purpose or enable them to deliver their services. We will consider the degree to which some of these sectors might benefit from more conspicuous project management guidance, and conversely, whether organizations struggling to deliver projects effectively might learn from these.

The development of this thinking will enable us to consider the project as a bridge between strategy and operations; this is an important aspect which is sometimes overlooked, yet is fundamental to the success of individuals, organizations and nations. There is potentially a large overlap of project management with other disciplines, and this theme will continue to be developed.

The practitioner world

In response to a desire to improve good practice and the success rate of projects, the emergence of practitioner-based approaches was introduced towards the end of Chapter 6. Nations have encouraged the development of member organizations, bodies of knowledge (BoK) and methodologies, and this in turn has spawned the wide availability of accredited training and development services. This could also be regarded as a response to fear of failure; failed or failing projects, as we discussed in Chapter 6, provide good material for news stories.

The bodies of knowledge

A number of the key parties in this area were introduced in the previous chapters. As it is one of the routes to help organizations to better deliver projects and also an area that has generated considerable momentum and critical mass, we will consider this from a strategic perspective.

Across the world, organizations provide support for the development of project management knowledge, skills and resources. A selection of these is shown in Figure 7.1.

Most of these organizations provide members with knowledge resources, accreditation, career development support and networking opportunities. Different organizations might provide 'good' or 'best practice' models or tools, with others providing training and development services. These are often tied together; for example, tool X developed by organization A is accredited by organization B, and approved organization C offers courses on tool X for the market (as shown in Figure 7.2).

There is a broad consistency of offering across geographies, as many of these are based on the generic project management methods introduced in Chapters 1 to 6.

FIGURE 7.1 Institutions and membership organizations

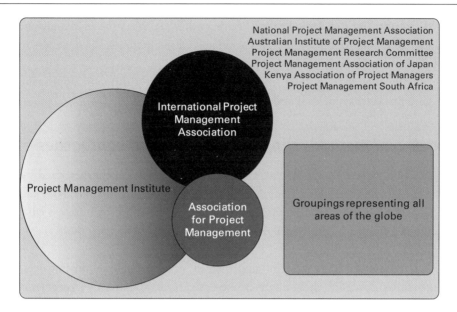

FIGURE 7.2 The relationship between owner, method, accreditor and training market

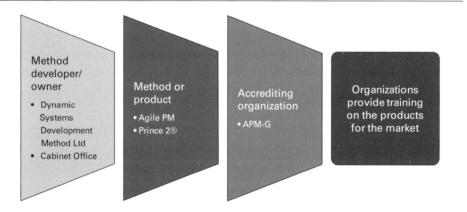

This is not to say that all offerings are the same, but the commonality is expected and also important, especially where a project manager is located in geography R, works on a project in geography S, delivering for clients in a further set of different geographies. For example, where the product is designed in the United States, development work takes place in India for a client with offices in China and Brazil.

In order to explain and discuss this further, we can focus on one region as an example of typical developments, benefits and arguments that arise. Let us look at the situation that has developed in the UK. There is a professional body (membership organization), the Association for Project Management (APM); a number of organizations provide methods products such as The Cabinet Office (for Prince 2®) and DSDM Consortium (for Agile Project Framework®), APM-G for accreditation, and a number of companies provide training on accredited methods for members of the APM. This is illustrated in Figure 7.2.

Reviewing this area usefully introduces two distinctly different approaches to managing projects: sequential and non-sequential.

Models and methods supporting sequential approaches

Sequential or 'waterfall' approaches typified by Prince 2® are characterized by following the lifecycle methods set out in Chapter 1 in a sequential manner. For example, the idea is followed by the development and then approval of the business case; the planning is followed by the staged delivery of the project outcomes; these are shown in Figure 7.3.

These are referred to as waterfall approaches, since, in such an ideal project, just as water flows downhill, these might be expected to flow similarly. However, in the real world of projects, often these steps cannot be followed in such a clear logical way. Frequently we need to move back a step, to repeat a stage of the project lifecycle. The waterfall is subjected to un-worldly forces and the result is the contortion of stages.

This is one aspect of the rationale behind the 2001 Manifesto for Agile Software Development, reported in *The Economist* (2001). The feature noted that 'a common cause of disaster in software development is that the end product is precisely what the customer ordered'. This provocative statement reveals much about the management of innovation-type projects, especially in the area of software development. Notwithstanding our comments made in Chapter 6 regarding the language used

FIGURE 7.3   Sequential project delivery

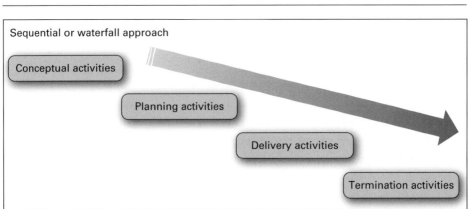

(in terms of using the word 'disaster'), this is a particularly real challenge that encourages us to consider other perspectives.

Models and methods supporting non-sequential approaches

The term 'agile' is used to describe iterative approaches that are based on flexibility and interaction; it is likely to include the breaking up of the project into smaller elements and ensuring that there is regular consultation with the client. The use of agile approaches is frequently promoted for innovative projects where a design specification is difficult to establish. Of course, in a genuine project (with some degree of newness) we could argue that establishing a clear design specification is always difficult.

As the world moves inexorably towards a greater reliance on (and appetite for) innovative software-driven products and services, we would expect the need for so-called agile approaches to have increased. Before we explore this new area further, since at first glance it seems to be a panacea (or antithesis, as the case may be), it is worth considering the significance of this development.

The recent manifestation of project management approaches has largely been derived from relatively more analytical methods arising in areas such as engineering, construction and defence. Widespread concerns about the need to ensure that soft skills are developed as effectively as these hard skills has seen the change in emphasis in content with the respective bodies of knowledge, admittedly subtle in some respects, conspicuous in others, such as in the growth of stakeholder management courses.

The agile development could be potentially seismic in undermining the established knowledge basis of project management, or it could be a realistic and timely reflection of the need for as much variety in approaches and style in project management as there is variety and style of projects.

Given that we explored project management in a sequenced style in the early chapters, leading us to recognize more immediately the characteristics of a waterfall approach, we will balance these insights by examining the agile style next. This will help us consider the area from a more balanced perspective. Is this something truly fundamental, or is it, like the emperor's new clothes, something we knew all along but were inhibited about challenging?

Continuing to explore this within the context of the UK, the DSDM Consortium (2008) developed a pocket-book-style approach called 'Atern', incorporating key sections covering an overview of the project lifecycle, key techniques, roles and products. To those with some experience of sequential approaches, this has some similarities in headings but contrast in terms of emphasis and focus. For example, the guide stated (2008: 5) that the approach '… avoids the cumbersome rigidity of "big design upfront" without the inevitable risks of "no design upfront".' This was followed by a statement regarding flexibility, that it can be 'used to complement other disciplines such as Prince 2®'.

By 2012 this approach had evolved into the 'DSDM Agile Project Framework' (DSDM Consortium, 2012: 5), a 'further-developed and refined approach' that has been accredited by APM-G International and is offered as a training product alongside Prince2® by a range of commercial providers. In addition to retaining the majority of the 'Atern' guide headings, this framework incorporates eight principles:

1 Focus on business need.

2 Deliver on time.

3 Collaborate.

4 Never compromise quality.

5 Build incrementally from firm foundations.

6 Develop iteratively.

7 Communicate continuously and clearly.

8 Demonstrate control.

Clarification of principle 4 ('never compromise quality') is achieved by arguing that in a '"traditional approach"'…, quality often becomes a casualty as projects struggle to deliver a fixed scope in a constrained timeframe' (DSDM, 2012: 17). They argue for the separation of the quality constraint into technical quality and scope. Further, they encourage prioritization (2012: 43) using the acronym 'MoSCoW' to represent 'Must have', 'Should have', 'Could have' and 'Won't have this time'. This is a useful mini-framework to adopt, since its use will clarify the priority level of the associated requests.

In contrast to sequential approaches, agile methods generally accept change as a constant and encourage strong client involvement throughout the process. The argument is that change requirements will be raised and addressed during the delivery period of the project. An approach such as Prince 2® is strong on control, and if an organization is most concerned about managing cost and risk, this may be a reason to utilize it.

Furthermore, agile methods emphasize people interactions, developing working solutions, customer collaboration and responding to change, whereas for Prince 2® the focus is on processes and tools, rigorous documentation, negotiation over contracts and planning to provide the route for project delivery.

In an article in *Project Manager Today* (2012), E Mitchell posed the question as to whether waterfall and agile techniques are mutually exclusive. This was evaluated in relation to a case in which the DSDM Atern approach had been used. In terms of a number of aspects, including governance and control, business need, buy-in and attitudes, a number of benefits were accrued and reassurance provided that control had not been lost. Furthermore, in terms of collaboration and communication, quality and the various techniques proposed were viewed as beneficial. Overall, the two different approaches were not deemed to be mutually exclusive, and the author stressed that the two are complementary. Other studies such as that by Socitm Insight (2014) have provided similar views.

Currently, the parties involved in promoting and accrediting these approaches are emphasizing the complementarity of both; within an environment where the specification is relatively more fixed, adopting a more traditional sequential approach might work better with the form of contract and the experience of the delivery team. In contrast, for projects that involve high levels of innovation or uncertainty about the final specification, the agile approaches lend some structure and formality to a style that we may in any case have no alternative but to adopt.

In terms of incorporating a model into our way of thinking, the practitioner world could well continue to change. To help inform our thinking further in this respect, it is helpful to consider the examinable schemes provided by the Project Management Institute; firstly, the Project Management Professional (PMP®) qualification is focused on performance domains (PMI, 2011a) that include task and 'cross-cutting knowledge and skills'. The associated domains are set out in the style of a sequential project (ie from initiating though to closing the project).

In contrast, 'PMI Agile Certified Practitioner' (PMI-ACP®, 2011b) sets out domains that include 'Value-Driven Delivery', 'Boosting Team Performance Practices' and 'Adaptive Planning'. This provides a usefully wide choice for practitioners who wish to further develop their knowledge and become appropriately qualified.

Integration of development approaches within organizational setting

This is a relatively common scenario: a practitioner model or framework is adapted to an organizational setting. For example, an organization sees benefits in formalizing various aspects of their project work, so they develop an underlying model that is adapted to the specific context of their own processes and cultural base. Some organizations have a strong project basis to deliver their services and so it is quite natural for this.

An example is found within the multinational petrochemical business Shell. An APM case study (APM, 2011) highlights that energy and petrochemical organization Shell counts around '3,000 project management professionals and a further 5,000 technical staff involved in project delivery in the 93,000 people employed in its global business'. It further discusses the 'mature project management approach, proven and developed over 100 years of experience'. Shell is a projects-business, with a project portfolio averaging 'US$25–30bn per year'. The case explains the establishment of the 'Shell Project Academy', which incorporates a competence development programme with a 'pentagon' of linked processes including 'learning, experience, networking, coaching and mentoring, professional accreditation and guidance for long-term competence development'. APM highlight that these are strongly aligned to their six dimensions of professionalism, breadth, depth, achievement, commitment and accountability.

This usefully highlights two aspects: firstly, the value of aligning institutional development processes with those in organizational schemes, and secondly, that some businesses are already projects-businesses, for whom projects are necessarily business-as-normal. As the key to successful production and distribution of hydrocarbon products, exploration projects are fundamental in such sectors. This leads us to consider the notion of projects-based organizations and similar organizational entities.

The context for projects-based organizations

There are many more examples of organizations (in the private, government and other sectors) that are primarily concerned with delivering projects. Bringing forward one of our definitions for a project from the PMI '… a temporary group activity designed to produce a unique product, service or result' and the associated aspects that 'a project team often includes people who don't normally work together – sometimes from different organizations and across multiple geographies'. Let us explore this aspect of business-as-normal through the eyes of news production and professional service organizations.

Both deliver activities that fit this definition. Both also deliver activities that range from relatively more standardized (recall paint-by-numbers projects) to those that are 'low-volume high-variety' activities. Perhaps it would be fair to say that both of these organization types depend on projects for some portion of their throughput.

Picking up a case from Chapter 6 highlights project-like characteristics; on 7 March 2008 the BBC covered the story that was unfolding associated with the baggage-handling debacle at Heathrow Terminal 5. This was unexpected; this was news. An increasing number of reporting facilities were established at the site, and much of the news reporting took place from the airport. 'Disasters' of the natural or artificial type inevitably attract a host of news organizations and, in order to get the breaking story, they need to get to the site, set up and start reporting quickly. While many of these scenarios act out in rapid form the typical ingredients and lifecycle of a project, they often incorporate a dimension worth articulating separately – danger. Multiple project-like activities of the type introduced in Chapters 1 to 4 will take place in a short timeframe.

Let us now consider the second example group, the professional service firms; success in this sector is associated with the successful delivery of projects, and the challenge of delivering projects is not new to them. Including lawyers, management consultants, human resources and compensation consultants, and accounting firms, the work of this group is diverse, spans virtually every sector of the economy and frequently incorporates international delivery teams. Again, these characteristics seem to fit our project definitions well. These firms provide outsourced work and elements of that work may in turn be subcontracted or outsourced. In the legal area, particular activities will have their own lifecycle stages. For example, Ohio State University (The Ohio State University Office of Legal Affairs, 2014) provides guidance on the stages that would be encountered within a litigation scenario:

1 filing of complaint;

2 answering the complaint;

3 discovery stage;

4 motion stage;

5 settlement/mediation;

6 trial;

7 appeal.

A further dimension to the work in this sector is that it is often international in content, delivery or in terms of resourcing. The significant opportunities provided by enhancements in communication technologies have helped to provide a platform for legal process outsourcing (LPO). Pangea3 provides an example of this. Founded in 2004 (Pangea, 2013a), they became part of Thomson Reuters in 2010, have headquarters in India (Mumbai) and New York and operations in Mumbai, Delhi and Dallas. Examples of services they provide are provided in the form of case studies, and these include supporting an AM (American lawyer) Law Global 100 firm mount a corruption trial defence (Pangea, 2013b) and also providing support to a leading pharmaceutical company with a complex document review. Both of these examples exhibit characteristics of projects and the second case narrative specifically highlights the '24-hour follow the sun coverage from India', a feature of international time zones.

Organizations that deliver projects

Let us focus on the notion of project-based organizations, and also consider the interpretation of projects as a means of delivering things, the value this creates, and the often inherently complex underlying structures that accompany this. We have already considered that some organizations exist to deliver projects. In addition to the two areas already mentioned, construction provides a wide variety of scenarios that are reasonably simple to visualize or understand, and these also often fit well with the established, more traditional perspectives of project management. Conceptually, we can perceive the breaking down of a large construction project into smaller components or stages; the lifecycle may be reasonably well understood (or anticipated); legal and contractual aspects will dictate various activities; teams are often composed of specialist contractors and temporary labour; although uncertainty will be associated with many facets of the project, the future outcome can be imagined through the use of drawings, designs and visualization systems; stakeholder groups can respond to these and the challenge of managing their expectations is an expected aspect; there will be problems; suing and counter-suing may form part of the project.

Related to the sectors previously mentioned, there is value in looking at some historical work that has a useful contemporary significance; research focused on the UK television industry (Starkey, Barnatt and Tempest, 2000) and on film making (DeFillippi and Arthur, 1998) set out a number of aspects of projects as business-as-normal activities that transcend organizational aspects.

Within the television industry (Starkey *et al*, 2000) there was a focus on networks, with individuals being brought in to work on a task-by-task basis, organized by a central permanent group that had a strategic focus. The industry was characterized by almost continual change. They refer to these (2000: 300) as latent organizations that '... come to exist when a central broker reconstitutes the same creatively unique set of agent partners on a recurring basis'. This model of temporal capability is popular in this sector and could characterize project-based organizations (PBOs) more widely.

The prior research by DeFillippi and Arthur highlighted that (1998: 126) 'film making is an industry where project-based enterprises have long flourished'; they also discussed the impact of uncertainty and demand volatility on the need to identify and recruit talented project participants. This industry also has complexities within the coordination of specialist resources (such as cast, production crews, sets, audio, visual and special effects technologies) that must be actioned effectively to deliver the production successfully.

This reveals the scope of the project management challenge, but there are a number of additional dimensions which are more focused in this field. For example, they go on to discuss 'wholly outsourced teams' and how 'the notion of temporary organizations sustaining a permanent industry presents a paradox'; teams are brought together for the making of the film, disbanding afterwards. This pattern is repeated many times. They also discussed that although situations such as software writing, construction and law exhibit similar characteristics, 'independent film-making may exhibit in relatively pure form a model of organizing that is broadly and increasingly applicable to other fields of strategic endeavour'.

If we move forward 16 years, we could observe that the temporary organization (in whatever form) has gained in popularity; for example, in the UK in 2014 there was a significant growth in self-employment and freelancing (Professional Contractors Group, 2014). The project-based organization continues to grow in popularity as a means of delivering things, and this is further enabled by the changes in communications technology.

Project-based organizations – definition

As we have considered a variety of scenarios that constitute 'project-based organizations', it is helpful to draw on existing work in order to formulate a definition that is practicable but sufficiently tight and delineating.

Hobday (2000) defined a project-based organization as 'one in which the project is the primary unit for production organization, innovation and competition'. Mindful that the wider interpretation of PBOs could include activities outside these categories, we will modify and adopt the definition as follows: a PBO is 'one in which the project is the primary means of delivering the product or service'. With this in mind, we can see that this would include a wider set of organizations, from media to engineering, sport to professional services, private sector to government and other sectors.

The following case focuses on some project management challenges associated with providing professional services support to a scenario that is centred on the embracing of private–public-partnership (PPP) principles. While this usefully highlights one of the many specialist areas in which PBOs operate, since PPPs may be of wider interest to readers the following explanation is provided. The Public–Private Infrastructure Advisory Facility (PPIAF, 2012) highlight that there is no single internationally accepted definition of a PPP, rather that there is a common understanding that a 'PPP is long-term contract between a government and private entity for provision of public service'. Specifically they highlight that a PPP means:

- full cost recovery from tariffs (such as that related to transport or sanitation);
- that governments are financial partners in the venture;
- asset ownership transfer to the private sector;
- supporting private-sector development.

CASE STUDY   International PPP scheme

Projects are business-as-normal to a professional services firm;
each project has its own challenges

Scenario

We see emerging or natural-resource-rich nations investing some of their export-generated income in much-needed infrastructure improvements. Initiated at a national government level, this is an undertaking of considerable scale, potentially incorporating projects in a range of sectors, from water and waste treatment to healthcare facilities and transportation systems.

In order to do this, a popular model is to deploy PPP mechanisms; joint investments of this type bring additional and sometimes innovative funding and incentives, but in turn these have associated considerations, challenges and risks that may be new to the host nation. At the outset of a large investment programme, before the projects commence, it is vital that legal, contractual and management frameworks are established.

Several professional services organizations will be appointed to undertake specialist roles at this early phase. At the centre of this new arrangement is likely to be a legal firm whose role is to provide support to the host national government. We will explore the role provided by an organization of this type, and the services they deliver can involve aspects of unexpected development work. Since this is a completely new project, we would anticipate that this might be the case; it is nevertheless worth highlighting the type of activities required, since a significant challenge may be presented by the project and project organization in addition to the legal matter (which we might expect to be the core service delivered). Urgency may be heightened owing to the need to complete specific activities to dates informed by a pre-existing strategic plan set out as part of the host nation's political process.

This scenario is drawn from countries rich in natural resources that want to utilize the opportunity presented by buoyant revenues to develop much-needed infrastructure.

Host nation

At the centre of this new programme of activities is a fictitious legal firm, LawFirm55, who are acting on behalf of the also fictitious host nation country, HNCountry1. The example has been developed from the perspective of LawFirm55, a professional services organization with many years of delivering international projects, and it is intended to reveal the types of issue that can arise during the initial period of establishing the project, with the process of resolving the inherent uncertainties and ambiguities.

HNCountry1 has a seemingly well-organized government, with a ministry for everything. Some sectors of the economy are well developed (such as retail); this contrasts with areas of state provision that are weak, and others that are underdeveloped, such as water and waste treatment. The need to improve is strong, not least politically. In order to manage the partnerships required to convert the five-year strategy into cohesive actionable plans, an intermediary office acts in an intermediary capacity. It is a point of contact between HNCountry1 and the various professional organizations that will enable the delivery of strategy, including LawFirm55.

Projects or programmes?

One of the challenges here is caused by the scale of the projects and how they are organized into programmes. Often something initially described as a project is in fact three or four different projects, each significant in its own right. Furthermore, each one may have a distinct set of PBOs providing core services, shown in Figure 7.4. There would seem to be some value in establishing a common vocabulary and classification framework for activities such as these to aid the project and programme management process.

FIGURE 7.4 Organization of key parties within PPP project

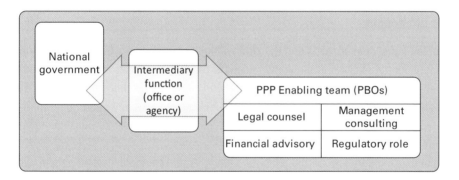

These are massive projects and HNCountry1 lacks experience in delivering these types of activity. At a practical level, there is often a project guide book, but the knowledge and skills required are not (initially) technical; rather, they are also about frameworks, roles and responsibilities – a broad set of activities requiring both hard and soft skills.

Structural considerations

The scale of hierarchy varies within the host government departments and some may not have many layers. The challenging part is getting access to the decision maker (or 'top man'). Often it is difficult to deal directly with this person, and an external party may need to go through intermediaries; these present access gateways. We need to be aware of a number of cultural aspects. One is that the host nation wants to benefit from the expertise being made available by external experts, but does not necessarily want to acknowledge the source since there are some underlying (historical) political connotations. Others may be specific to the geography in which the activities take place.

Cultural aspects

The environment is very competitive in some respects, with cultural traits magnifying the style of interactions and negotiations; there are clear divisions in role status between genders. Often an external party will need to spend a lot of time with the more senior (and powerful) members of the HNCountry1 team. It helps to think in the same style as the person that we are dealing with. If language is not a barrier, relatively more time can be spent explaining concepts relating to legal and management aspects.

When hierarchy provides a barrier, it may be possible to improve the communication flow by focusing on specific individual groups where it is possible to establish common ground. For example, in some scenarios, gender might provide the differentiator; this may be unexpected given the male dominance in some of the cultures. However, where women are numerous in terms of project management roles, this can provide an opportunity to establish rapport in some areas where the hierarchy seems impermeable.

Some challenges

One of the many challenges is that the staff within the intermediary office, and others from the host country involved in the management of the projects, have limited insight into the inherent complexity of the implementation of PPP projects on this scale. Largely due to inexperience (this is a first-timer to them), they lack insight as to the approach required for this type/scale of project activity and the inherent frameworks and management arrangements.

Sometimes magnified by the cultural setting, understandably some people will be nervous about taking responsibility for things they didn't start; there is therefore a need for trust within and outside the established project management group. The cultural base of the host country staff may inhibit the asking of questions, and some might become aggressive when nervous.

Timetable / schedule aspects

HNCountry1 has put in place a schedule that is linked to the five-year planning period (Figure 7.5). External parties providing support have to act in accordance with this.

FIGURE 7.5 Time-frame arrangement of project activities

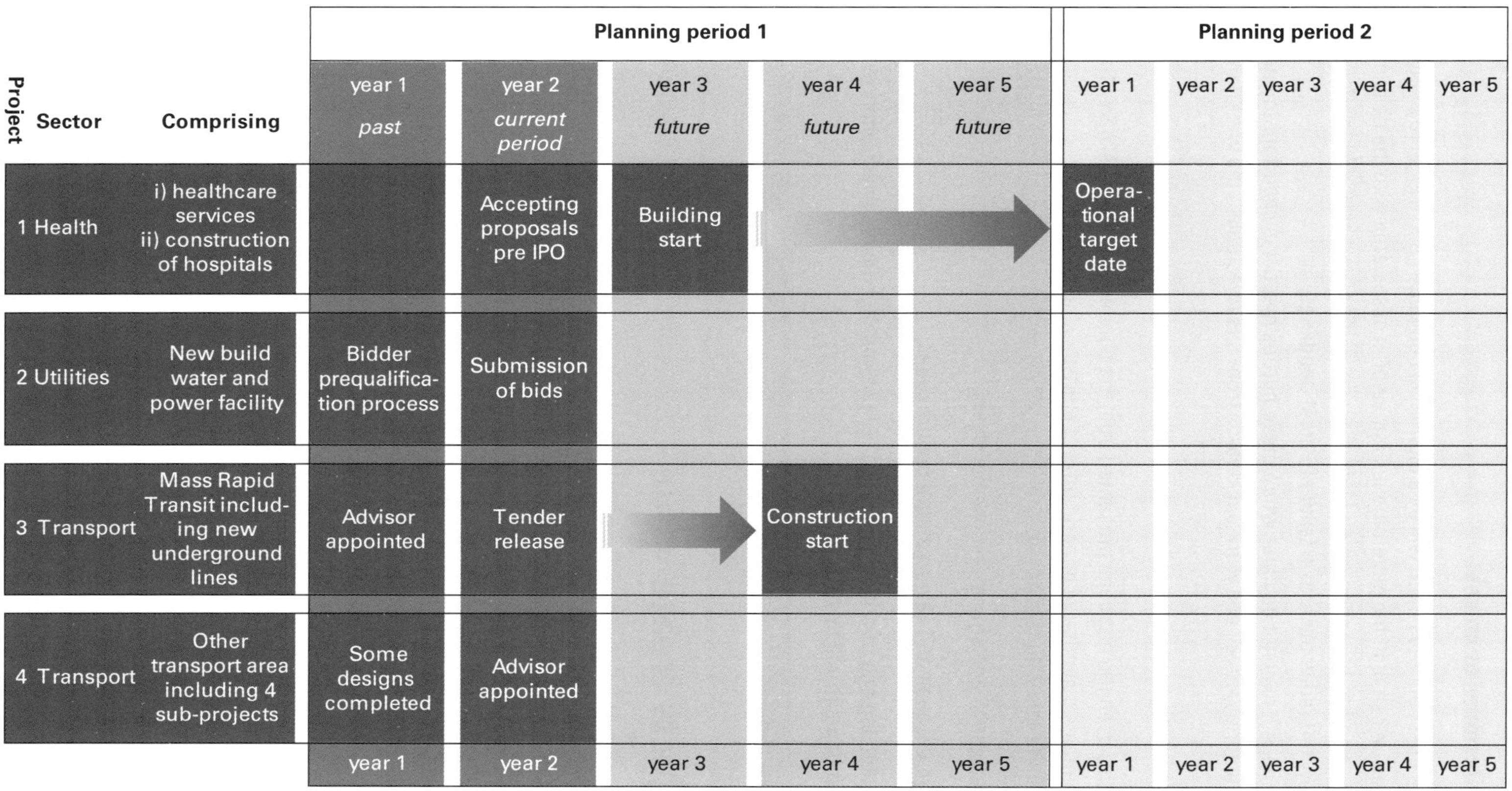

		Planning period 1					Planning period 2				
		year 1 *past*	year 2 *current period*	year 3 *future*	year 4 *future*	year 5 *future*	year 1	year 2	year 3	year 4	year 5
Sector	**Comprising**										
1 Health	i) healthcare services ii) construction of hospitals		Accepting proposals pre IPO	Building start			Operational target date				
2 Utilities	New build water and power facility	Bidder prequalifica-tion process	Submission of bids								
3 Transport	Mass Rapid Transit includ-ing new underground lines	Advisor appointed	Tender release		Construction start						
4 Transport	Other transport area including 4 sub-projects	Some designs completed	Advisor appointed								
Project		year 1	year 2	year 3	year 4	year 5	year 1	year 2	year 3	year 4	year 5

Key milestones or stages

In some host countries there will be a high-level committee and a legal regulatory body that operates on behalf of the government. Frameworks associated with the delivery of the PPP projects need to be approved by both of these parties, and staff within HNCountry1 may have low tolerance towards a failure to meet deadlines.

Although it may not be clear when these parties meet, it is important to understand the deadline for approval, and work backwards from this to establish the work-flow.

Case reflection

While this scenario has been presented from the perspective of a legal party, the role of this PBO contains a number of generic project start-up challenges.

Evaluate this with respect to:

i   organization and structural considerations;

ii   value-creation and value-capture opportunities;

iii sequencing and priorities; where is the initial project development effort focused, and what benefits will this bring?

Projects create value

Having established an understanding of the PBO, it is now helpful to consider the value created by the projects themselves; it is important to recognize that this can be extended to all projects. Projects and programmes should be considered as value-creation processes. In their work in 2007, Winter and Szczepanek (2008), in part based on reinterpreting the work undertaken by Normann in 1993, observed an evident 'conceptual shift, away from the traditional engineering view of projects, towards a more value-centric view, in which the primary concern is no longer the capital asset... but increasingly the challenge of creating value and benefit for multiple stakeholder groups'.

This is a powerful observation and statement, since it helps the deliverer of the project better understand the pressures proffered by expectant stakeholder groups, and is a basis to reflect more strategically on the value of the work undertaken. Why does this matter? Because we are often held to account against a set of performance parameters that are formed from a more traditional view of project management, when we probably know that the overall perception of the value of the project will be different, even with an effective review process in place. Reprising our discussion in Chapter 6 recalling the Flyvbjerg *et al* (2003) research and the associated observation by *The Economist* that 'if we were going to cancel infrastructure projects when they start to run more than 25% over budget, **we'd never build any infrastructure**'.

This fundamental change in perspective is particularly helpful; it provides a different basis to review the mid- or longer-term effectiveness of a project and helps us visualize a strategic basis to manage stakeholder expectations. Indeed, we could argue that this provides the insight that helps us to understand better why some projects, despite being interpreted as failures, in fact exceed some of the original performance objectives and are 'taken for granted' for generations after delivery. A word of caution, too: this does not necessarily change the arguments in the original business case, where the justification for the investment was based on returns over a particular period.

Furthermore, Winter and Szczepanek (2008: 103) argued that the projects (or programmes) 'do not, by themselves, create value, and that the perspective should be more of contributing to value creation'. They also reiterate that 'the goal of a project or programme is not to create value but to mobilize customers to create their own value from the project or programme's various offerings'.

The final point is particularly apposite for those who are involved in the delivery of an asset that will be used operationally long after the period of the project. The Snowdon Summit building (Chapter 1), Heathrow Terminals 2 and 5 (Chapter 6) and Airbus A400M (Chapter 5) may all be examples of this. A building provides an opportunity for visitor revenue generation, an airport terminal likewise; an aircraft will form the basis of an organization's operational assets, to generate revenue from customers (in the private sector) or to provide long-term cost-effective cargo-lifting capacity (in the public sector).

Value creation and value capture

The previous discussion leads us to the next observation, namely the discrimination between value creation and value capture (Figure 7.6). In 'value creation and value capture: a multi-level perspective' (Lepak, Smith and Taylor, 2007), the authors succinctly observe that 'the process of value creation is often confused or confounded with the process of value capture or value retention', and argue that value creation should be regarded as a process distinct from value capture. Again, this resonates with our experience of projects: we build the asset, it is delivered, it provides long-term value.

It is worthwhile reflecting upon the difference between the targets or users 'for whom value can be created', the set who might have originally specified the requirement, and finally the set who ultimately capture the value. This might in fact be three different sets of people or stakeholder groups. Focusing on the first element, it seems

FIGURE 7.6 Perspectives of value creation

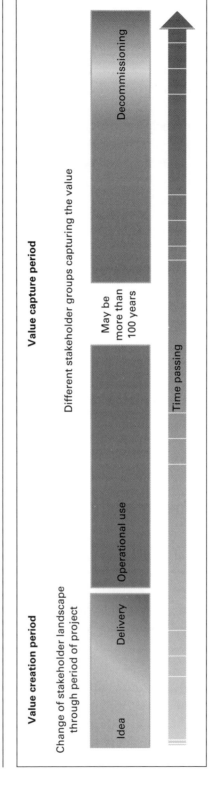

that value creation means different things to different people, yet in a project scenario we may be trying to manage all of these together.

This takes the stakeholder analysis into a further dimension, since, when we then consider value capture, one group of stakeholders are part of the project creating the value, a second possibly different set might be involved in the capturing of this value from the delivered project. We should also remark that Lepak *et al* (2007) also noted that value creation refers to both the content and process (of new value creation). Again, in a number of respects this is quite significant, since we may not normally place a value on the processes developed within the project. We know that they are important (in order to increase the likelihood of success), but we could reflect that this know-how element could have a quasi-asset value.

Value lag

A further dimension to this consideration is that there is a slippage between the 'value created by one source or at one level of analysis' and the fact that it 'may be captured at another' (Lepak *et al*, 2007). Looking at this candidly, there is likely to be a time lag between the creation and capture of the value. For example, if it takes three years to build, commission and hand over the asset (such as a new product) and the contract has been fulfilled and monies paid, the value has been created, but there will be a project value lag of one or more years – the subsequent period of captured value.

Aspects of this should have been captured in the original business plan, but for many projects, especially those of a speculative or innovative nature, this will be difficult. The world's first underground train travelled between Paddington and Farringdon in 1863 (Transport for London, 2014). Over a period of 150 years, using the average length of a generation as 25 years, this suggests that six generations of users have captured value from that created by the building of the London Underground (Ancestry, 2014).

Carrying over 3m passengers per day in 2012, the London Underground was approximately midway through a 15-year upgrade plan to address the problems created by the age (of infrastructure), capacity and cost limitations, and ongoing repair and maintenance challenges. This upgrade also responds to the needs (and opportunities) resulting from collocated infrastructure projects such as the Crossrail line. Associated with this development, the London Underground plan included the development of a new ticket hall at Tottenham Court Road, six times the current size (Transport for London, 2013). It is worth reflecting that this is a significant investment activity that will generate value to be captured during a subsequent, perhaps unknown, period. Stakeholders currently affected by delays caused by the current works may not be the same stakeholders that benefit from the lagged value.

To summarize this section, we have considered that a project is an instrument to create value, and that this value will be captured; there may be a lag between the creation and capture of this value. By creating value from strategy and providing value to be captured during the subsequent operational period, the project therefore provides the bridge between strategy and operations.

A project should not be viewed simply as a mechanism to deliver an output or outcome, nor should it be regarded in an over-simplistic triple-constraint style; while they have value in terms of providing metrics during the planning and delivery phases, projects should not be measured solely against a narrow set of parameters including time, cost and quality, or specification. Projects are powerful, central mechanisms that enable organizations and societies to achieve things. The use of the 'bridge' as an example of a project is perhaps prophetic, as the project is itself the bridge between strategy and operations.

A cycle of value and liability creation

It is important finally to reflect that while some projects successfully create long-term value, this is not a one-way process. There has to be a balancing action at some future point, when the outcome of the project creates a corresponding liability. A good example of this is the 'Atomium'. Rising above the landscape on the outskirts of Brussels, this structure was built for the World's Fair in 1958 (*The UNESCO Courier*, 1957). Depicting an atomic structure, it was intended to stand only for the period of the exhibition. However, it was so popular that it was still there nearly 50 years later, its spheres greying and tarnished. A €23m renovation project began in 2004, and it reopened in 2006. The shine of the spheres once again lights up the Brussels skyline. The initial project created long-term value, captured by a variety of stakeholder groups. The refurbishment project creates new value and heralds the next phase in the capture process.

Summary

Building on what is sometimes prompted by a fear of failure or a desire to move towards a projects-as-normal state, this chapter has explored the development of practitioner support and the emergence of alternative approaches to those that tend to reinforce the relatively more traditional sequential forms of project management. While initially more popular in project environments with relatively high levels of innovation, agile approaches have found popularity elsewhere.

We have also recognized the prevalence of the 'project-based organization' that exists in many sectors. Without espousing conspicuously much of the project management vocabulary, these organizations routinely deliver projects, as it is their business. The chapter has considered that while projects create value, many of the metrics that are used to measure project success are based on those that are used to control the project during implementation. These are often wholly insufficient to measure the long-term success of a project.

The chapter has also explored the notion of a lag between the value created by a project and the ultimate capturing of that value. Associated with this is the realization that the stakeholders that play an active role during a project may not be the same stakeholders that benefit from the outcome of the project. Although a subtle observation, this does highlight the project management challenge in respect of planning for and evaluating success, and managing the processes that enable the navigation of stakeholder groups. The closing example in the chapter highlighted that projects can create liabilities as well as value.

References

Ancestry (2014) How long is a generation, retrieved on 10 September 2014 from http://www.ancestry.com.au/learn/learningcenters/default.aspx?section=lib_Generation

Association for Project Management (APM) (2011) Corporate accreditation case study: Shell, retrieved on 25 August 2014 from http://www.apm.org.uk/sites/default/files/ Shell%20_%20APM%20Corporate%20Accreditation_case_study.pdf

DeFillippi, R and Arthur, M (1998) Paradox in project-based enterprise: the case of film making, *California Management Review*, 40 (2), pp 125–39

DSDM Consortium (2008) *DSDM Atern Pocketbook*, Ashford, Kent

DSDM Consortium (2012) *The DSDM Agile Project Framework*, Ashford, Kent

The Economist (2001) Team spirit: agility counts, 20 September

Flyvbjerg, B, Holm, M and Buhl, S (2003) How common and how large are cost overruns in transport infrastructure projects, *Transport Reviews*, 23 (1), pp 71–88

Hobday, M (2000) The project-based organisation: an ideal form for managing complex products and systems, *Research Policy*, 29, pp 871–93

Lepak, D, Smith, K and Taylor, M (2007) Value creation and value capture: a multilevel perspective, *Academy of Management Review*, 32 (1), pp 180–94

Mitchell, E (2012) Are 'waterfall' and 'agile' project management techniques mutually exclusive?, *Project Manager Today*, 22 March

Normann, R and Ramirez, R (1993) From value chain to value constellation: designing interactive strategy, *Harvard Business Review* (July–August)

Pangea3 (2013a) About us, retrieved on 29 August 2014 from http://www.pangea3.com/ about/company-overview.html

Pangea3 (2013b) Case Studies, retrieved on 29 August 2014 from http://www.pangea3.com/ the-journey-from-project-to-partnership.html

PMI (2011a) Project Management Professional (PMP®) qualification, retrieved on 27 August 2014 from http://www.pmi.org/en/Certification/Project-Management-Professional-PMP/~/media/PDF/Certifications/PMP%20Examination%20Content%20Outline_2010.ashx

PMI (2011b) Agile Certified Practitioner Examination Content, retrieved on 27 August 2014 from Outlinehttp://www.pmi.org/Certification/~/media/Files/PDF/Agile/PMI_Agile_Certification_Content_Outline.ashx

PPIAF (2012) The World Bank Public-Private Infrastructure Advisory Facility, retrieved on 18 November 2014 from http://www.ppiaf.org/sites/ppiaf.org/files/documents/Note-One-PPP-Basics-and-Principles-of-a-PPP-Framework.pdf

Professional Contractors Group (2014) Economic outlook: the freelancers perspective, retrieved on 15 November 2014 from http://www.pcg.org.uk/sites/default/files/media/documents/RESOURCES/Economic_Outlook_Jan2014.pdf p5

Socitm Insight (2014) Agile or PRINCE2 – a need to choose?, Issue 66

Starkey, K, Barnatt, C and Tempest, S (2000) Beyond networks and hierarchies: latent organisations in the UK television industry, *Organisation Science*, **11** (3), pp 299–305

The Ohio State University Office of Legal Affairs (2014) Life cycle of a court case, retrieved on 29 August 2014 from http://legal.osu.edu/help_litigation.php

The UNESCO Courier (1957) Brussels 1958: The Atomium, symbol of a peaceful world, July

Transport for London (2013) Our upgrade plan, www.tfl.gov.uk

Transport for London (2014) London Underground, retrieved on 17 October 2014 from https://www.tfl.gov.uk/corporate/about-tfl/culture-and-heritage/londons-transport-a-history/london-underground

Winter, M and Szczepanek, T (2008) Projects and programmes as value creation processes: a new perspective and some practical implications, *International Journal of Project Management*, **26**, pp 95–103

Within and outside projects

08

LEARNING OUTCOMES

By applying the topics within this chapter you should be able to:

- recognize the aspects of aggregation that take place in the project environment;

- reflect upon the impact of aggregating people in projects, in the form of groups and teams;

- explain the challenges associated with locational aspects;

- understand the need for the extended terminology of portfolio–programme–project;

- recognize the articulation of projects within the deployment of organizational strategy;

- explain the need for support in project environments and the value of project management office functions.

Introduction

Adopting a central theme of aggregation, this chapter will explore both the need for and value of grouping in project environments. We will examine the impact of opportunistic and systematic groupings of people and consider associated locational considerations, reflecting on this from an organizational perspective. The challenge of balancing autonomy and control is introduced in relation to aspects of structure and governance.

Projects and project-based organizations (PBOs) are fundamental building blocks in the development of our society. The examples introduced have ranged from small to large, yet we still use the term 'project'. In this chapter we will extend our thinking within and outside the project; we will consider the people part in terms of size and structure, related locational aspects and different forms of aggregation of projects as programmes and portfolios. We will revisit a number of themes already introduced in previous chapters in relation to these new topics.

This will prompt a consideration of the additional management challenges presented by these aspects, such as governance and stakeholders; we will discuss the need for balance between autonomy and control and consider the distinct feature of internal and external forces that drive the project. This will lead to a final section concerned with the consequences of needing almost perpetually to expect the unexpected.

Aggregation within and outside projects

Projects are rarely, if ever, a single-person undertaking. Unless we are commissioned to undertake a piece of illustrative artwork or generate a sculpture, it is more likely that a project will involve more than one person, department or stakeholder group. Even the examples just mentioned could have those characteristics. Almost inevitably there is some form of aggregation, of people into groups or teams or locations, or across locations.

In Chapter 2 we introduced the notion of the work breakdown structure (WBS); in order to deliver our new project activity we proposed the value of breaking it into smaller parts so that we might better be able to undertake the planning and related activities. We were encouraged to disaggregate the challenge into smaller steps. We might also have seen the use of an organizational breakdown structure (OBS) or a product breakdown structure (PBS). Now we may observe that the activity that we are delivering as our project is in fact part of a bigger project. We will consider this aspect later in the chapter.

For our own project we will often find that we need the involvement of people from different departments, centres, organizations or locations. In the course of delivering projects, teams are formed. We need to consider this aspect fully, as this affects a variety of things, including decision making and communication. Some of these attributes can be grouped and expressed in terms of 'project autonomy'. In other words, how much freedom is there to act independently?

The degree of autonomy affects the speed of progress of individual stages of a project (and therefore the project overall) and this can also present a strategic problem. However, if decisions are taken counter to general organizational guidelines or other forms of compliance, this provides a risk of operating out of control.

We will focus on two aspects of aggregation, of people and locations. This will help to provide a basis for the further consideration of the challenge of choosing the right structure, bases for control and governance, the form that both facilitates effective decision making and also optimizes other aspects such as motivation. This will help us develop insights for Chapter 9 in which we will direct our attention to the cultural and demographic dimensions presented by global projects.

Number of people; where size matters

Projects come in a variety of sizes, from small to large. By size we could mean budget, numbers of activities, stakeholders, scale of ambition or economic impact. We can compare the size of projects using a variety of measures. If we consider the number of people directly involved, a very small project might comprise one or two individuals, such as a scenario in a small business, single department or a personal activity with a specific goal.

Moving up the scale slightly, if the number of people directly involved is three to six, perhaps as a small team within an organization or business, there are some changes in the dynamics. Upscaling again, the project might comprise two or more teams, and so on. In a particularly large project, the number of people involved might be in the thousands.

Consider the projects involved in the delivery of a mega-event such as an Olympic Games. The International Olympic Committee (2011) published a range of facts and figures for the Winter Games that took place in Vancouver in 2010. Summary statistics are presented for two areas of success; the second group includes legacy benefits relating to:

- transportation;
- sports;
- environmental sustainability;
- economic and housing;
- tourism;
- social;
- cultural.

Immediately this list reveals the likelihood that a substantial range of projects took place to provide delivered activities in all of these areas. If we focus on 'social legacy', one of the key highlights reported that 'more than 75,000 people volunteered to help with the Games'. This is a significant number of people who would have been recruited and deployed across a range of projects.

Similarly for the Sochi Winter Games, in February 2013; just less than one year before the event, '80% of the 25,000 volunteers had been recruited' (Russia Beyond

The Headlines, 2013). Encouraging people to apply for the remaining 20 per cent, the feature highlighted a recruitment process that included:

- the application form process;
- candidate testing to cover diligence and linguistic skills;
- interview process (to evaluate suitability, work experience and spoken English);
- selection.

By considering the significant number of people involved in these two examples, we gain an insight into the scale of these activities; the recruitment of volunteers is one of many processes that contribute to the delivery of something new, as it was in the Sochi Winter Games project.

Size matters, because the number of people and teams affects the scale of the management challenge. More management will be required with larger numbers, who will be organized in a particular way that reflects the project management requirement, style and impact of the underlying organizational culture, often in respect of structure adopted.

Figure 8.1 illustrates how the project management challenge rises with an increasing number of teams (which normally equates to people). A corresponding characteristic

FIGURE 8.1   Relationship between number of teams and complexity of project management

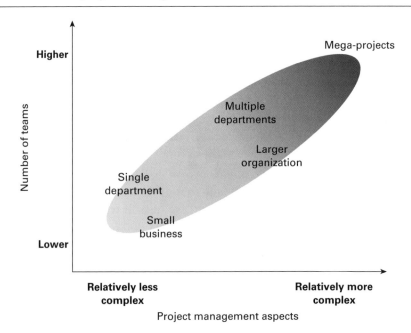

of these scenarios is that often the degree of autonomy enjoyed by project teams will vary in a similar but opposite way. By autonomy we mean the degree of independence or freedom, of organization and rule setting. Within a social system this could also include being self-governing. In a project scenario, self-governance provides concerns, as we will discuss later. Gemunden, Salomo and Krieger (2005) discussed the autonomy of projects using four constructs:

- goal defining;
- structural;
- resources;
- social.

They argued (2005: 367) that 'project organizations do not have (full) autonomy to define their goals'; with structural autonomy they observed that this is intensively discussed in project management and venture management literature, with the latter recommending separation from the routine organization; they argued that 'structural autonomy is a necessary but not sufficient condition for project success', and reduced their discussion of social autonomy to aspects related to location. This last area is highlighted as having a 'significant positive influence on project success'.

Of course, this may not be true for all situations, but, in terms of general management control, many organizations will be naturally concerned to extend this to cover all activities, including project work. The decision-making speed for a small business in the private sector can be dramatically different from that in a highly centralized and hierarchical government organization, especially if the organization has been subject to a period of extraordinary scrutiny (the same might hold for private-sector organizations, such as that following any publicized corporate scandals).

This stems from the need to ensure that the organization operates within the rules stipulated in the form of laws or regulations, and these could emanate from a variety of sources. The development of these rules (and the degree of compliance with them) is often stimulated in the external environment. For example, the need to 'restore public confidence in American business, which has been shaken by huge corporate scandals, such as those which led to the bankruptcies of Enron and WorldCom' (*The Economist*, 2007) led to the signing into law of the Sarbanes–Oxley Act in 2002. This incorporated 'tough new rules' and was followed by a sharpening-up of the scrutiny of companies by auditors.

Referring to the OECD Principles of Corporate Governance (2004), the Association for Project Management argued 11 principles for the 'governance of project management' (APM, 2004). This sought to address the issues arising from weak governance with others associated with poor project management. A whole topic on governance is now provided in the context section of the APM Body of

Knowledge (2012). Project governance is combined with stakeholder as a dedicated section in the Project Management Institute (PMI) PMBOK Guide (PMI, 2013).

The organization needs to be confident that it is managing its business-as-normal processes dutifully, and this requirement will extend to the delivery of projects (which may or may not be business-as-normal). This presents a challenge for the project manager in terms of balancing autonomy with control.

Influence on choice of structure

Although it is not the only factor, in this respect size does matter. A combination of overarching general management principles and associated cultural factors may cause the organization to be inherently unsuited to delivering projects. An organization may find itself in a halfway house, where market opportunities encourage the fulfilment of activities with strong project characteristics, but the underlying organizational structure is more traditional or bureaucratic.

In practice, an example of this situation emerged within a service-agency-type organization (comprising 100–125 people); the traditional structural model that had been adopted initially served the business establishment period well and enabled the delivery of smaller self-contained projects. Although without many layers, the hierarchical management arrangements and associated thinking style nevertheless inhibited the effective adoption of practices needed for the delivery of a hybrid range of projects that required higher strategic prominence and cross-functional input (Figure 8.2).

FIGURE 8.2   Organizational structure inhibiting project development

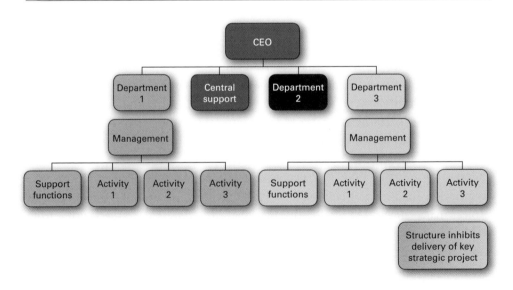

One feature of this particular scenario was a resistance to reforming bureaucratic management systems that emphasized functional focus. Ultimately the organization was unable to respond to the simultaneous demands presented by dissimilar projects, the need to significantly enhance internal project capability and revenue pressures; ultimately the organization ran out of cash and was bankrupted. A contributory factor in the failure was an inability to adopt the platform that was needed to support a burgeoning portfolio of projects (this was not seen as a strategic priority quickly enough). An investment in project management practitioner-based training (introduced in Chapters 6 and 7) might have helped, certainly in terms of the drawing out of distinct roles, responsibilities and idealized project management structures, but the underlying drag inherently associated with the type and characteristics of an organization may inhibit efforts to transform it into one that is project based.

Aspects of this type of situation are described from the perspective of governance by Zenger (2002) and Lindkvist (2004); Zenger (2002: 80) highlights that 'hybrid governance forms that seek to meld the virtues of both market control and traditional hierarchical control are alluring' and discusses the limitations of overlaying of new structures without new (pay) systems, the failure to restructure or develop new measures of performance. Lindkvist (2004: 5) discusses that 'since projects enjoy great autonomy they easily become separated from each other' and further highlights that a firm risks becoming a series of 'disconnected projects'.

Learning point

The sometimes contradictory need to balance autonomy in the project environment with an effective (and appropriate) management basis for the projects delivered yields a challenge; this can also present a significant risk to the project and project parent (or host) organization.

One final dimension to consider here relates to the size of the potential project team population. By this, we mean the total number of people within the project landscape who could have an involvement in the project. As the potential project team population increases, the need for clarification of role, responsibility and acknowledgement of the need for dedicated project structure rises, as shown in Figure 8.3.

In scenarios where this has been overcome, and where projects are moving forward with a relatively higher degree of freedom, this can create a variety of other problems, such as the aforementioned concerns about governance and compliance. We will review these further after a brief consideration of another source of aggregation challenge, one of location.

FIGURE 8.3   Impact of size of potential project team population on project management organization

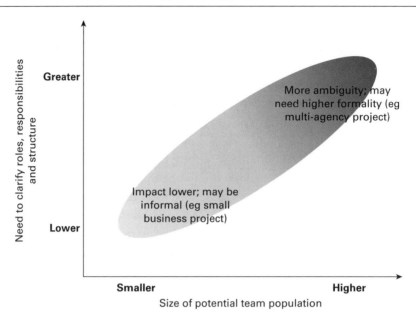

Location: a sense of division

While continual improvements in technology provide an ever-widening platform for communication, the physical location is still the key shaper of who we are and what we are; the environment in which we live or work provides the basis for the development of relationships, perspectives and prejudices. Although it is possible to communicate and interact globally, our physical being can be in only one place at one time. Our virtual presence is almost unlimited; potentially this is positive for participation in projects but can be a problem in a variety of associated ways, such as encouraging over-commitment and being seduced into believing that the always-on 24/7 world will help us to manage everything better.

A physical location is a home to individuals, departments, centres or organizations. As many organizations operate across many locations, this will inevitably have an impact on the management of a project. For a project that incorporates parties from different organizations, location may well be a driver in the overall success of the undertaking, however success is measured.

The impact of enabling technologies has contributed to a proliferation of virtual project teams, to the extent that the word 'virtual' may be itself becoming unnecessary, perhaps soon even obsolete. As we introduced the term 'virtual team' earlier, it is helpful to extend our understanding of the types of team we might encounter in projects. These are summarized in Table 8.1.

TABLE 8.1　Terminology for types of project teams

Traditional	Co-located; close proximity of team members; interaction face to face
Hybrid	Some team members co-located, some remotely based
Virtual	Completely dispersed

A note of caution here: within an increasingly connected world, in time we may see the term 'traditional' more closely associated with teams that are currently of the hybrid or virtual forms. The terminology assumes that there is a home base for the project. We could also use the terms 'co-located', 'hybrid' or 'dispersed'.

A traditional team would be co-located; for a project that is centred on one key physical area, this is relatively easy to visualize. The converse of this is the virtual team, where all members are located in different places. Hybrid teams describe the scenarios that fall between these extremes. These definitions will become blurred, since we might regard a project team as traditional when it comprises members who are located at different sites but within a similar geographical area (ie where the distances are small and there is movement of staff across sites). Like many other areas, the definition may become difficult to apply.

More importantly, combining locational characteristics with technology enablement, we do need to consider the important area of team dynamics. Clearly there is a difference between wholly co-located teams and those that are completely dispersed. A global virtual team (GVT) will encounter challenges associated with communication that are completely different from those in most traditional scenarios. For example, we need to consider the impact of time zones, culture, or both.

Often we hear people claim that face-to-face interaction is the most effective form of discussion; body language and facial expression in full three dimensions can contribute to the telling of the truth, which may be more difficult in the compressed form of a video conversation. Yet as this latter means of communication becomes ever more popular, we may be adapting to these new forms without realizing that anything has been lost.

The possibility that we miss something important may be manifestly worse if we are working with people from different global locations, who each have their own culturally based expressions, mannerisms and style. Conversely, if video technology limits some of the expression mentioned in the previous paragraph, then as the lowest common denominator this could contribute to an equalizing of these aspects of communication. Working on projects using this communication medium could be a positive development.

Shachaf (2008) described the positive and negative impacts of cultural diversity on GVTs. An important aspect of this is associated with the use of e-mail, which was described as a 'lean medium'. As it cannot include language accents and non-verbal misinterpretation, e-mail was seen to reduce miscommunication. Further, the research revealed that information communication technologies (ICTs) can help to overcome some aspects of cultural diversity.

Therefore, it is important to consider the dimension of aggregation in terms of location, since this will introduce a heady mix of culture, style, standards and behavioural norms. We may also see the exhibition of variable levels of motivation and trust, but this is not exclusively associated with projects and project managers. Groupings of people in departments not co-located may be a source of mistrust and jealousy.

For example, while working in a small office employing 15 people that comprised three or four small teams, these developed to be well motivated and particularly effective. Good interpersonal relationships also contributed to the location becoming the home of a highly cohesive social group. During occasional absences of essential services staff, temporary cover was sent over from the main headquarters. Suspicions that the cover staff were in fact being sent over to observe what was happening seemed to be confirmed when it was discovered that the office was colloquially known as 'the wild west'. A belief that fun and games were taking place was amusing but supported a view of potential jealousy by people outside the location.

The aggregation of people into teams, the integration of teams into bigger teams, or the need for teams to work interdependently are all potential scenarios during the project, and the associated management is potentially demanding. Certainty that those involved will be able to implement exactly what is required (in the plan) is difficult to achieve; removal of this would be a major source of uncertainty (and hence risk). What people do will reflect how well they understood the request, whether they are capable of doing this, and whether they are focused on achieving the particular task. This in turn will reflect the related elements such as whether they are distracted (attempting to do several things simultaneously), and if they are, to what extent they are motivated to maintain a high focus on the completion of this key (to the project) task. Clearly location plays an important role in the management of projects, and some key areas are highlighted in Figure 8.4.

There has been a subtle change in emphasis for the project manager. The ability to understand people and organizational behaviour is a valuable skill in the toolkit of the effective project manager, perhaps in turn reflecting different people, personality, cultural context and leadership modes. We should also consider that the aggregation of capabilities, as well as people or locations, can have unexpected and unintended effects, both positive and negative. A deeper understanding of this may provide a better platform to deliver projects; this area is important and will be developed further in Part Four.

FIGURE 8.4   Multiple locations and some project management dimensions

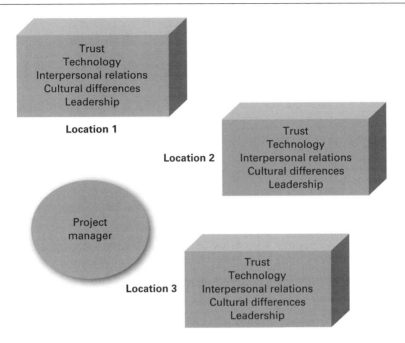

Projects, programmes, portfolios

The term 'project': we had some difficulty finding an adequate definition for a typical project in Chapter 1. Why was this? In part, this is because projects have different forms and emphasis. Recall that some have a stronger emphasis on the time dimension in terms of deadlines, therefore fitting well the definition that emphasizes start and end points. Others will have a strong cost or budget focus, and these will also lend themselves well to the more specific form of definition that highlights cost, value or resource.

We also acknowledge that there will be a group of activities that we refer to as a project, but these are more ambiguous and more difficult to fit into a definition. Some of these will be large projects, seemingly comprising a multitude of different activities that themselves could be regarded as projects. We might sometimes refer to these as 'sub-projects'. This is another of our difficulties, in that we use the term 'project' and a component of that project could also be a project... or projects.

An example of this could be an international sporting event, the development of an airport, the delivery of a new vehicle, the implementation of a new system or the establishment of an energy facility. All of these activities are likely to be multiple-project scenarios. The following case highlights a scenario that exhibits multiple projects, multiple organizations, conflicting stakeholder interests and is also related (at a portfolio level) to the case included in Chapter 2, by dint of being a component of the national energy supply portfolio.

CASE STUDY   Sun Moon Lake

Tourism and energy[1]

The mountains rise above blue waters; walkers, cyclists and sightseers mingle in a warm exotic setting. This area is a magnet for tourists. Perhaps few will notice that Sun Moon Lake provides two distinctly different but wholly coupled contributions to the national economy: tourism and energy.

Two dams on the western side of the lake provide water for hydro-electric power schemes below, at Takuan and Mingtian. As a key contributor of renewable power generating 1,602MW, this is the largest pumped storage power plant in Taiwan (Taipower, 2013). Unless the visitor follows the signpost to the dams, the bluish-green waters do not reveal this secret; swimming, however, is permitted only once a year, when at least 10,000 yellow-capped swimmers enter the lake for the annual swimming carnival (Keeling and Minnigh, 2011).

Although the management of these two distinct activities is undertaken by different parties, the common element is the lake. With associated projects taking place in either tourism or energy, this provides several examples of portfolio–programme–project segmentation at different organizational and activity levels.

At a macro level, the portfolio could be twofold, comprising firstly the establishment and maintenance of hydro-power assets and systems, and secondly the development of tourism market opportunities, as shown in Figure 8.5.

Alternatively, concentrating solely on tourism, the Sun Moon Lake National Area Administration public information regarding projects describes the background (high-level three-point statement), objectives (including four programmes) and specific project objectives. This provides an opportunity for a portfolio–programme–project interpretation as per Figure 8.6.

The evidence for the enactment of activities within programme 3 of this strategy is seen within a wide range of associated marketing campaigns, at a local, national and international level. For example, this includes activities such as cycling, walking and music festivals, promoted in a variety of media and formats. The Eva Air in-flight magazine carried a 10-page insert; a full-page advertisement in *The Economist* featured Sun Moon Lake as a central element in the promotion of Taiwan as a 'biker's paradise'. These activities are also likely to be structured on a portfolio–programme–project basis.

FIGURE 8.5 A portfolio–programme–project analysis of Sun Moon Lake

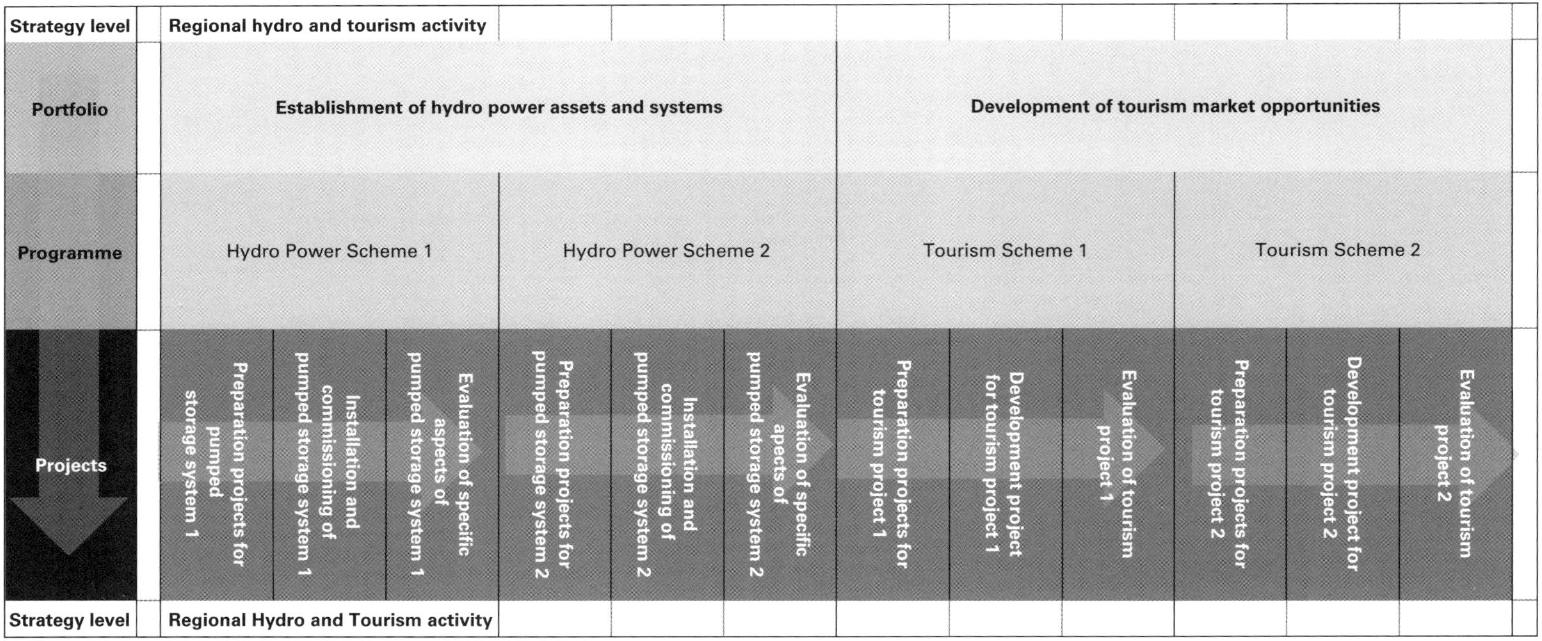

Strategy level	Regional hydro and tourism activity		
Portfolio	Establishment of hydro power assets and systems		Development of tourism market opportunities
Programme	Hydro Power Scheme 1	Hydro Power Scheme 2	Tourism Scheme 1 / Tourism Scheme 2
Projects	Preparation projects for pumped storage system 1 / Installation and commissioning of pumped storage system 1 / Evaluation of specific aspects of pumped storage system 1	Preparation projects for pumped storage system 2 / Installation and commissioning of pumped storage system 2 / Evaluation of specific apects of pumped storage system 2	Preparation projects for tourism project 1 / Development project for tourism project 1 / Evaluation of tourism project 1 / Preparation projects for tourism project 2 / Development project for tourism project 2 / Evaluation of tourism project 2
Strategy level	Regional Hydro and Tourism activity		

SOURCE: adapted from Sun Moon Lake National Scenic Area Administration (2008)

FIGURE 8.6 A portfolio–programme–project tourism-based analysis of Sun Moon Lake

Strategy level	Sun Moon Lake National Scenic Area Administration: adapted terminology and description of activities			
		Statement 2	Statement 3	Statement 4
Portfolio	'Background statements'	1. Doubling Tourist Arrivals Plan: National Development Plan		
Programme	'Objectives: National Development Plan'	1. The programme aims to establish a tour route focusing on Thao culture and mountain lake resources to develop the area as a mountain lake vacation destination with international appeal. This objective will be achieved by developing four large-scale recreation systems offering high-quality facilities and services.	2. The programme aims to create a new image of the urban and rural areas of Sun Moon Lake and create a tourism-friendly environment that can attract international visitors through the reduction of built structures and development of bilingual guide systems.	3. Programme statement regarding specific international markets and eco-tourism.	4. Programme statement
Projects	'Project objectives'	(1) Establish leisure facilities and enhance the quality of tourism service facilities	(2) Establish a comprehensive bicycle and trail system and expand areas for public leisure, sports and recreation	(3) Enhance landscaping, beautification, and eco-engineering work to improve the landscape along road corridors	Further project objectives

This structuration presents a simplification of what are often inherently complex organisms. In the case of Sun Moon Lake, the proliferation of government and commercial organizations generates objectives which may be conflicting. This contributes to a challenge of coordination, and is magnified at the macro level; the expectations of visitors (stakeholders) may not be compatible with the usage parameters defined by the operators of the hydro-electric power generators.

Case reflection

Evaluate this scenario from a portfolio–programme–project perspective in terms of:

i   the core project opportunities for each organization; what conflicts will this create?

ii the impact on organizations that share the same resource base but have completely different strategies, objectives and priorities;

iii taking into account the wider involvement of parties in the tourism and energy markets.

This challenge of categorization is not unique to projects. For example, if we talk about markets, we could describe food as a market. We might then refer to dairy production, a subset of food, as a 'sub-market'. Or is dairy production the market? Similarly, we will see this type of terminology challenge when we are discussing things such as products or in engineering ('sub-assemblies' as a pre-assembled component of a larger device).

Let us therefore introduce more formally the terminology project, programme and portfolio. The term programme was defined in Chapter 1 as 'a collection of more than one project (connected formally or not), or a combination of projects plus other organizational or project-like activities'. It is now opportune to explore further the notion of not only programmes, but also portfolios, as examples of the establishment of terminology that is often used to clarify aggregated activities, build associated management frameworks, and in turn help disaggregate expectations and targets.

However, there are some problems with this approach. For example:

i   There are different understandings of what a programme constitutes.

ii As the associated frameworks developed for programme management will be based in part on these definitions, these will vary depending upon the (agreed) definition.

iii Roles and responsibilities associated with project and programme management will sometimes come into conflict.

iv We may see an activity described as programme management where the underlying vocabulary is almost entirely project management based.

We can further complicate this by carrying a similar four concerns into portfolio management. On the other hand, we could look at this from a different perspective, one of organizational strategy. This will help to rationalize the vocabulary and clarify relationships between activities.

Organizational perspective

An organization exists to deliver things – products, services – whether in the private or government sectors. 'Strategic capability is the resource and competencies of an organization needed for it to survive and prosper' (Johnson, Scholes and Whittington, 2008: 95). The organization will be faced with making strategic choices, and one or more of these choices will relate to the products or services that it delivers. In turn, the outcome of these choices might result in the delivery of a completely new product or service, or the entering of a new market; this will be achieved through some form of project, associated with product development, or through some form of venture.

Learning point

Exploiting strategic capability leads to projects. Whether related to retailers, manufacturers, services, government departments or multinational organizations, sporting concerns or micro-businesses, one or more projects will inevitably form part of strategy deployment.

Before we take the next step, the deployment of organization strategy, we need to consider the impact of changes in the broader environment and the ever-increasing expectations of stakeholder groups. Organizations increasingly have to ensure that they are robust in terms of corporate governance; Johnson *et al* (2008: 133) used an adapted definition: 'corporate governance is concerned with the structures and systems by which managers are held accountable to those who have a legitimate stake on the organization'.

This was introduced earlier in the chapter but is reintroduced for two principal reasons. Firstly, this is a core principle at the heart of running an organization, as we have discussed earlier in the chapter. Secondly, we need to be cognizant of the principles of stakeholders, as organizations find themselves increasingly accountable to wider interests. In Chapters 1, 2 and 3 we argued that the stakeholder is a significant component of project management; from an organizational perspective the stakeholder is a key component of delivering strategy.

FIGURE 8.7   Simplified governance chain

Let us pursue this further and consider a chain of governance. In a simplified form it could look like Figure 8.7.

It is shown and referred to as a chain since there are linkages between each group. This also represents the organizational entities that will set out and provide direction for the portfolios, programmes and projects that will ultimately deliver the strategy. Some will be closely involved with setting out the strategy and instigating the projects that enable the delivery of the strategic objectives. This is further developed in Figure 8.8, which shows the cascading of vision and organizational strategy, which will be organized in order to deliver the projects.

How will the organizational strategy be delivered? Consider an example we mentioned earlier, Shell Exploration. Typical of many multinational organizations,

FIGURE 8.8   Deployment of strategy

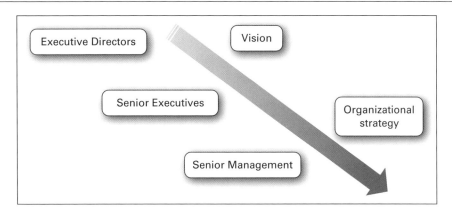

FIGURE 8.9   Generic portfolio, programme and project breakdown

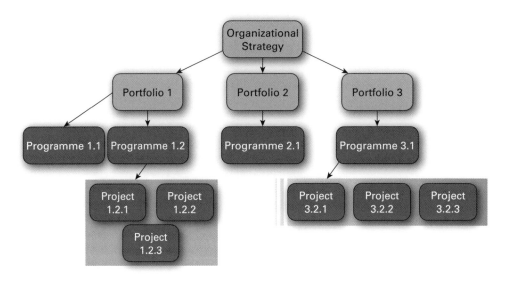

its activities are delivered in a number of generic areas, 1, 2 and 3. We can refer to these as portfolios. In turn, these portfolios will be delivered through a number of activities, which we have called programmes. Further, each programme might comprise one or more projects. This is shown in Figure 8.9.

Immediately we can see similarities with a work breakdown structure. While it is neat, clear and concise, from an analytical perspective this is another way of breaking things down, this time in terms of the delivery of strategy. But, of course, things are not that simple. A large (enough) organization will have a number of portfolios; each will have a head. Each portfolio will have a number of programmes; each programme will have a head. Each programme will have a number of projects; each project will have a head. The overall terminology adopted could look like Figure 8.10.

FIGURE 8.10   Potential directing and managing roles

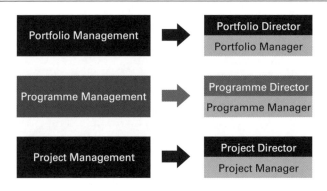

Consider this as an ideal model. We have developed this top-down (similar to our discussion regarding estimating in Chapter 3), and the lines of command and control seem relatively clear. Vision becomes strategy becomes deployment though a portfolio–programme–project process that ultimately delivers the strategy and hence the vision. But in the real world of organizations, often the idea comes from the people closest to the market, perhaps at the project level within this hierarchy. The delivery of a key project could transform the fortunes of a business and alter its course. This does not follow the intended logic, but is a pragmatic possibility.

This discussion helps to reveal the position and value of projects in creating value, but doesn't necessarily confirm that the project has followed from the antecedent process of strategy making. The strategy-making and deployment model illustrated in Figure 8.7 is another example of a sequential (or 'waterfall') approach. This might imply that the project is on the receiving end of organizational strategy when in fact events at the project level might continue to remake the original strategy. Furthermore, does this mean that we need to reflect four or more levels of strategy, for organization, portfolio, programme and project?

In a number of respects, this may already be taking place within the organization or, for multi-partner projects, perhaps some of it needs to be established. Typically, the cascading down of strategy might look like the model proposed by Maylor (2010: 51), where he argues that:

- the chief executive officer has the vision;
- the senior management team develop the organization strategy;
- portfolio management is responsible for the portfolio;
- programme management focuses on the programmes;
- project managers are responsible for the delivery of the projects.

This model can be applied to most situations; although for small organizations some of the levels are redundant (ie not required or not relevant), the degree of applicability nevertheless can be high, even in micro-businesses where the services are offered by a multi-skilled single business person. In such a case, the person generates the idea and strategy (as both CEO and senior management) and may offer services in quite distinct portfolio markets (eg as an illustrator, developer and teacher), and organizes the projects into logical groupings as programmes, working with other parties as appropriate. The terminology works well, as portfolios reflect an organization's different interests or services offered.

Ambiguity may surface, though, when discussing projects and programmes, and it is this area that has seen multiple interpretations. However, this should not present any difficulties if there is consistency of internal definition and therefore a common understanding of all terminology. This is an important point, since an investment in the training and development we mentioned in the previous chapters might help to generate a critical mass of understanding within the organization.

Interpreting the organization of projects in this portfolio–programme–project way in fact reveals some secondary considerations. Firstly, there are more layers than we might have expected, and in some respects this has provided an opportunity to remake some of the hierarchies that may have been removed in previous eras of reorganization and delayering. If we look to one of the practitioner sources for instruction, we see guides that articulate the introduction of particular roles associated with the playing out of the portfolio–programme–project architecture.

This can cause a cooperation–competition paradox such as that highlighted in the Amsterdam Metropolitan region by Buuren, Buijs and Teisman (2010); they discovered that 'too much programme management can undermine the potential of project management, but the opposite is also true' in revealing a genuine cooperation and competitive relationship between the two management groupings. Furthermore, the need to ensure effective management and organization within this type of structure often provides a justification for the establishment of project or programme management offices. Overall, there is a need to manage a grouping of project-like activities as efficiently and effectively as possible. How this is achieved will vary from scenario to scenario.

This section has introduced more fully the additional terminology of programme and portfolio by presenting it in terms of the deployment of organization strategy. While we will continue to use this wider phraseology, the main unit of delivery vocabulary remains the 'project'.

Providing support – project management offices

As projects become an increasingly popular mechanism to deliver things, this generates an accompanying rise in the number of people who have the skills and knowledge to enable organizations to do this successfully. With success comes further demand for this know-how, and organizations may find that supporting this is challenging. They might also find that their portfolios and programmes make such demands on their core human resources that the capacity is exceeded. A further aspect should be considered: successful delivery through autonomous project management brings some additional risks in terms of breaking rules within and outside the organizational boundary. These three areas often provide a justification for the deliberate articulation of support for project activities in the form of an office function.

To provide additional practical context for this, I would like to include six personal examples of scenarios where questions were raised in different organization settings; these highlight the need to fill a gap of missing knowledge:

Scenario 1:

Role: Management of two newly developed and approved slow-start first-timer projects
Setting: Service organization

The building of a unique management and analysis spreadsheet table over a half day is opportunistically observed and adopted by co-located staff as their standard, as they also lack the same tool in their projects. With some final modifications the spreadsheet starts its journey around several other new first-timer projects that had all started around the same time.

Scenario 2:

Role: Interim project manager for a client relationship management system
Setting: Government agency

A question to a particularly effective subcontracted management consultant: 'Mike, this document is really helpful with establishing the underlying basis for this new project; where did the template come from?' He replies that it was a project initiation document from a practitioner approach, and added 'not to worry too much about it at this time'. This conversation was revisited several times as the benefits of using a structured method in an ambiguous multi-partner project environment became increasingly apparent.

Scenario 3:

Role: Information provider
Setting: Conversation in a social setting

'Do you know anyone good that could help us manage this new project, as it is quite an unusual activity for us?'

Scenario 4:

Role: The opportunist
Setting: Conversation with an ex-colleague

'Can you show me how you put together that business case... we've got a similar project coming up... I can do the descriptive part but am struggling with all the mathematics of discount factors and those calculations.' Having talked through it, after 10 minutes my colleague concluded it was going to take too much of his time. The development of the business case became two days' subcontracted work.

Scenario 5: Three questions that get asked frequently

1 'Do you think our staff should be trained in a project management software tool?'

2 'Do you think I should get a project management qualification?'

3 'Do you know who can provide a project management qualification in this area?'

Scenario 6:

Setting: Discussion with two former colleagues
Setting: Tourism business
During a catch-up lunch with two former colleagues, the discussion becomes increasingly focused largely on the frustrations they are experiencing in their engineering section. Drawing a diagram on a napkin reveals an undiagnosed 'two bosses' problem. On seeing the drawing they went quiet for a moment and then said: 'That's obvious! Why didn't we see it?'

All of these are examples of problems that are not difficult to solve, but frequently occupy organizational staff as they lack the time, insight or experience or are just not sure where to look to get the right type of support for their projects. Aggregate these occurrences within an organization faced with delivering multiple projects and there is a business case for a dedicated project support function. All of them represent the types of questions that could be addressed (or circumvented) by establishing a 'project management office' (PMO).

Project management support exists as a formal office function in some organizational settings, informally elsewhere, as the cost to a small business might be prohibitive. A larger organization might also find it difficult to justify the expense of this. We could, of course, argue that if this is an essential service, it is worth paying for. The important thing is to recognize that support may be required, as the inability to support projects might contribute to a much bigger strategic problem.

Summarizing these points to provide an indication of services often provided by PMOs, it is important to ensure that:

- common templates exist where appropriate (scenario 1);
- suitable methods are deployed (scenario 2);
- there is access to effective specialist resources, analytical skills that enable risk-mitigating approaches (corporate or otherwise), insights and judgement;

- support for appropriate training and development;
- consulting-style problem solving and knowledge.

These are some of the useful roles that can be provided by a project support function. It can be centralized or distributed, heavyweight (in terms of undertaking a command and control role) or lighter (more agile approaches), personal or virtual, concentrating on hard or soft skills and finally, it may be valuable… or not.

Emergence of PMOs

The concept of the PMO has been developing over a number of years. In 2004, Dai and Wells highlighted that 'a standard set of PMO presence features have yet to be agreed upon in theory or practise' but identified the following broad categories of support:

The development and maintenance of:

- project management standards and methods;
- project management archives;

and providing:

- project administrative support;
- human resource/staffing support;
- project management consulting and mentoring;
- arranging project management training.

This analysis matches the example scenarios mentioned in the previous section well. They drew some pertinent conclusions from this research, including the following:

- Since many organizations were establishing (or planning to establish) PMOs, this demonstrated confidence in the concept.
- Project management standards and methods seemed to correlate highly with project performance.
- The use of historical archives showed a significant correlation with project performance.

By 2013, Muller *et al* (2013a) remarked on the implementation of 'multiple PMOs, each one having different mandates, functions and characteristics'. In their research they also noted that 'PMOs are extremely heterogeneous (diverse in character or content)… varying in size, mandate, function and so forth, and they are very ephemeral (lasting a short time) in nature'. They identified different PMO roles in examples within specific sectors across three 'basic roles' of 'serving', 'controlling' and 'partnering'

TABLE 8.2   PMO roles; adapted from Muller *et al* (2013a) research

Role	Characterized by...
Serving	Providing expert and administrative support for functions
Controlling	Supporting through control and enforcement of standards
Partnering	Cooperative style; lateral communication between PMOs

(Table 8.2). Some PMOs would exhibit characteristic strength associated with one of these roles – others would be more 'balanced'.

These perspectives are valuable in a number of respects; for example, it would help us to choose the appropriate form of support based upon the context of a particular project delivery environment. If compliance is weak, a relatively more controlling PMO could support the addressing of this. In contrast, where menu-like support is required, this could be organized within a serving type. It is likely that a partnering style would be appropriate in other contexts, especially where the overall culture is more cooperative and consensually based.

Also in 2013, the same core of authors provided some additional valuable insights (Muller, Gluckler and Aubry, 2013b), researching a pharmaceutical research and development company in China. Looking at 'knowledge flows amongst and between project managers and project management office members', they noted that the exchange of knowledge occurs in clusters and 'contrary to expectations, PMO members are not identified as the most popular knowledge providers in the company's community of practice'. They highlight instead that 'knowledge was requested from earlier collaborators'. In other words, the staff preferred to get support from colleagues (other project managers) with whom they had worked previously. While this is not surprising, it highlights the potential value of encouraging project-focused staff to share their knowledge, enthusiasm and concerns. This is a form of virtual project management office support.

Although associated with a specific sector (pharmaceutical) in a specific geography (which brings in certain cultural aspects), these insights are helpful. In this case, as 'the most popular knowledge providers are not PMO members but seemed to be based upon the prior collaboration of individual project managers', this reminds us of the value of strong, supportive and effective communication mechanisms within the overall project delivery environment.

If we hold this final point, let us complete this section by considering briefly the example of a small education-based service business from the same geographic region (Asia-Pacific). Comprising around 15 staff and 3 office locations with student-destination markets of the United States, Western Europe and Australasia, the organization needs to ensure that its staff have adequate knowledge of higher education institutions (such as a university), national institutions (for example, concerned with the approval of entry visas) and local accommodation (in the would-be target country), among other key areas. These are important, since each of the students could be regarded as an individual project with their own lifecycle that includes:

- enquiry from student;
- counselling support for student;
- application to study in destination country;
- study and completion of degree scheme;
- return to home country.

In this type of business, the development and delivery of an internal training day is a means of providing knowledge support to the staff and achieves some of the goals of a PMO. Notably, it is the staff who provide the material and presentations, based on their experience of the particular aspect or topics above. As project managers who have collaborated with others within their organization, they are transferring dynamic and valuable information in a collective, constructive and value-adding forum. It is unlikely that this will have been consciously designed as a PMO, but it is achieving the same goals.

Expect the unexpected

We have considered the notion of projects, project-based organizations and generalized support that exists in certain project environments. It is also worthwhile recognizing that a project (and its attendant structure and organization) might emerge from an unexpected event. This presents a somewhat extreme counterpoint to the plan–deliver perspectives developed so far.

There are many examples that could be used to highlight this phenomenon, with natural disasters being an extreme form and significant contributor, if not in volume then certainly in terms of human, economic and emotional impact. While perspectives developed often reflect a cultural position (there is a marked difference in awareness and expectation between someone who lives in an area subject to frequent seismic events and those who never experience this phenomenon), the natural disaster may be expected but timing unknown, or the impact of the event may be particularly difficult to predict (such as the effect of an earthquake). Even with significant planning, nations can be overwhelmed by the scale of the events.

Organizations exist to provide support for such events, but the timing of their mobilization may be completely unknown, demands for services extremely high and access to affected areas difficult. Are these another form of project-based organization? We could argue that they have similarities to the latent network discussed in Chapter 7 (regarding media/production), but the unpredictable timing adds dimensions that are quite different.

A mountain rescue team provides an example of this. Often comprising volunteers, they are likely to be called upon at short notice. While familiar with the equipment, geography, climate conditions, other team members, general protocols and having practised for such emergencies, each call-out will nevertheless be different, with its own set of challenges. Some rescue scenarios will require coordination and support from other services (such as providing aerial support).

Unexpected events are in fact a feature of projects everywhere. The route we plan may not be the route we take during project execution. Soderholm (2008) provides some insights here; investigating 'unexpected events and environmental events not normally planned for', this provides some useful insights. Concluding that project managers in such scenarios 'engage in a number of practices in order to stay on track while constantly being exposed to unexpected events', this included the following (2008: 84–85):

- innovative action;
- extensive meeting schedules and short-term coordination;
- detachment strategies;
- negotiation skills and project-safeguarding.

Having strengths in these areas is not universal; we may find that there are particular types of people who are invaluable project managers or team players in these circumstances.

Summary

This chapter has introduced and explained some of the issues concerned with the inevitable forms of aggregation that occur in the project environment. Focusing on people and location, some fundamental dynamics have been discussed.

The aggregation of groups of people into teams has presented a perpetual challenge within the management of organizations and our discussion encouraged the reader to consider the additional value of understanding perspectives from organizational behaviour and human resources management, and the potential conflict between autonomy of project teams and the potential loss of control by the parent organization, a challenge often prevalent in project environments.

Our consideration of locations included some reflection concerning the challenge of co-located and virtual teams, and touched on the opportunities presented by mature communication technologies and the impact this may be having on the style of project management. This helps to set out some of the bases for a deeper reflection in the final chapters of the book.

The concept of the portfolio–programme–project terminology was introduced in order to establish coherent vocabulary and also from an organizational strategy perspective; the terminology of project management remains core.

Our final section explored the need to provide support for projects and the means of delivering this, through so-called project management offices and other in-situ approaches.

Note

1 This case study draws upon information from the following sources:

The Economist (2014) Taiwan: The bikers paradise, full-page advertisement,
    6 September
EVA Air (September 2013) En Voyage
Keeling, S and Minnigh, B (2011) *The Rough Guide to Taiwan*, Rough Guides, London
Sun Moon Lake National Scenic Area Administration (2008) National Development
    Plan, retrieved on 2 November 2014 from http://www.sunmoonlake.gov.tw/infoEng/
    GovInfoEng/ProjectsEng.htm
Taipower (2013) Operation and Management, Taiwan

References

Association for Project Management (APM) (2004) *Directing Change: A guide to governance of project management*, APM, Princes Risborough, Bucks
Association for Project Management (APM) (2012) *APM Body of Knowledge*, APM, Princes Risborough, Bucks
Buuren, A, Buijs, J and Teisman, G (2010) Program management and the creative art of coopetition: dealing with potential tensions and synergies between spatial development projects, *International Journal of Project Management*, **28**, pp 672–82
Dai, C and Wells, W (2004) An exploration of project management office features and their relationship to project performance, *International Journal of Project Management*, **22**, pp 523–32
The Economist (2007) Sarbanes–Oxley: Five years under the thumb, 26 July
Gemunden, H, Salomo, S and Krieger, A (2005) The influence of project autonomy on project success, *International Journal of Project Management*, **23**, pp 266–373

International Olympic Committee (2011) Vancouver facts and figures, retrieved on 28 January 2015 from http://www.olympic.org/Documents/Games_Vancouver_2010/ Factsheet_Vancouver_legacy_February_2011_eng.pdf

Johnson, G, Scholes, K and Whittington, R (2008) *Exploring Corporate Strategy*, 8th edn, Financial Times Prentice Hall, Harlow

Lindkvist, L (2004) Governing project-based firms: promoting market-like processes within hierarchies, *Journal of Management and Governance*, **8** (3), pp 3–25

Maylor, H (2010) *Project Management*, Pearson Education, Harlow

Muller, R, Gluckler, J and Aubry, M (2013a) A relational typology of project management offices, *Project Management Journal*, **44** (1), pp 59–76

Muller, R, Gluckler, J, Aubry, M and Shao, J (2013b) Flows in networks of project managers and project management offices: a case study in the pharmaceutical industry, *Project Management Journal*, **44** (2), pp 4–19

Project Management Institute (PMI) (2013) *A Guide to the Project Management Body of Knowledge*, PMI Inc., Newtown Square, PA

Russia Beyond The Headlines (RBTH) for the *Daily Telegraph* (2013) Volunteers get into the Olympic Spirit, 26 February

Shachaf, P (2008) Cultural diversity and information and communication technology impacts on global virtual teams: an exploratory study, *Information and Management*, **45**, pp 131–42

Soderholm, A (2008) Project management of unexpected events, *International Journal of Project Management*, **26**, pp 80–86

Zenger, T (2002) Crafting internal hybrids: complementarities, common change initiatives, and the team-based organization, *International Journal of the Economics of Business*, **9** (1), pp 79–95

A global stage

LEARNING OUTCOMES

By applying the topics within this chapter you will be able to:

- reflect on the presence of international aspects within many project scenarios;

- explore how comparable management disciplines reflect international dimensions;

- understand some of the inherent in-situ challenges of international projects;

- evaluate some core dimensions based on culture, communication and commonalities;

- examine specific aspects of these as they affect individuals and organizations and influence national perspectives;

- explore the implications for key underlying project management models and frameworks.

Introduction

This chapter will explore the global aspects of projects, in terms of both those that are cross-border activities and those that are more local, manifested through culture, language or factors associated with the delivery process. For example, communication in this chapter will largely focus on language. Topics will be introduced in a relatively diffuse style to encourage cross-topic reflection.

Although needing to focus on a limited number of geographies and using examples from a limited number of areas, we will promote a more generalist thinking and reflection with regard to the more generic considerations identified. The chapter is structured around a number of core themes. By making comparisons with other management disciplines, we will consider whether international project management is an upscaling of project management, or if it is something quite different.

By building the context for international aspects, we will then focus on culture, communication and the commonalities that may help to overcome the challenges often inherent within these project scenarios. We will discuss the implications of this for some of the core areas of project management already introduced and draw some initial conclusions that we will carry forward into Part Four.

Many projects have international elements

Context

In order to prepare the mind for embracing the challenge of the international dimension, we will first explore the dynamics of management at a relatively high and reflective level. In Chapter 8 we argued that projects are rarely, if ever, a single-person undertaking. It is also unusual for a project not to have some international dimension. For example, Table 9.1 shows some of the international aspects associated with the cases introduced in the first six chapters.

TABLE 9.1 Review of some international aspects within examples in first six chapters

Ch	Case	Typical international elements
1	Visitor attraction	Element of external funding; sourcing materials; tourism markets
2	Wind energy project	Supplier of turbines and engineering; specialist consultancy
3	Mega-event hosting	International events; significant proportion of stakeholder groups
4	Motor vehicle/SUV	Supply chains; international standards and clients
5	Airlifter	Pan-European developer; international standards, clients and markets
6	Airport terminals	International hubs; significant proportion of stakeholder groups

Most of these projects are transnational, incorporate international resources, conform to international standards, are deployed in international markets, involve international stakeholder groups or incorporate some international ingredients. This analysis is not exhaustive. If we subjected our more local projects to analysis, it is likely that we would see quasi-international characteristics in them, too. This is because they will have some components that are multinational, multicultural, multilingual or multi-ethnic. Of course, this will not be true for all scenarios, but even within a single-nationality monolingual project, there will inevitably be different cultures either within the stakeholder groups or within the organization.

Understanding these aspects provides a valuable insight for anyone involved in the management of projects. By starting from a more informed perspective we are better equipped to find the right course of action. If we understand the reason for a problem, we can often find the way to resolve it, or sometimes realize that it is not the problem we had initially perceived. This is a further key area that the project manager needs to be aware of. Projects are demanding in this respect as well as in many others, and the project manager needs to be a versatile skilled generalist.

If project managers resolve to develop skills, awareness and knowledge of these areas, where would they look? They might find suitable discipline-based insights within the areas of international business, international management, international human resources management (IHRM) or in other specific areas focused on culture, diversity or a combination of all of these. This raises a point to consider: as a comparator to project management, to what extent is HRM different from IHRM? In terms of activities such as workforce planning, recruitment, training, management development or compensation, how are these truly different in an international context?

To help answer this, let us consider training and management development. Briscoe, Schuler and Tarique (2012: 255–56) discuss the training and development (T&D) topic from the perspective of the multinational enterprise (MNE). They argue that since 'human capital may be its most important source of competitive advantage' (2012: 255), there are a number of important considerations, such as:

- thinking and acting globally;
- establishing equidistance – not see anywhere as overseas;
- focusing on the global system rather than its parts – breaking down silos, country and customer/supplier boundaries;
- developing global leadership skills – requiring a set of competences different from those of a domestic marketplace;
- empowering teams to create a future that is global – using cross-border and virtual teams;
- making learning a core competence for the global organization;
- a constant reinvention of the global organization and its members.

This advocates an approach which would foster the adoption of a broader mindset, since a global organization might look very different from one that has a domestic-only focus. However, arguably these points have relevance within all organizations if they are involved in the delivery of global projects or use projects to deliver products for an international market.

We can adopt this by changing the vocabulary to consider some of these points in relation to an international project rather than an organization. Thinking and acting globally is vital; establishing equidistance would help us not to regard any location as 'home' or 'overseas'. Breaking down silos and country boundaries is an essential consideration in delivering a project, as the structure might otherwise provide an inhibitor to our progress. The development of global leadership skills, the empowerment of teams and prioritizing learning are salient and relevant to an international project. Finally, the 'constant reinvention' is an attribute that might well be associated with project environments, since projects are always likely to change something.

This highlights the value of embracing a model, framework or approach from a complementary management discipline; other approaches can be adopted or developed in an indirect form by transposition into the vocabulary of projects. Be aware, of course, that this has some limitations, such as in areas that have completely different legislative frameworks.

Building on the previous discussion, it is likely that cultural differences will influence the design and deployment of learning and development support; if support is delivered through training, a traditional approach might mean different things in different cultural settings. We would then need to consider learning styles, which provides another example of an area that we need to be aware of in our project role, but in which we may or may not become relatively more expert. This will depend on the context in which we are working, our role and the availability of appropriate expert support from elsewhere. This is just one area that we have considered; while it is not necessary for the scope of our book, there are many other areas worth further exploration.

The significance to projects

We will often find ourselves vacillating between two poles of thought. On the one hand, global projects take place successfully, despite the potential difficulties that could arise when undertaking them. For example, in international banking and commerce, commodity sourcing, and the bringing to market of fashion or automotive products, multi-partner development projects take place. It can prompt us to think: 'Why is there so much concern about the cultural aspects?' On the other hand, by being unaware of specific customs or behavioural styles, it is unfortunately easy to make a mistake at an early stage of a project, and the *faux pas* might significantly contribute to the ultimate failure of an activity. This could happen during a key negotiating stage.

Like so many other areas with which the project manager needs to be familiar, this is yet another – a complex fusion of things that range from real practical challenges (such as that relating to visa arrangements for members of the team) to potentially stereotyped cultural, attitudinal and behavioural traits. A better knowledge of these topics will contribute to increasing the likelihood of success with the project. It is also worth highlighting that such awareness is not uniquely associated with spanning far-away lands; it is often just as prevalent in our local area as anywhere else. Given the continual establishment (and/or re-establishment) of global diaspora, multi-ethnic, multilingual and multicultural environments may be the norm for many of us.

These areas touch many others too, such as discrimination, politics, gender or ethics. For some project teams, project managers, project directors or affected stakeholders these represent significant levers for motivation, leadership or attitudes to change. The management of any project where these aspects are pertinent but not considered will run into some difficulties. A good and thorough evaluation of stakeholders will provide much of the insight we need. However, we run the potential risk of exposing ourselves to blind spots, where our inadequate knowledge becomes associated with complacency or arrogance or is regarded as dismissive.

Project management: international perspectives

We discussed that if we are undertaking something that has an international dimension, it could be approached as if it were an extension of what we considered in a relatively more domestic sense (for example, IHRM, international business). While this might be sufficient in setting out initial frameworks, there is a risk that we have the wrong emphasis or are adopting the wrong framework. The rationale for highlighting this is reinforced by insights from research such as that provided by Muriithi and Crawford (2003). They highlighted the wariness in Africa of adopting concepts of western origin; a number of reasons for this were cited, including an underlying resistance following political independence and also that there was strong evidence that western methods were partially or wholly inapplicable. They argued that this was associated with human behaviour and highlighted the need to recognize the cultural context. This is pertinent.

There are many lenses or perspectives that help to frame the challenge and therefore to facilitate or support the deployment of the right approach. As the context and objectives change from project to project, we find that we need to continually modify our approach, and this implies that there may not be a single ideal one. This should not come as a surprise, but emphasizes the danger of adopting a one-size-fits-all approach to managing projects.

The notion of 'international project management' can suggest problems, issues, conflict and risks. Key topic areas would include stakeholders, culture, ethics and aspects relating to geography and nationality. Culture is inherently part of the study of strategic management; cultural and international differences present challenges to students of international management; in order to undertake international business we need to understand multinational organizations, international strategy and core functions such as production, marketing, finance and HRM. In order to deliver international projects, we need to understand some or all of these.

Culture is a component of several of the aforementioned topics. It could be the sole focus in a study, where we evaluate its impact on communication, negotiation, learning, motivation and change management, but this could also include a consideration of leadership and the need to understand how to conduct business in a particular regional area; this in turn could reflect the particular aggregation of people in terms of ethnicity (a social group that has common national or cultural traditions). This is a complex landscape.

In order to develop the core elements of a framework, let us consider a couple of examples of project scenarios to inform our critical reflection. There are numerous examples where the organization got it wrong. In Chapter 6 we discussed the 'lessons from Jindal's Bolivian failure' (Gateway House, 2013), where in 2007 the Indian company Jindal Steel and Power Ltd had secured a contract for an integrated mining and steel project in Bolivia intending to invest $2.1bn, but by 2012 terminated the contract citing issues over the supply of gas. Disputes between Jindal and the Bolivian government escalated (*The Wall Street Journal*, 2012), leading to an arbitration judgment in 2014 (Bloomberg, 2014).

Gateway House (2013) identified four areas that contributed to the failure as:

- complex political relationships;
- a misjudgement of political power;
- disproportionate size of investment raising unrealistic expectations;
- a failure to evaluate the scenario sufficiently.

They also emphasized that a 'thorough political and risk analysis is necessary' and also remarked that 'understanding local politics and culture is critical'. Let us highlight the second of these, 'culture', and use it as a one of a three-part focus within the next section.

Culture, communication, commonalities

This section will focus on three areas that tend to be general in terms of organizational management, but we need to articulate them specifically in relation to projects and how they relate to project management. We will explore:

- Culture; this is pertinent to almost every project we undertake.

- Communication; this will include a focused consideration of the areas that will affect projects directly, for example in terms of linguistics.

- Commonalities; this is includes the sometimes disparate common characteristics of clanship, ethnicity, cultural and facets of tradition. While articulated separately, there is some overlap with the first two. It is important to note that these reflect the world that we live in… and the one in which projects are delivered.

We have already highlighted that some of these are regarded as barriers, problems or issues for project management, but this is not always true: one example that we will consider later is the potential value of bicultural team members – it may instead reflect narrowness of thinking, unwarranted stereotyping or prejudice. While this may not impair activities in a limited domestic environment or single geography (and it is not endorsed), we have argued that many projects are international, so we need to find ways to accommodate, accumulate and understand the particular aspect of difference, expectation or action.

The following example is provided as context for this. In Chapter 6, I described the scenario of working in the small office of a larger service agency, and that the 15-strong team was sometimes referred to as 'the wild west' by employees located in the main headquarters. Within the staff team, the local language was Welsh; it was the business language for certain projects. Strong cultural factors transcended many aspects of the organization and business environment.

Part of my role was to lead two distinct projects; the first of these involved establishing a support service for regional businesses, with a focus on new information technologies. In this project, the key constraint was funding (ie cost), as this was set at a threshold value by an external government department; the time constraint was based on the period of funding, so this was also anchored. The scope of the service needed to be developed but, owing to a number of constraints prevalent at the time of the project (since largely overcome through changes in technology and user-knowledge), this demanded local provision, with services delivered at a physical location.

Existing physical centres, operated by partner organizations, were distributed round an area that covered 40 per cent of the country (roughly equivalent to 8,500 km^2) but had a sparse population of just over 200,000 people. Many other nations with equivalent population densities provided models for decentralized service provision, but in this case the argument by the fund-holder was that this should be used to establish one (and only one) centre, in keeping with other similarly funded (but urban) geographies. By this time I had worked across the region and understood that it had a wide variety of cultural and linguistic characteristics, ranging from industrialized English-speaking to highly rural Welsh-speaking areas with an agricultural-based economy and relatively poorer transport infrastructure.

Cultural aspects were almost as diverse as the aforementioned economic activity and language. In this particular project scenario, understanding the geography, economy, demographics, culture and language seemed to be as important as the core project-planning skills, especially as this informed the initial framing of the project. Importantly, the success of the project depended upon joint delivery with four partners; although fragile, this stakeholder partnership was crucial. The external funding stakeholder (client) intended the use of the money to establish a single centre; critically, all assessment of the external environment for the project, which provided a novel arrangement of constraints, forced the proposed solution to be delivered in a decentralized style (in a virtual way). The funding stakeholder had strong interest and power which could have resulted in an impasse.

Each project lead was invited to present and argue their case (or proposal) at a neutral venue; by this time I had started to absorb some highly motivating aspects of the regional culture, had become impassioned by the project and, most importantly, I was representing the stakeholder partnership. The presentation included a map of the respective geographic areas, and the discussion became increasingly focused on this aspect, as it became the basis for constructive arguments about the need to provide services in a decentralized way. The argument was won, and the project took place on this basis.

To reflect on this example, we might immediately comment that the process was laboured and a conclusion should have been reached earlier. True, but often we will be faced with scenarios that require some effort to establish the correct starting basis for a project, and in this case it was influenced strongly by the cultural setting, geography and demographics and also by a number of political aspects that were associated with all of these. The delivery of this project demanded an approach that was suitably tuned to all of these things, but it also reflects the style of the person running it. Much of this can be amalgamated into an extensive stakeholder analysis and process, but it is well worth articulating separately here.

All of the above could be relevant in a comparable but completely different international setting, or conversely in an urban situation, where there are many cultures, languages and ethnic groups co-located. Nations can try to remove some of this diversity, but the advance of technology continually brings together different groups, so it remains prevalent in project environments. These types of scenario will be the typical landscape of projects, providing challenges for many project managers.

We can summarize that the demographic, cultural and linguistic aspects were reflected in the following project management areas:

- adaptation of project concept;
- communication and presentation of ideas;

- negotiation style and basis of rationale for the adopted project approach;
- framing the planning;
- informing the cost and budget planning and composition of the project team;
- stakeholder engagement and partnership.

A scenario such as this highlights the areas of culture, communication and the vital need to find commonalities that bridge gaps within the project.

Cultural influences

Culture means different things to different people; although this has had a strong emphasis on the arts and other manifestations of collective human intellectual achievement, this section will focus on culture in two senses: firstly, as stated by Hofstede and Hofstede (2005: 2–3), we will regard it as 'culture as mental software' – what we have learnt so far, how we think, and in many respects also how our brain is programmed, in terms of culture being a 'collective phenomenon'; secondly, according to Trompenaars and Hampden-Turner (2005: 6), who introduce culture as 'the way people solve problems'. These two definitions encapsulate the experience shared in the previous example. We should be careful also to distinguish this from when we are taking into account individual character, temperament and personality, for which we will use a different set of frameworks.

We might feel some certainty with our perspective on the world, over whatever period we have learnt and absorbed these things. What seems strange to you might seem quite normal to me. It is important to acknowledge that strangeness does not equate to wrong, but differences can present some challenges, and in the global world of projects this is likely to be a regular occurrence.

One basis for challenge within the project environment is the disparity of understanding associated with a pre-existing familiarity with different cultures. Whether this is working in a team initially as an outsider (including a difference of language, customary behaviour or religion) or misunderstanding the impact of a product in an alien market, these are some of the things that a mismatch can contribute to the failure of a project.

There is a significant body of knowledge associated with learning about and understanding culture (Hofstede, Trumpenaars, Hall, Adler for example); depending on the type of project, this BoK might be as valuable as any that have a specific focus on technical project management. Why is this? We need to remember that our world is based on people, not only in substantial aggregated geographies, but also in distributed diasporas. Where this affects behaviours, perspectives or management/working style, this will show in project environments.

Learning point

We could argue that our experience is broadening and the world seems smaller every day; communications tools are universal. As we discussed earlier, we may vacillate between two poles: on the one hand it is important, on the other hand the world functions; nations trade, projects are delivered. Keep a sense of perspective.

Insights for project management: uncertainty and power

Maintaining our focus on how this affects project management, which areas or aspects are going to be important to us? Some examples will help us to answer this question. This will be presented from the perspective of the specific cultural construct; since we all have a different position, it is up to us to apply this effectively within the project management environment.

On the basis of a survey of 36 Singapore managers, Tran and Skitmore (2002) evaluated a number of Hofstede's characterizations of national cultures. Their analysis yielded conclusions relating to 'low uncertainty-avoidance' and 'high uncertainty-avoidance', 'individualist and collectivist societies' and 'masculinity' cultures. They highlight that 'respondents from a low uncertainty avoidance culture appear to be associated with a communication process that is based on trust and therefore is less formal and standardized'. This insight is helpful, since it can be used to inform approach and style within a project environment and also help us better understand some characteristics of stakeholder behaviour.

But what does this mean? The term 'uncertainty avoidance' is used to reflect the degree to which a nation generally is comfortable or uncomfortable with uncertainty (Hofstede and Hofstede, 2005: 164–65) – in *Cultures and Organizations* (Hofstede and Hofstede, 2005: 164–65) the writing of Peter Lawrence is referred to; he describes travelling on long-distance trains in Germany, how seemingly important it was for passengers to check the progress of the train against the arrival and departure times, and that a foreigner might notice the high importance of punctuality. The point made is that different nations react to levels of uncertainty in different ways. This is one basis for the characterization of national cultures; references to individualist versus collectivist societies are framed in terms of the power of the group, and masculinity versus femininity are labels for 'the desirability of assertive behaviour against the desirability of modest behaviour' (2005: 116).

Let us consider an example relevant to uncertainty avoidance. Japan's Shinkansen trains also form the basis of the high-speed rail (HSR) system in Taiwan; however, Taiwan's HSR system has some differences from its counterpart in Japan. A passenger who also frequently travels between Japan and Taiwan stated that, 'The cars Taiwan's high speed rail uses are the same as those on Japan's Shinkansen… the difference between the two is that in Japan, the JR (Japan Railways) are much stricter about ticket inspection and it's a real pain… in Taiwan, it seems there is no ticket inspection, only when you board and alight the train' (Yueh-lin, 2012).

According to the Hofstede research (2005: 168–69), Japan scores more highly (ranked 11–13) than Taiwan (ranked 39) on the uncertainty-avoidance scale. If we accept that this relative measure is relatively true, what are the practical implications in terms of the project? Returning to the HSR scenario, Yueh-lin further explains: 'but what Tsusui doesn't know is that it's not necessarily a lack of ticket inspection on HSR trains, it's just that the system employs Taiwanese technology to check tickets unobtrusively'. It seems that the project has characteristics of an 'as-but' type, in that it was delivered with largely similar aspects but also incorporates dissimilar aspects that reflect a different national requirement.

Acknowledging uncertainty avoidance as a construct in cultural programming, this example highlights the incorporation of a modified design in a project of significant scale. We should also consider this at an individual or personal level, since it will help us to adopt our own responses during the delivery of a project. We could further argue that this adoption and accommodation are likely to be a universal challenge since, as Trompenaars and Hampden-Turner assert, 'the one best way of organizing does not exist' (2005: 13).

Uncertainty avoidance can be expressed in a way that might be misunderstood; during a cycling trip with a colleague we shared our breakfast table with a friendly German who was doing the same route as we were. We exchanged views and experiences in a particularly convivial atmosphere. An hour later, having loaded up the paniers on our bikes, my colleague Simon and I were about to ride away when we spoke again with our new German friend who was about to do likewise. He glanced at my tyres and said to me firmly 'you must not ride your bike; the front tyre needs more pressure…'. I thanked him for the advice and reassured him that I would do this after cycling a short distance.

I have since worked with Russians, many of whom I find have a similar direct style. These are the types of thing we may experience in a multinational or multicultural team; our style, the one we are most familiar with, is neither better nor worse, wrong nor right; it is just different. Where some of this is characterized by the various frameworks of Hofstede or other researchers, it is up to us to learn and understand better the facets of people that enable us to work together in project environments.

The construct uncertainty avoidance exists, but this characteristic is not always predictable since this will depend upon the specific context and scenario, and can be influenced by particular personalities or linguistic abilities. In the previous example it is possible that the advice would not have been given so strongly if the person had been more introverted or if language had been a barrier.

An insight into other aspects of culture may be useful to the project manager, so we will draw on one final construct from Hofstede: 'Power distance' is defined (Hofstede and Hofstede, 2005: 46) as the 'extent to which the less powerful members of institutions and organizations within a country expect and accept that power is distributed unevenly'. Institutions ('basic elements of society') are distinguished from organizations ('the places where people work'). To what extent does this construct affect our projects? Potentially in many ways.

We would expect a project that is being delivered in a society with high power distance to exhibit relatively strong planning and control characteristics, since the stereotyped response from members of the project team (and potentially some stakeholder groups) could include degrees of acquiescence. Reviewing the London Olympic Games, *The Economist* (2012) compared the style of delivery of different events. The London Games had been 'a "nudge" Olympics, where locals and visitors had been coaxed'. They attributed the successful 2008 Beijing event to a different approach: 'in 2008, China staged a command and control games...' These views are intriguing.

As such, good planning and control is important; we may not always agree when it is the highest priority in our approach, nor the extent to which it is as transparent as the style. This is due in part to our cultural setting, either as an individual or in aggregate as a diaspora, society or geography. And, of course, some of this may well be changing, as it may become more difficult to ensure that the planning is followed with the same vigour into implementation. In 2012, Ting-feng (2012) reported that young workers are 'averse to authority and often prodigal'. They stated that '... members of the Post-90 Generation are no longer merely workers on an electronics goods assembly line... they are voracious consumers of technology products...' and 'during working hours they may well be satisfied employees... but they are relatively worldly and knowledgeable...' and 'companies are finding it harder and harder to get a feel for who they really are'. This hints at change within a demographic group, and the implication is that they will be more difficult to manage; the newspaper crew reported from Wuhan in central China.

The areas mentioned in this section are part of a broader cultural landscape and are of relevance to a project manager, not only in the Asia-Pacific area, but in projects everywhere. Two further cultural constructs are worth considering here: degree of individualism and time orientation.

Insights for project management: other aspects of culture

One of the many benefits that can accrue from living in different geographies is the insight into how societies function. A tourist may not notice the degree to which a society is based on 'I' or 'We'. Studying, working or an extended visit helps us to observe what seems to be fundamental differences in the way that societies are based upon collaboration and collectiveness in contrast to a society that has a relatively strong individual focus or emphasis.

International students may be surprised at the differences between living in South America or China and studying in the UK. But why would they not be surprised? These are different nations; students are likely to be younger and this may be their first time to visit. But the inevitable stereotyping has some currency. Our personal examples bear out the theoretically established position, and insights such as these can be particularly helpful.

Trompenaars and Hampden-Turner (2005: 67) provide guidance for communitarians doing business with individualists and individualists doing business with communitarians. This includes:

- speed of decision making (quick decisions vs consultation and consensus building);
- decision-making autonomy (individual can make decision vs needing to consult);
- levels of status or esteem (conducting business alone vs bringing helpers);
- drivers for deal making (aiming for quick deal vs building lasting relationships).

All of these points are useful for project managers, but the last one is worth drawing out further; this reinforces the importance of spending time to establish the relationship platform. Although it has been referred to in a number of sections, this is the most explicit manifestation so far.

A project environment might incorporate the assembling of a team that is multinational and multicultural. Members of a relatively more individualist society may approach dealing with conflict differently from those used to living in one that is relatively more collectivist (or communitarian). In *Managing Cultural Differences* (2011: 236–37), Moran, Harris and Moran discuss the 'patterns of behaviour toward conflict from individualistic… and collectivistic cultures', highlighting orientation towards action and communication styles as a number of different approaches that a team member might adopt.

My observation is that the difference in learning styles of international students is sometimes very wide. Personality and linguistic capability also play a part in this. A final point here, in some respects often seen in learning teams of international students, is how we perceive time. Moran *et al* (2011: 11–14) set out the following 10 categories intended to help understand a macro or micro culture:

- sense of self and space;
- communication and language;

- dress and appearance;
- food and feeding habits;
- time and time consciousness;
- relationships;
- values and norms;
- beliefs and attitudes;
- mental processes and learning;
- work habits and practices.

In 'time and time consciousness' they highlight how 'sense of time differs by culture – some are exact and others are relative'. They compare the degree of precision of different nations, and how, in some cultures, 'promptness is determined by age or status'. Understanding these inferred characteristics may also have a value to the project manager, even if in indirect form; for a project where meeting the time component is critical, a better understanding of how the team will react to associated pressure will help with the management. Often this will not solve the problem but will help us to understand how better to deal with the problem from a more informed perspective.

All of these characteristics are relevant to project management if the project takes place in an international setting. We could argue that they are important in any setting. Some are more practically oriented (such as dress, food and feeding habits), some will be more difficult to understand (such as beliefs and attitudes), and some organizations will provide training and development courses to help; for all of us, it is important to bear in mind that these are one group of potentially many groups (of management considerations). Depending on the context of the project, we may consider the need to extend our knowledge and insights via an appropriate means.

Learning point

The diversity in the aforementioned characteristics provides a challenging landscape. This could manifest itself in the inappropriate adoption of planning style. Where cultural differences affect perspectives regarding time, this will be reflected in the planning too.

Communication: language and linguistics

The previous discussion included communication and language as one of a number of key dimensions for us to consider. In many respects this is obvious; a difference in language perhaps presents us with the first barrier when we encounter someone whom we expect to speak the same one. The European Union has 24 official languages, with many more used daily across all the member states (European Union, 2014); the inhabitants of the UK are quite fortunate that the English language has been adopted as the lingua franca of many multinational enterprises, that it is commonly a language of commerce, and that it is a legacy from a previous period of history. This also presents potential complacency: a complacency of learning other languages competently, and also a component of assuming that everyone who speaks the same language actually understands it to the same level and can respond in challenging environments with the same level of consistency as those for whom it is the mother tongue (ie first language).

As one component of a broader heading of communication, language may provide more barriers than we realize. When we consider non-verbal types of communication and body language, this presents a further set of potentially difficult considerations for the project manager. For example, if the project management role requires the successful incorporation of resources from international centres, the naïve project manager might have some difficulties with style of greeting, negotiation, and relationship building.

There are, of course many other areas of potential problems, but this is where good diagnostic skills are valuable; the project manager should assess the requirement and deal with the associated issues in the most efficient and effective manner.

Specific issues associated with language and linguistic ability

In the early years of my working career I was frequently disappointed to hear my colleagues reflect that, despite working in a European geography, they found it too difficult to learn a language such as French or German. Often I would hear people remark that 'there are so many languages, we don't know which to learn... and, of course, English is used nearly everywhere'. They were right, at least on the final point. However, as I came to work in different places I realized that the first, about difficulty, was not true. Curiously, while working in a bilingual environment (Welsh and English), I recall a colleague say: 'I can't speak French or German... I'm not very good at languages.'

There are some important perspectives here; in a busy working environment the pressure to get the communication right (ie correct) is very important. The success or otherwise of a particular process would depend on this. This brings us back to the world of projects. In a global project it is likely that there will be a mix of languages: a host or local language; the business language; the language of an individual team member. The common denominator may be the English language; equally it might be Mandarin Chinese, French, Arabic or Spanish – or one of many others. As the common language, it will only be as good as the speakers are good. Of course, this will present difficulties, and in project environments the consequences might be disastrous. This therefore presents a risk; this could be significant.

To provide further context for this, Tenzer, Pudelko and Harzing (2014) explore 'the impact of language barriers on trust formation in multinational teams'. The research concerned the members, leaders and senior managers within 15 multinational teams, in 3 German automotive corporations. They discussed (2014: 525) how professional competence can be impaired due to language barriers and found that 'respondents of all nationalities associated team communication in a foreign language with "insecurity", "embarrassment", "feeling stupid", "feeling threatened", "showing weakness", "losing face" and "having no self-confidence". Taken together, these emotions created a 'pervasive language-based anxiety'. Each of these expressions is powerful in its own right. These could apply to any multinational project team. They also remarked that 'these feelings become salient in MNTs (multinational teams) of all functions, sizes, and regardless of the language policies in place'. This has direct application within the project environment.

It is worthwhile considering these challenges further. Feely (Communication across language barriers, in Tayeb, 2003: 216–18) highlighted the following problems for a second language user:

- 'Failure of rhetorical skills' (interpersonal skills such as humour, sensitivity, negotiation or persuasiveness).

- 'Face' (for example, nobody wants to look stupid… so will continue to look as if they understand even if they don't).

- 'Power/authority distortion' (power or authority could be lost due to a disparity in the competence of the language spoken).

- 'Miscommunication' (this is self-evident).

- 'Attribution' (for example, if the confidence of the non-native speaker is misjudged by the native speaker, encouraging the native speaker to project a number of ideas, concepts and feelings; the reaction by the non-native speaker then surprises the native speaker). There is an unrealistic expectation that can generate subsequent mistrust.

- 'Code switching' (second language speakers need to confirm their understanding, so switch to native language during a key moment in a meeting; this switching can be interpreted as suspicious).

All of these things can manifest themselves as problems in a project environment. A form of this will even take place among teams that have only native speakers but who may have a relatively limited ability with some aspects of the language. It is possible that technology might one day help to resolve this by providing real-time translation (currently tools can help, but this can provide a different form of confusion, as it may encourage the introduction of multiple languages rather than one). Clearly challenges exist, and in a project environment we need to take a pragmatic approach to dealing with the problems that emerge. Understanding that the problems exist will help to resolve them.

Commonalities

As the third component of our consideration of the typical international project, this section will be used to briefly explore the opportunities provided through common areas of nationality or ethnicity, as well as those presented by culture and communication. In many respects, these can be viewed negatively; we have some evidence for this in the preceding sections. Yet there are many areas in common, and these provide the glue for the capability that ultimately contributes to the successful delivery of projects. There are, of course, other opportunistic areas that provide this, such as personality, which we will consider separately.

Ethnicity, as a social group that has common national or cultural traditions, can help to overcome barriers caused by language. An understanding of these aspects will help the project manager to navigate the right course through difficult scenarios. Insight into contemporary regional politics could reveal a reason why specific individuals do not work together well; if the parties originate from areas that are in conflict, this will inevitably have some effect on their feeling and perspectives.

It is also important to highlight the strength of commonality of purpose, interests or personality. The development of productive and effective relationships can help to overcome barriers that are presented by conflict of objectives, structure, competition for resources, or perceived cultural mismatches. Seeking commonalities is also to urge disparate parties within the project environment to find mechanisms that will overcome these barriers. It is putting soft skills, at the appropriate time, in the vanguard of project management.

CASE STUDY   Shoe projects: from design to store

If we do not have any insight into the background development processes, the arrival of the latest season's fashion into the stores is something that 'just happens'. We may or may not be able to find what we want in the shop (online or offline), but most of us will neither consider the projects that will have taken place prior to some shoes being on display nor be aware of the tight development-to-market project timescales.

FIGURE 9.1 Interrelated sequence of activities required to manufacture a shoe

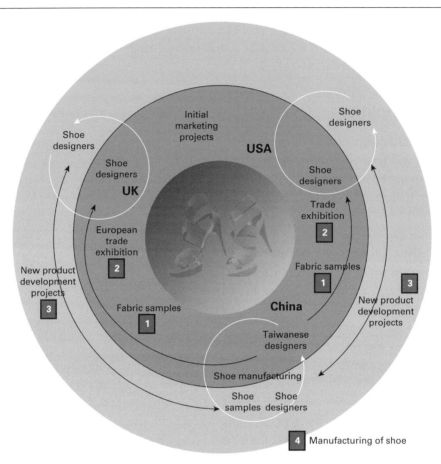

To consider this, we will look at one aspect of this cycle, the design of a new shoe. Figure 9.1 reflects the need for an interrelated sequence of activities that take place prior to the manufacturing of the shoe. There are three core geographic locations marked on this; it is as if we are looking down on the world, and in this world China provides shoe manufacturing capability, and the United States and the UK are the home of brands that will ultimately utilize this capability to deliver shoes internationally.

The inner ring represents 'initial marketing projects'. By this we mean the earlier exploratory marketing that takes place involving the respective teams of fabric and shoe designers:

1 Selections of fabric designs are sent from Taiwan to shoe designers in the United States or the UK in the form of a swatch (a book containing samples of fabrics).

2 In addition to this, the fabric designs may be exhibited at the trade fairs that take place either in the United States or in Europe. This is an opportunity for the fabric designers to sell to the shoe designers.

3 If the fabric designers successfully attract the interest of the shoe designers, the outer ring represents the new product development projects that are likely to take place. The fabric is incorporated into a sample shoe; this is subject to a development process that will involve extensive testing; if this is successful, and the negotiated price of the fabric is suitable, the shoe will go into production.

4 The shoe is manufactured in China and then sold to the world. After this stage, the process moves progressively into operations management. There will, of course, be a number of further development actions that will result in subsequent project activities.

This sets out some projects that typically take place in this market. The process will often need to take place in a period of only 18 months (from start to finish as a manufactured item), as the shoes need to be ready as part of a product portfolio that will be marketed for a particular grouped season (ie spring/summer or fall/winter).

Case reflection

The challenges in this scenario are typical of many retail markets:

i Within the projects mentioned, identify the key international dimensions in terms of the type and scale of challenge.

ii Determine the associated practical issues and means of addressing them; does this cause business case issues?

iii Success in these projects brings products to markets on schedule; identify stakeholder groups, change issues and risk areas that affect this type of market.

Implications for project management

While discussing some international aspects we have drawn attention to relevant areas of project management within each section. In order to provide an overall focus for this chapter, it is worthwhile bringing forward some of the core project management building blocks. In Chapter 1, we introduced the notion of a project; recall '... so a project team often involves people who don't usually work together – sometimes from different organizations and across multiple geographies' (PMI, 2014). In the latest sections we explored this dimension further in terms of the challenges presented by culture and communication, and the need to maximize commonalities in terms of these, through nationality, ethnicity or other 'glue'.

At the start we also introduced risk as an ever-present aspect of projects. This chapter has extended the range of uncertainty through the potential mismatches and barriers that sometimes arise in projects with international dimensions. With respect to this aspect, we have examined some areas presented by culture and language. There are, of course, many more. We could use the risk analysis to reveal specific areas that need further or deeper attention, and use that as a guide to give us direction. For example, political risk arises in relation to nationality and culture, and we will examine this further.

Figure 9.2 shows the diagram that was introduced in Chapter 1; this gives us a framework to reflect on the components of a project from an international perspective. Each of the blocks is considered in terms of the international context. This is intended to prompt and provoke further thinking and reflection, and this process is initiated in Table 9.2.

There are, of course, a number of specific aspects that need to be considered at a strategic level. One key area is stakeholders; a second example would be risk. In terms of the first of these, we would need to evaluate the stakeholder landscape through an enhanced or further informed perspective, especially when there are strong cultural influences. This may help us to justify taking an approach with which we are not entirely comfortable (for example, such as the recruitment of specific types or gender of project manager in a particular geography). This is a significant aspect of the project management challenge.

In terms of risk, we have argued that it is ever-present in projects and we have also explored the relationship between perceived certainty and risk. But what if we subject to scrutiny these perceptions that arise in different regions or geographies: Do attitudes to risk vary across regions? How will this affect the planning and delivery of a project?

FIGURE 9.2   The project represented as a journey

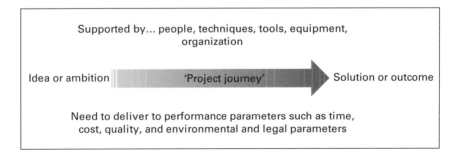

TABLE 9.2   Impact of international aspects on a typical project

Heading	Some questions include...
Idea or ambition	In a global project, what is the impact of culture? How well does the idea or ambition translate?
Performance parameters such as time, cost, quality	What is the impact on these performance parameters? For example, if a key priority is time, have we considered the impact of a regional or cultural dimension on the team? Do we (or the stakeholders) share the same view of the other parameters (such as those concerned with environmental aspects)?
Supported by people, techniques, tools, equipment, organization	What are the barriers to establishing effective teams? How will the diversity of team members affect the project? Have we planned the project sufficiently in terms of adopting tools and techniques, and do we understand the response to these? Do we understand the impact of cultural 'norms' on the project?
Solution or outcome	Will we see the outcome similarly? Will stakeholder perspectives vary across different regions?

To provide insight, here are two contrasting examples: in the UK I witnessed the surprise of a department manager on realizing that a wire shopping basket on top of a cupboard had been identified as a serious health hazard; in the Asia-Pacific area I see climbing walls in public areas without any conspicuous warning or disclaimer notices. Are these trivial, or do they reflect different attitudes?

It serves as a reminder that we consider risk from different perspectives. Trompenaars and Hampden-Turner (2005: 39) highlighted that 'weighty contracts are a way of life in individualist cultures', but may provide a rough guideline or approximation elsewhere. If, in such an environment, there is a desire to make the contract vague, reflecting a genuine desire for mutual accommodation, then the idea that the contract is a risk-mitigating mechanism may need to be revisited.

General types of risk in international business

While we discuss risk in relation to international business, the following insights are useful. In their 'examination of the vulnerability of international projects to political risks', Khattab, Anchor and Davies (2007) reasoned that general risks comprise:

- political;
- financial;

- cultural;
- natural.

If we explore one of these, within political risk they articulate the following:

- government interference with business operations;
- occurrence of political or societal events.

If we use this as an initial framework to assess category risks, the likely outcome will be to identify risks in several domains that could range from restriction of import/ exporting, ownership or personnel, credit or taxation, to the possibility and impact of civil unrest or violent expression of views or pursuit of political views. If we are tasked with delivering a project in a region that we perceive has a high level of risk, this might lead us to feel that the risks are too high to undertake the project.

However, *The Economist* (2014) describes the limited impact of things that we might find as overpowering reasons not to undertake a project in an area perceived to be particularly high in political risk and perceived danger. The article highlights the measures taken by multinational organizations when they operate in an area subject to high perceived risk of this type. In addition to considering the scope for profitable activities in areas affected by war or conflict, one aspect they consider is that 'the sub-prime and Eurozone crises inadvertently helped; big firms carry more cash than before, making them less exposed to a credit market freeze'. Risk is ever-present; it is likely that the uncertainty in international projects will be higher than in those we feel we know better, but this does not stop projects from taking place.

Keeping a sense of perspective – cultural friction

We have explored the international nature of projects, both as a cross-border international activity and also recognizing that there are degrees of international aspects in almost all projects we deliver. Common to this is the discussion of cultures, and this aspect is often seen as a barrier, for example by being referred to as 'cultural distance'. Earlier in the chapter we remarked on the vacillation between yes, this is important and worthy of specific elicitations and strategy, and no, this is something that we just deal with, at an individual, organization, national or international level.

Taking this latter point, the diversity of culture often provides a positive basis for the creation of new ideas, processes and inspiration. Shenkar (2012) argued for the replacement of the term cultural distance with 'cultural friction'; this is a more positive reflection and is something we should promote and carry forward into project environments. We will always see some friction between different cultural surfaces; 'by friction, we mean the scale and essence of the interface between interacting cultures, and the "drag" produced by that interface for the operation of those systems'.

By viewing projects as a bridge between strategy and operations, we could argue that the project manager (or project management function) needs also to provide a bridge, and this needs to be sufficiently robust to accommodate the friction caused by the incorporation of different cultures, be they of the organizational or national type. At an individual level, members of the team will reflect their own cultural position, as we have discussed in this chapter; they are also individual people who have a particular personality, ability, style and contribution. The role they play will reflect all of these things.

Summary

This chapter has considered the likelihood that all projects are international to some degree. In addition to those that take place as a cross-border international activity, others within a single region will contain multi-ethnic, multilingual and multicultural elements.

We have asked the question whether project management can be upscaled to the international form, as is the case with other management disciplines; while in many respects this is true, the best perspectives can be gained from viewing this the other way round: examining and understanding international dimensions such as culture, and exploring commonalities that exist, enable us to ask the right questions, in turn enabling us to deliver projects on an international basis.

References

Bloomberg (2014) Jindal Steel wins $22.5 million verdict against Bolivia, 23 August, retrieved on 1 October 2014 from http://www.bloomberg.com/news/2014-08-23/jindal-steel-wins-22-5-million-verdict-against-bolivia.html

Briscoe, D, Schuler, R and Tarique, I (2012) *International Human Resource Management*, Routledge, London

The Economist (2012) The London Games: the joy of the nudge Olympics, 11 August

The Economist (2014) Profits in a time of war, 20 September

European Union (2014) EU administration – staff, languages and location, retrieved on 25 September 2014 from http://europa.eu/about-eu/facts-figures/administration/index_en.htm

Gateway House (2013) Lessons from Jindal's Bolivian failure, 19 July, retrieved on 23 August 2014 from http://www.gatewayhouse.in/lessons-from-jindals-bolivian-failure/

Hofstede, G and Hofstede, J (2005) *Cultures and Organizations: Software of the mind*, McGraw-Hill, New York

Khattab, A, Anchor, J and Davies, E (2007) Managerial perceptions of political risk in international projects, *International Journal of Project Management*, **25**, pp 734–43

Moran, R, Harris, P and Moran, S (2011) *Managing Cultural Differences*, Butterworth-Heinemann, Oxford

Muriithi, N and Crawford, L (2003) Approaches to project management in Africa: implications for international development projects, *International Journal of Project Management*, **21**, pp 309–19

Project Management Institute (2014) [Online] retrieved on 12 November 2014 from http://www.pmi.org/en.aspx

Shenkar, O (2012) Cultural distance revisited: towards a more rigorous conceptualization and measurement of cultural differences, *Journal of International Business Studies*, **43**, pp 1–11

Tayeb, M (2003) *International Management: Theories and Practices*, Pearson Education, Harlow

Tenzer, H, Pudelko, M and Harzing, A (2014) The impact of language barriers on trust formation in multinational teams, *Journal of International Business Studies*, **45**, pp 508–35

Ting-feng, W (2012) Managing those difficult young workers, *Commonwealth Magazine*, 20 December

Tran, D and Skitmore, M (2002) The impact of culture on international management: a survey of project communications in Singapore, *The Australian Journal of Construction Economics and Building*, **2** (2), pp 36–47

Trompenaars, F and Hampden-Turner, C (2005) *Riding the Waves of Culture: Understanding cultural diversity in business*, Nicholas Brealey Publishing, London

The Wall Street Journal (2012) Jindal Steel exits Bolivia project, 17 July, retrieved on 1 October 2014 from http://online.wsj.com/news/articles/SB10001424052702303754904577532592283910030

Yueh-lin, M (2012) HSR: the new benchmark for travel culture, *Commonwealth Magazine*, 19 July

PART FOUR
Developing a capability

Managing and leading in project environments

LEARNING OUTCOMES

By applying the topics within this chapter you should be able to:

- consider the extent of differences between general and project management;

- explore whether there is a universal specification for the project manager;

- examine appropriate competence frameworks;

- evaluate the role of leadership in project environments;

- reflect on some of the practicalities associated with leading and managing in project environments;

- understand the character and value of diversity within project management.

Introduction

As we arrive at the final part of the book, we will start by understanding better the challenges presented by managing and leading in project environments. Many areas of management were explored indirectly as project management within the first four chapters; although primarily defined as dealing with or controlling things or people, the term management has many connotations and is used in different ways.

The generalist project manager has to be able to incorporate knowledge of a wide variety of specialist areas; the need to ensure delivery of the project for expectant stakeholders reminds us of the need to make sure we are capable in every area required. This also requires effective leadership.

In this chapter we will focus first on the two key areas, management and leadership, in project environments. By establishing a set of broad principles for each, we will also be able to determine where our strengths lie, and help to inform our own strategy for future development. This chapter will consider what managing and leading are concerned with, what we need to do to be successful when managing projects, the challenge of sourcing an effective project manager and value of diversity in resources.

Managing and leading; distinct and complementary attributes

We all come into the project environment with different experience, knowledge, expectations, attitudes and capability. We are all different people with a variety of characters and personalities and we deal with things in a unique style. It is important to recognize the value of enhancing, developing or understanding better our profile, as this will help us to build the capability required in project environments. It is helpful to start this process by considering two related points:

- What is managing and leading?
- What do we need to do to be effective at managing and leading in project environments?

It is worthwhile considering that while some management is specifically associated with project management, some is general management and some is international management, leadership is universal.

Management in project environments

In order to help us answer these questions, let us start by checking our understanding of management. Hitt, Black and Porter (2009: 5–6) describe management as:

- a process; activities such as planning, deciding, evaluating;
- assembling and using resources; human/financial/material/informational;
- goal-directed; purpose and direction;
- carried out in an organizational setting; achieving common purpose through coordinated intentional structure.

Correspondingly, they highlight that managers are concerned with planning, organizing, directing and controlling. Alternatively, 'management' is set out as four functions

FIGURE 10.1   Relationship between project and general management

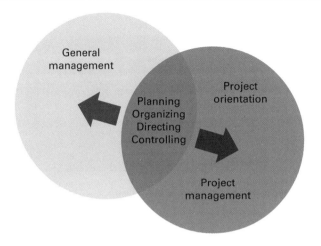

of planning, organizing, leading and controlling (Robbins and Coulter, 2012: 37). They also discuss efficiency (getting the most output from the least input) and effectiveness (doing the right things).

Other than the type of process concerned, it is difficult to see distinct separation of these general management frameworks from project management at this level, unless we reflect upon the specific notions of effectiveness and efficiency and specific traits associated with orientation towards projects (such as creativity). This is shown in Figure 10.1. Although we would want to do the right things when managing a project, sometimes how to do this will be difficult to envisage, as we may be faced with additional uncertainty within project environments. More critically, we could argue that while the general principle of using resources efficiently holds in all circumstances, we may find that the specific emphasis within the project actually sets the criteria for how resources are deployed and utilized. This discussion started to reveal some subtle differences.

Would we then expect management to be different from project management? It is within the high-level headings that we notice the difference. For example, within management, 'planning' comprises the foundations, decision making, tools and techniques. This is not dissimilar. 'Organizing' incorporates different aspects relating to organizational design, human resource management (HRM) and groups and teams. This reveals some separation of focus, since for the project manager the emphasis is likely to be with the design of a project organizational structure; this could be distinct from, or related to, the existing organization design (or organization designs). HRM knowledge is expected from the project manager; how an individual fulfils that requirement will vary. Getting it wrong can be very costly.

FIGURE 10.2   Communication actions

Communication headings	Activity and action			Communication headings
A plan to meet increased demand	Rationale	Plan	Progress	The upgrade is underway
How it benefits you	Positive impact	Stakeholder	Negative impact	How our works may affect you
How you can check what's coming up	Coming	Communication	Completed	What's been done already
Our plan for your line	Impact	Specific aspects of plan	Impact	Our plan for your stations

SOURCE: adapted from London Underground upgrade programme

In term of 'controlling', the foundations are often explored through measurement, comparison, corrective actions; control is discussed in relation to organizational performance and performance-measuring methods. It will often also include a review of operations and supply chain management. In this respect there appears to be a greater divergence in focus, since we argued in Chapter 1 that projects tend to be new activities and therefore at the opposite end of the spectrum to operations management. However, the project might be concerned with the implementation of a new supply chain or aspect of it; the project might depend on this for the provision of resources.

The logic and argument could also hold for operations management. If our responsibility is for the operational management of a route within an MRT (mass rapid transit) or metro system, a new project that is concerned with upgrading the line or infrastructure will certainly have an impact on our activities, and of course vice versa. For example, Figure 10.2, adapted from the London Underground upgrade plan, shows the eight key headings from their information bulletin; this highlights a number of impacts on stakeholder groups. Within the organization and transport network there is a need for significant coordination between operations management and project management.

This usefully highlights one of the recurring difficult-to-address facets of project management: a project could be in one or more sectors, one area, or all areas, requiring knowledge and know-how in a potentially very wide range.

We have argued that a project manager needs to have a wide range of management skills and knowledge, but the range and depth of this will vary from scenario to scenario, reflecting both the type and context of the project. For example, a project manager concerned with the development of a new home management system will need to be aware of a host of building-specific and legislative dimensions that will be quite different from those experienced by the project manager who is concerned with developing a new product for an export market. This presents a challenge, since

FIGURE 10.3   The need for three dimensions of capability

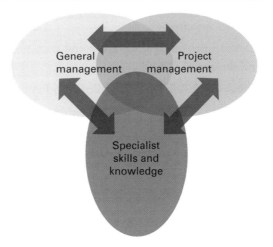

it is therefore difficult to arrive at a generic specification for leadership and management skills. There are three dimensions of capability, shown in Figure 10.3.

The shape of this will depend on the person, their experience, and the particular requirement of the project and its environment; the role and style will vary between general and project management; in highly specialist roles, the needs within the bottom ellipse are very important and this would be dominant in defining the role and person specification.

Project manager: a specification

Is there a specification for a good project manager? We can develop some perspectives from HRM, project management, body of knowledge bases, or from organization-specific sources. While these come from distinct areas of perspective, there is of course an overlap. Let us look at an example from the *Human Resource Management Journal*.

Cheng, Dainty and Moore (2005) sought to reveal the underlying competences associated with 'superior' project managers. Focused on the construction sector, the research suggested that the following 12 'core behavioural competences' underpin effective project management performance:

- achievement orientation – towards improving performance, entrepreneurial and innovative behaviour;

- initiative – being proactive with respect to problem aversion in order to enhance job results;

- information seeking – being proactive to explore issues and seeking solutions outside immediate environment;
- focusing on the client's needs;
- impact and influence – providing inspiration and with proficiency in team coordination and direction;
- strong directiveness – ensuring team complies with intended demands;
- strong teamwork and cooperation attributes – influencing desired team performance;
- appropriate team leadership – style and balance in terms of cooperation versus command and control;
- analytical thinking to inform management decisions – in terms of conception, analysis and reasoning;
- conceptual thinking – switching between details and strategic perspectives;
- good self-control – calm under pressure, maintaining performance levels;
- flexibility and adaptability – in terms of problem solving.

This is useful but it raises a couple of points for reflection. Firstly, as the research was conducted in a particular sector, we need to consider how applicable these competences are in a more general project management role. Secondly, how does this relate to the specific knowledge and skill-base within our potential project management pool (that is, what does this mean in terms of particular development activities at an individual or corporate level)? To what extent are these being developed in the existing frameworks within the organization (or by the individual)? This is an opportune moment to look at the development in the practitioner area.

Practitioner and body of knowledge bases

This area provides valuable insights for a couple of reasons. Firstly, as this is often based on an understanding of developed project management and human resource management theory, it is likely to reflect a strong practical basis. Secondly, in many cases the BoK organizations have established qualifications associated with these profiles, thus providing a potential source of suitable qualifications (or suitably qualified individuals).

Given the extraordinary diversity of project management roles, these mechanisms cannot provide a complete solution to all needs, but competence frameworks and accrediting processes help to support individual and corporate development. It is worthwhile taking a look at the IPMA Competence Baseline (IPMA, 2006) and APM Competence Framework (APM, 2009); both group competences into the following areas, shown in Figure 10.4:

FIGURE 10.4   Comparison of APM and IPMA competence groups

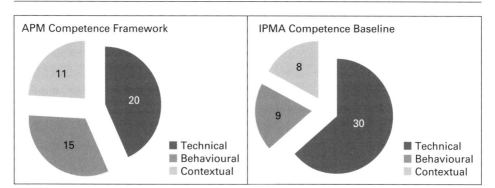

- contextual;
- technical;
- behavioural.

The contextual elements focus on orientation and implementation with regard to project, programme and portfolio and 'the project manager's competence in managing relations with the line management organization and the ability to function in a project focused organization' (IPMA, 2006: 9). The technical elements have relatively more emphasis on hard skills such as project requirements, objectives and quality; the behavioural competences comprise a range of elements that includes leadership, results orientation and negotiation, conflict and crisis, and also values and ethics.

Although each framework has different numbers of items in each category, there is commonality in many of the individual competences. For example, within the technical group, we see 'requirements management' (APM) and 'project requirements and objectives' (IPMA). Within the behavioural groups, we see leadership and negotiation common to both, with similarities in many of the other competences. The greatest diversity is in the contextual grouping; other than 'legal awareness' (APM) and 'legal' (IPMA), the others have a different phraseology, with the IPMA emphasizing project, programme and portfolio orientation. Nevertheless, this is balanced overall, since it is expressed in other areas of the APM framework.

The strong overlap of the headings is helpful for organizations that operate or deploy projects in multiple territories. We would expect the derivation of competence frameworks in other geographies to be developed on a similar basis; for example, Project Management South Africa (PMSA) have worked to integrate the PMI framework (PMI, 2001) with the context and demands of the South African environment.

The value of adopting a framework

Chapter 8 included a section that described how a number of questions, once posed, had in fact highlighted the lack of insights associated with a need for a project management support (or office) function. One of these questions was: 'Should I get a project management qualification?' This is relevant here; our previous discussion introduced competence frameworks and these are the basis for some of the qualifications or certifications available for individuals to pursue.

It is useful to consider this, since it helps us to reflect upon the scenarios, direction or choice associated with respect to investing in qualifications. There is also linkage with the important areas of management and leadership. But is this an effective route to improve the capability of the individual or the team? Based on research undertaken with project management practitioners, Crawford (2005) reported that there was 'no statistically significant relationship between performance against the standards selected for study, in their entirety, and perceived effectiveness of workplace performance'. This sample reflected the four areas of engineering and construction, information systems/information technology and telecommunications, industrial process and business services. It was framed in terms of senior management perceptions of competence and suggested that different perceptions were held.

Subsequent research, undertaken in 2010, compared the hiring criteria between IT recruiters and IT executives (Stevenson and Starkweather, 2010) in the United States; this revealed some key differences in perspective. Where the recruiters regarded education and experience as the most valued criteria for hiring, the views expressed by the IT executives were quite different (regarded as 'marginally important'). The study found that IT executives valued the 'critical core competences' of leadership, an ability to communicate at multiple levels, verbal and writing skills, attitude and the ability to deal with ambiguity and change. This sample disagreed over the value of a formal project management certification – over half of the IT recruiters thought it was important, but most IT executives thought it 'irrelevant'.

Other studies have endorsed the value of formal certification, such as that reviewing usage within the Finmeccanica Group (Buganza et al, 2013). In this study, the impact of the deployment of PMP® (Project Management Professional) within Italy's high-technology manufacturer was deemed to be positive, conveyed as (2013: 296) '... the PMP can be considered a best practice'. This was within a corporate training programme that had been developed and delivered through collaboration with an academic partner.

We may never know the complete answer to the question posed regarding project management qualification, but clearly there are scenarios where the adoption of a common framework brings benefits and there are other scenarios that need more development. Clearly a project manager needs to have a wide set of managing and leading skills, and the competence frameworks introduced by IPMA and APM high-light leadership as a key element. The sample of research mentioned also confirms the importance of effective management and leadership skills – in order to do that most effectively, we need to clarify what we mean by leadership, distinct from management.

Project managers need to lead in addition to manage

The argument for project management to be about management and leadership is easy to make; by definition, the project manager needs to manage. Leadership skills are vital too, but when, how and what does this actually include?

Kent (2006) provides a useful clarification of this. The framework can be utilized effectively in the area of project management in a number of ways. This applies to the most commonly mentioned role, project manager. But this also applies to project leader, developer, and the host of other roles that are associated with the project... and, of course, for programme and portfolio roles. Most of us need to both manage and lead – in projects, outside projects; in working environments and outside working environments.

Secondly, it is difficult to disaggregate the terminology when it is applied in the real world. We often have to switch roles, preference and behaviours. This is apparent in sporting contexts – the management of the team practicalities requires a different approach from the positive encouragement before play when team members need to be inspired to perform at a high level. Kent highlights the idea that:

- managers do things right; leaders do the right things and also that
- managing is an authority relationship; creating stability whereas
- leading is an influence relationship; creating change.

We can substitute project manager or project managing in these expressions, but for what do we substitute leader – is it project leader? In reality, in projects or in general management, it is the manager who needs to switch hats, being able to both manage and lead, sometimes simultaneously.

So, although these statements provide helpful pointers, they are not sufficient to build our framework. Kent (2006) further argues that the 'two processes, while distinct, cannot operate without each other working in tandem'. This subtle statement is key to the development of a project manager, whatever their job title. Furthermore, he defines the two areas: leading and managing.

We can see that the emphasis of project management is in the top part of Table 10.1, but this cannot take place effectively without the associated bottom part. This is the challenge with which we often find ourselves faced. It could be two different roles, project director and project manager. It could be two similar roles, project director

TABLE 10.1   Leading and managing; adapted from Kent (2006)

	Purpose	Products	Processes
Managing	Choosing most efficient alternatives for product or goal	Resources, effort, performance awareness and progress monitoring; establishing efficient mode of working, dealing with problems and scenarios associated with purpose	Planning, organizing, directing, controlling
Leading	Creating direction and unified will; developing thinking and valuing	Thrust toward purpose or end; creation of associated social context; engendering higher state of behaviour and thinking	Visions, alignment, inspiring

and project manager, who each have different personalities and find that they naturally exert, exhort or provide management to the project; equally, it could be two roles that do not have 'project' or 'manager' in the title.

Andersen (2008) introduced leadership styles in the context of project management and discussed different approaches that include trait-based (based on personality), behavioural (what we do and how we do it), power-influence (including democratic models), situational (considering contextual factors) and integrative (combining several approaches). Since project leadership 'should take account of project type and project environment', Andersen (2008: 239) argues that as a general rule, 'situational leadership will help the project manager achieve project success'. This is a useful reinforcement of the need for another aspect of project management: to be contingent upon the circumstances. Bringing forward our previous discussion of cultural dimensions would provide several potential examples of this.

Let us look more closely at leadership style in relation to project scenarios, referring to Antonakis, Avolio and Sivasubramaniam (2003), who summarized this in three groups:

- transformational – proactive;
- transformational – based on fulfilment of contractual obligations;
- non-transactional laissez-faire – regarded as passive and ineffective.

It is likely that all project managers need to be proactive, though the degree or emphasis will vary depending on the stage of the lifecycle. For example, it may be inappropriate to adopt a proactive 'get it done' style during a key creative stage that, importantly, determines the right idea or basis to undertake the project. We have discussed the overall need for contracts within project environments; notwithstanding our reflection of cultural variations, this is an important aspect of the project manager role, and in some sectors it is absolutely critical. The laissez-faire style is not normally one that we would necessarily expect in a project environment, since it would seem to be at odds with the higher emphasis on (admittedly narrower) project performance metrics of time, cost and quality. This could be misinterpreted, since it is possible that an individual personality provides the basis for a more relaxed leadership style appropriate during certain phases of a project.

These styles reflect our own character; being aware of the effectiveness of different approaches is helpful, but we may find it difficult to act or behave in a manner or style that is not our normal preference. Understanding this is helpful, since the emphasis required at different stages of the project lifecycle may require us to act in appropriate ways, ranging from consultative and consensus seeking towards adopting a more coercive position or style.

Leadership in project environments (specific focus)

Having introduced leadership, we need to understand more specifically the impact of this in project environments. Drawing on the Dulewicz and Higgs' (2005) definition of intellectual (IQ), managerial (MQ) and emotional (EQ) groups of competences shown in Table 10.2, Muller and Turner (2010) examined the leadership competence

TABLE 10.2   Competence groups; adapted from Dulewicz and Higgs (2005: 111–12)

Intellectual dimensions (IQ)	Critical analysis and judgement Vision and imagination Strategic perspective	Managerial dimensions (MQ)	Engaging communications Managing resources Empowering Developing Achieving
Emotional and social dimensions (EQ)	Self-awareness Emotional resilience Motivation Sensitivity Influence Intuitiveness Conscientiousness	Is there an ideal combination of these?	

of successful project managers. Analysing by project application area, complexity, importance and contract type revealed that different profiles contributed to success.

Intuitively this is not surprising, given the likely significance of contextual and strategic factors. For example, Muller and Turner (2010: 444) reported that 'project managers of most successful engineering projects show strong competences in critical thinking (IQ), developing (MQ), as well as influence, motivation, and conscientiousness (three EQ competences)'. This contrasted with the project managers of successful information and communication technology projects who showed a consistent strength in all competences except vision (IQ group).

Muller and Turner (2010: 444) argued that their results 'should be of interest for organizations with a relatively homogenous set of projects but variation in terms of perceived project complexity'. The analysis provides results for three dimensions of IQ, MQ and EQ and the work also includes a useful five-step suggestion (2010: 446) for organizations:

1 Recognize the type of project and the appropriate leadership style.

2 Assess your leadership skills.

3 Develop these in line with 1.

4 Match the leadership style of the project manager to that required by the project.

5 Value your project manager.

The value of having an appropriate leadership style has been discussed, and we have seen that the specific mix of attributes will often depend on the context and requirement of the project. While this is not surprising, it presents some challenges. With a small pool of project managers (or one that is biased towards a particular type), it may be difficult to find the right match. It will of course be possible, through training and development, to help people increase their self-awareness and influence the nurturing of a different approach, but we are moving into a more difficult area which is concerned with personality and character.

At this stage, it is worth reminding ourselves that there may be a limit to how far we can expect an individual to be reformed, developed, coaxed and re-presented. One of the key learning experiences one can take from studying an MBA is that it is difficult to be good at everything. This can lead us to two conclusions: firstly, the value of having the right person with the right skills, knowledge and character; secondly, that there are people who can (learn how to do something) and do (they generate the solution), but that there are others who struggle, despite supportive development and accommodation, and find this difficult. These are realities.

To provide an example of the first reflection, consider a generalist project manager who has the goal of leading the development of a business plan; the discussions with the start-up venture team lead to the drawing together of a strong case for funding, but the critical questions regarding the proposed investment relate to the analytical areas dedicated to the presentation of the financial aspects. In this case, working closely with a finance expert can make the difference between success and failure in that aspect of the project. Of course, a project manager who is a practising financial analyst will be able to approach this type of project from a different perspective and position of relative strength. However, such project managers still may find that there are areas with which they do not feel as comfortable (such as marketing) and again benefit from appropriate expert support in that area.

Considering the second reflection in relation to a project scenario, we may not have the luxury of waiting for the key resource (the person) to manage/lead in a style that is needed for the match and which he or she finds alien. It is important to keep a sense of perspective in reflection and in practice, especially if the demands of the project are high; we may need to act in order to keep the project in control.

It is helpful to consider the specific areas of intellectual, managerial and emotional competences further in relation to the project environment.

Intellectual competences (IQ)

Let us consider each of the three competence areas discussed by Muller and Turner (2010) in relation to project management topics that we have already introduced. The first of these, **critical analysis and judgement**, could be applied to any or all of the topics. We subjected the introductory topics, the lifecycle phases of planning, delivery and review, and the project lifecycle itself to critical thinking and analysis; in Chapter 6, a view that many projects would end in failure provided an opportunity to think more objectively and constructively about the overall or long-term performance, and indeed the role of projects. Acknowledging that value creation is an output of a project provides an insight into the dimensions by which to measure its success. These go beyond the more obvious (and more easily measurable) traditional measures that are time, cost and quality based.

The second, **vision and imagination**, is important at the outset, but the uncertain and changing aspects of a project continually provide a scenario that benefits from these perspective-enhancing traits. If the delivery follows the plan very closely, we could argue that this is relatively less important (and might be an unwelcome source of change), but this could also show itself in the form of innovation or improvisation in relation to problems.

Taking a **strategic perspective** is crucial. When the pressure is high and the focus is on what is very close or immediate in the plan, we can lose the important broader perspective that helps us see where we are. When perplexed by what seemed an almost continual sequence of barriers to progress at a key stage of a project, a colleague would say to me 'but look at how far we've come… the progress made so far is significant', helping me to focus instead on the longer-term strategic aspects of the activity.

While this helps, it doesn't always overcome the sense or scale of challenge. A variation of this can be used to help members of the team who are finding it difficult to overcome a particular challenge and who experience a feeling similar to lurching from one direction to another until the solution is found. It may help them to be reminded of where we are all going and why.

The team may also find reassurance and inspiration from a project manager who can maintain and present the strategic perspective. The project is a journey, and the detail is likely to be unknown until each stage is completed. We can all reflect on the traits of a good leader. One final point of reflection relates to the circumstance of the micro-business, a situation where the core activity of a project could genuinely be a one- or two-person undertaking; providing or maintaining a strategic perspective may be challenging in this type of situation, and entrepreneurs may find the input of lateral experts more beneficial in this respect than in other scenarios.

Managerial (MQ)

Of the five MQ competence areas highlighted in the Muller and Turner (2010) research, **engaging communications** and **managing resources** have been considered in earlier chapters. The need for an engaging communication style is manifest, as the reach required is potentially significant: within and outside the team, up and down hierarchies, with a wide variety of stakeholders. For some, this may be the most challenging part of a project management role. The importance of effective resource planning and management has also been discussed in Chapters 2 and 3.

In terms of **empowering** and **developing**, these aspects of personal competence have high prominence within the team dimension. While the need to **achieve** may be important personally, it is vital in project environments, since the project will have been established to deliver (and therefore achieve) something. One additional consideration here is the potential need to moderate this aspect when circumstances dictate that a project should be stopped rather than pursued further. Whether this is due to economic, political, resource or other factors, if a strong urge to achieve to pursue completion is manifested as inappropriate persistence, this may be the wrong approach.

Emotional (EQ)

Within the final set incorporated in the Muller and Turner (2010) research are the emotional competences of:

- self-awareness;

- emotional resilience;

- motivation;

- sensitivity;

- influence;

- intuitiveness;

- conscientiousness.

This set includes several of the interpersonal skills, known as 'soft skills', highlighted in the PMI BoK (PMI, 2013: 275) and it has particular relevance to cross-cultural, multi-ethnic or multilinguistic projects or teams; **self-awareness** of things such as our own capability, personality or beliefs, the **resilience** required to deal with a wide range of situations, remaining calm under pressure, and anticipating the appropriate **motivation** required are traits that can be nurtured, but will also directly reflect our personality style.

Our degree of **sensitivity** will also reflect personality and, while many of these competence components can be learnt and developed, changing our style may be limited by our inherent character or personality. This also applies to the degree of **conscientiousness** and **intuition**, as we shall explore in Chapter 11.

Influence is a powerful word. In many project scenarios, influence may be the best we can achieve given a position of limited control within the project. It is essential to recognize the importance of this likelihood and the associated value of having – or being able to exert – influence.

We also need to consider the importance of culture, stated earlier. Should this be represented as a key competence group (CQ) for leadership or is this a subset of the emotional group (EQ)? Is cultural empathy a component of sensitivity, an MQ dimension? These are also difficult questions to answer, since this area has generated different views on the diversity or dissimilarity of international leadership.

If global leadership depends upon culture, the norms and values that underpin this will have an effect on it. Based on a sample of 12 nations, Bigoness and Blakeley (1996: 8) highlighted that their analysis 'offers support to those who believe that values are becoming increasingly homogenous across nations and those who believe that value differences continue to exist across cultures'. Furthermore, Morrison (2000: 120) remarked that 'national leadership models generally work well as long as the leaders deal primarily with individuals from the same culture. As companies become more exposed to global markets, however, national leadership models no longer work as well.'

> ### Learning point
>
> From a global perspective, cultural values have become more similar, yet leadership approaches need to be contingent upon a particular culture. Given the potential significance of this to the outcome of a global project, it is something we need to revisit periodically and by combining information and reflection from elsewhere. This usefully brings us to a point to continue our development and reflection; framing the challenge in projects that will often incorporate mixed cultures encourages us to look at the project management role from a relatively more 'global' leadership perspective.

It is valuable to consider the impact of emotional and cultural intelligence on the symbiotic leadership and management role. This enables us to bring together another set of different topic strands developed in earlier chapters, and also to reflect upon the important aspect of gender.

Gender diversity and leadership

Introducing this as an explicit topic presents some challenges; we have already discussed the impact of culture and cultural diversity, and we have to recognize that across global projects the degree of diversity will vary, and that this will also reflect attitudes to gender. In order to circumvent the alienation of any group, I would like to focus on an example from my own experience and present this from the following perspective: with my 'cultural settings', people are perceived as the person rather than being influenced by any labels that are assigned through societal or cultural setting. I tend to judge the effectiveness of people; whether they can do the job and how they do it. In the pressured situation of projects we need people who 'can do' and 'will do'. I would like to highlight the following example of an inspiring leader who helped my understanding more fully.

Working for Nia was quite tough. She would often take on too much and was always trying to meet the expectations of all of her stakeholders. With a particularly principled style, she would take exception to the organization's decision to serve notice on a community-focused client that was experiencing cash-flow difficulties. She set challenging goals for her team, seemed to know how to get them to see these the same way, and had a style that endeared her to all stakeholders, including external clients and internal staff. When there was a battle, this was undertaken with mutual respect.

Nia was part of a cohesive high-performing team, a scenario that is rare. When she died suddenly in a car crash, the impact was extraordinary. There weren't enough seats at the church where her funeral took place and the wake that followed filled the boardroom in the office; it seemed to be appropriate, but everyone knew the name of her son whom she adored. The team and the organization were a reflection of her principles and ethics. An inspirational leader.

Eagly (2013) discusses 'a way in which female and male leaders differ – their typical values and attitudes'. She contrasts the relatively more democratic and participative style of female leaders with the top-down command and control approach adopted by more men.

In terms of balance, we can argue that both approaches are important, irrespective of whether they are associated with either gender. Good planning is valuable; good people skills are essential. We need to combine the two and more. Any form of diversity provides an opportunity to build a heterogeneous team. This may not be appropriate for all situations, but we must be aware that biased or prejudiced views may cloud our judgement as to who is, or who are, the best people to lead, manage, contract with, collaborate with, or participate. The project has goals. We want to succeed with this; recognize the strengths and the risks of adopting a particular strategy. Keep things in balance.

Negotiation and cultural intelligence

It is worthwhile understanding some specific practical aspects of cultural intelligence; Brislin, Worthley and McNab (2006) introduced cultural intelligence as having various meanings, including intelligent behaviour in relation to specific cultures and also relating to the adjustment by an individual to a culture different from the base in which they developed their socialization and experience. They set out some important higher-order skills associated with cultural intelligence.

Firstly, 'a critical skill of people who are culturally intelligent is the expectation for misunderstanding' (Brislin *et al*, 2006: 48) between the individual and host. Furthermore, they highlight that the culturally intelligent will consequently lower their stress during the interaction in order to wait until they can understand and signal this. Throughout the process, the culturally intelligent will be looking (or listening) for patterns that will help to establish whether the interactions are likely to be typical of a broader population.

Learning point

In international settings the culturally intelligent can usefully establish rapport using body language and confirmatory communication. While this is invaluable, beware if this is a component of a process leading to a common understanding of a critical area such as project scope.

Within a project scenario where activities are taking place at different regional or international locations, there is scope for separate teams to develop, with distinct norms and different behavioural bases. This can take place despite strong efforts to coordinate activities and engender an overall team spirit, leading to misalignment of approach and disunity. It is helpful to have people in the overall team who can make linkages with all relevant individual or group participants. These are the chameleons, those who can blend into different surroundings; they make linkages, facilitate the flow of communication and can bring potentially disparate stakeholder groups to-gether. These provide a form of lubrication for the project.

One valuable skill that the culturally intelligent member or culturally diverse team can bring is negotiation. An important aspect of projects, negotiation skills will be needed throughout the lifecycle. From the moment the idea is presented, it will gen-erate enthusiasm from some but will also be less appealing to others; within the life-cycle, from the idea, during the planning; in the delivery, the reviewing and quite possibly in the period afterwards. We will need to negotiate for more time, resources, the right people, within the setting out of a contract, during any procurement, or in the marketing process. Reflecting different character and personality styles, some will have well-developed negotiating skills, others will not.

Cultural bases provide part of this challenge. Adair, Brett and Okumura (2001) highlighted the different styles of negotiation between US and Japanese managers. Revealing a significant difference in terms of intracultural relations (2001: 380) and style, their research confirmed 'a prediction based on hierarchical and egalitarian cultural differences'. Given the difference in culture we have already explored, this highlights the likelihood of difficulties in negotiation between dissimilar sets.

Other researchers (Fitzsimmons, 2013; Branen and Thomas, 2010) have high-lighted both the rise in a new demography of employees identifying with more than one culture, and the internalization (Branen and Thomas, 2010) of more than one culture through immigration (Fitzsimmons, 2013), long-term migration and personal relationships. Aside from the political noise that this creates inside and outside nations, we need to recognize that this may provide an opportunity to overcome difficulties of the type introduced earlier (negotiation between US and Japanese managers).

With a greater awareness of the 'other' culture, the bicultural individual is likely to understand better the style of thinking, recognize signals and respond in a more synergistic manner. Liu et al (2012) highlighted that 'successful cross-cultural nego-tiation can be fostered by the selection of people who, despite fully understanding their own culture, are open to change' (2012: 192). While our intuition might have suggested something similar, these findings are a powerful reminder of the potential value of our team members. This has application in direct negotiating situations (such as that within the deployment of a project manager into a foreign environment), in teams, in the whole area of working with stakeholders and inside organizations.

We could argue that if any of these present a substantial risk to the project, the value of their contribution could be substantial.

The Economist (2011) reported that, despite the temporal unpopularity of being foreign, diasporas help spread ideas and money, and help companies from their host country set up business activities in their home country. These are ingredients of projects. A final point here: we can, of course, also use the term culture in connection with the context of the organization and apply the same arguments – a member of the team who understands the culture of a collaborating organization or unwilling participant department can help to unlock the barriers that occur. This also touches on social networks; it is an important area in the project environment.

CASE STUDY   Africa and projects[1]

Push and pull

The headline of the feature concerns the investment of the world's technology giants, but my attention is drawn to the quote 'I don't understand. Why is it that the media only seems to talk about Africa when bad things happen?' (BBC, 2013). This comment is powerful. Only four months previously (IDG, June 2013), a different article covered the failure of rural technology projects in South Africa. Describing the collapse of digital village projects, this highlighted the disparity of markets adopting this concept across the continent. Quoting the vice chairman of Africa ICT Alliance, 'the succession of ineffective Ministers of Communications has meant the failure of our network infrastructure to be as accessible and affordable as it should be', and '(South Africa is) small on delivery, poor at executing the plans, lousy at monitoring progress and ironing out the problems that arise along the way'.

In the *Project Management Journal* (2012), Ika discusses the persistent problems faced by international development projects in Africa. Highlighting that 50 years after independence, 'many African countries have seen their economies overtaken by those of countries that were worse off in the 1960s' and noting the use of a push as an effort to improve the situation (2012: 27), the article also discusses that the implementation context is different in managerial, economic and political terms from those in the developed nations. The analysis culminates in the drawing out of and need to break four 'traps' (2012: 36–37):

- 'One size fits all' – needing to draw insights from alternative project management approaches.

- Accountability for results – refocus international development (ID) project management on managing objectives for long-term results.

- Lack of project management capacity – improving project supervision by aid agencies (ID).

- Cultural disparities – tailor project management approaches to African values and cultures.

Within the fourth point, the work of Muriithi and Crawford (2003) is referenced with a consideration that Africa may be more collectivist, have a higher power distance and have other cultural traits dissimilar to the West (where the management concepts and approaches were developed). We can draw a bleak picture.

Yet, highlighted in the first report referenced in this case (BBC, 2013), Africa was 'booming', with growth of 5.6 per cent predicted. In 2014, McKinsey & Company reported that Africa was the world's second-fastest-growing economic region; although having benefited from a surge in commodity prices, the majority of this has come from wholesale and retail trade, transportation, telecommunications and manufacturing (2014: 2).

The growth is attributed to improved stability in macroeconomic and political terms, and the structural reforms that have taken place within the economies of Africa. Privatization, openness of trading, and tax and regulatory reform are some of the factors that have contributed to this. As Africa's largest economy, Nigeria (McKinsey Global Institute, 2014) has seen gross domestic product (GDP) grow to $510bn, with over 80 per cent coming from 'beyond the resources' sector (2014: 2). There are some significant challenges (for example with respect to poverty and other associated indicators), but this points to a different emerging picture.

In 2011, *The Guardian* reported on the economic revolution in Africa that was taking place in the use of mobile telephones: 'half of Africa's one billion people has a mobile phone – and not just for talking'. This highlighted how the mobile phone was helping to forge a new enterprise culture, and that Africa was at the centre of using these in ways different from the developed world. For example, in mobile banking, this was a great benefit to a billion people who had limited access to electricity to charge a computer (nor the funds to buy one).

Safaricom exploited already-existing developments in mobile banking, created in other countries but exploited in Kenya. By 2013 they had launched a $40bn project to connect major cities and towns to their fibre-optic network (Ventures Africa, 2013). This form of network project brings us back to the start of this case (networked digital village projects), but the context is quite different. There is pull from the African economies; a significant portfolio of projects are being developed and managed in Africa.

Case reflection

This two-part case scenario is intended to stimulate reflection – evaluate:

i   Whether the challenges faced in delivering projects in Africa are universal.

ii The underlying project management and leadership styles; are we seeing a need for contingent approaches that reflect different contexts, environments, or stakeholder expectations?

iii Is there an opportunity for a new strategic approach? Are there other factors that need to be considered?

Summary

This chapter has explored the sometimes subtle differences between general and project management; the project manager needs to be able to understand how to undertake a wide range of management functions and also to display an appropriate style of leadership. Some appropriate competence frameworks were explored, and these inform the underlying composition of skill-sets and knowledge areas.

While we discussed leadership styles, this included a consideration of the synergistic relationship between both management and leadership, and the review of some core components of each. By exploring leadership, managerial and emotional dimensions we also considered the potential impact of gender and cultural diversity in project environments.

Note

1 This case study draws upon information from the following sources:

BBC (2013) Why the world's technology giants are investing in Africa, 15 October

The Guardian (2011) Africa's mobile economic revolution, 24 July

IDG Connect (2013) South Africa: why have all the rural tech projects failed?, 21 June, retrieved on 28 September 2014 from http://www.idgconnect.com/ blog-abstract/2292/south-africa-why-have-all-rural-tech-projects-failed

Ika, L (2012) Project management for development in Africa: why projects are failing and what can be done about it, *Project Management Journal*, **43** (4), pp 27–41

McKinsey & Company (2014) Lions go global: deepening Africa's ties to the United States, August

McKinsey Global Institute (2014) Nigeria's renewal: delivering inclusive growth in Africa's largest economy, July

Muriithi, N and Crawford, L (2003) Approaches to project management in Africa: implications for international development projects, *International Journal of Project Management*, **21**, pp 309–19

Ventures Africa (2013) $40m 'Safaricom Digital City' to boost connectivity in Kenya, 25 November, retrieved on 29 November 2014 from http://www.ventures-africa.com/ 2013/11/40m-safaricom-digital-city-to-boost-connectivity-in-kenya/

References

Adair, W, Brett, J and Okumura, T (2001) Negotiation behavior when cultures collide: the United States and Japan, *Journal of Applied Psychology*, **86** (3), pp 371–85

Andersen, E (2008) *Rethinking Project Management: An organisational perspective*, Pearson Education, Harlow

Antonakis, J, Avolio, B and Sivasubramaniam, N (2003) Context and leadership: an examination of the nine-factor full-range leadership theory using the Multifactor Leadership Questionnaire, *The Leadership Quarterly*, **14**, pp 261–96

Association of Project Management (APM) (2009) APM Competence Framework, retrieved on 23 October 2014 from http://www.apm.org.uk/sites/default/files/APM%20 Competence%20Framework%20-%20sample%2040%20pages.pdf

Bigoness, W and Blakeley, J (1996) A cross-national study of managerial values, *Journal of International Business Studies*, **27** (4), p 8

Branen, M and Thomas, D (2010) Bicultural individuals in organizations, *International Journal of Cross Cultural Management*, **10** (1), pp 5–16

Brislin, R, Worthley, R and McNab, B (2006) Cultural intelligence: understanding behaviors that serve people's goals, *Group & Organization Management*, **31** (1), pp 40–55

Buganza, T, Kalchschmidt, M, Bartezzaghi, E and Amabile, D (2013) Measuring the impact of a major management educational program: the PMP case in Finmeccanica, *International Journal of Project Management*, **31**, pp 285–98

Cheng, M, Dainty, A and Moore, D (2005) What makes a good project manager, *Human Resource Management Journal*, **15** (1), pp 25–37

Crawford, L (2005) Senior management perceptions of project management competence, *International Journal of Project Management*, **23**, pp 7–16

Dulewicz, V and Higgs, M (2005) Assessing leadership styles and organisational context, *Journal of Managerial Psychology*, **20** (2), pp 105–23

Eagly, A (2013) Women as leaders: leadership style versus leaders' values and attitudes, Research Symposium: Gender & Work: Challenging Conventional Wisdom, 28 February–1 March, Harvard Business School, Boston, MA

The Economist (2011) The magic of diasporas, 19 November

Fitzsimmons, S (2013) Multicultural employees: a framework for understanding how they contribute to organizations, *Academy of Management Review*, **38** (4), pp 525–49

Hitt, M, Black, J and Porter, L (2009) *Management*, 2nd edn, Pearson Education, Harlow

IPMA (2006) IPMA Competence Baseline: ICB, Version 3.0, retrieved on 23 October 2014 from http://ipma.ch/certification/competence/ipma-competence-baseline/

Kent, T (2006) Leading and managing: it takes two to tango, *Management Decision*, **43** (7/8), pp 1010–17

Liu, L, Friedman, R, Barry, B, Gelfand, M and Zhang, Z (2012) The dynamics of consensus building in intracultural and intercultural negotiations, *Administrative Science Quarterly*, **57** (2), pp 269–304

Morrison, A J (2000) Developing a global leadership model, *Human Resource Management*, **39** (2/3), pp 117–31

Muller, R and Turner, R (2010) Leadership competency profiles of successful project managers, *International Journal of Project Management*, **28**, pp 437–48

Project Management Institute (PMI) (2001) A national dilemma, retrieved on 23 October 2014 from http://www.pmi.org/learning/securing-stakeholder-commitment-practice-local-implementation-7937

Project Management Institute (PMI) (2013) *A Guide to the Project Management Body of Knowledge*, PMI Inc., Newtown Square, PA

Robbins, S and Coulter, M (2012) *Management*, 11th edn, Pearson Education, Harlow

Stevenson, D and Starkweather, J (2010) PM critical competency index: IT execs prefer soft skills, *International Journal of Project Management*, **28**, pp 663–71

Transport for London (2013) Our upgrade plan: improving London's Underground, TfL, London

A spectrum of project management roles

Introduction

In this chapter we use the word 'spectrum' to emphasize the wide variety of roles that are associated with, or inherently part of, project management. This is a wide scale; aside from the various managing or leading aspects, we see a variety of internal and external roles with specialist and generalist aspects.

Following the previous discussion on management and leadership in project environments, this chapter will consider individual and team roles; this will include the review of established views of traditional teams as well as the particular challenges associated with the virtual or disparate types.

There will be a focus on the type of person that we are, a look at the use of profiling frameworks and an opportunity to reflect on the value of using these. We will explore the challenges commonly faced by teams and also introduce some of the more unusual difficulties presented by delivering projects though teams.

The chapter will also consider particular types of project management roles; we will look at some areas of this spectrum to provide insights into the variety of responsibility, emphasis and focus in a number of sectors. Different expectations are reflected in different roles.

Teams in project environments

Context

In the previous chapter we focused on management from an organization or project perspective and leadership from a more individual standpoint. By considering a number of qualities, we were able to discuss the characteristics of leadership and introduce some widely accepted models. We were also encouraged to consider our own style and character. We are all different: thinking differently, acting differently, with different personalities. Yet, in the project world we rarely work alone, needing to share our time, energy, ideas and activities with others. It is likely that we need to lead, manage and participate in a team activity.

The use of the word 'we' is emphasized; this is our project, we own it. Although this is perhaps idealistic, we must seek to adopt this as a default in order to reflect on our position in the project from both an individual and a team perspective. At either end of the spectrum, it helps if we understand the psychology, level of ambition and underlying dynamics within the project team (or teams).

Teams within the project lifecycle

A team is required in order for the project to take place; recruitment of members is an important activity, but how does this take place? A task-based approach (introduced in Chapter 3) uses the developed planning to inform the development of an associated resource plan. In this scenario we would expect the recruitment of team members to take place in a systematic manner.

Alternatively, for an innovation-based (or change) project, sufficient details may not be known in advance; that is, the circumstance of the innovation may yield a project scenario that has high ambiguity in terms of the requirement for the types of people (skills, experience and personality).

Both scenarios present challenges. In an ideal scenario, we will know how many people and the combination of skills, experience and personality. We would then recruit the team. How will we do this? One scenario is that we draw on existing human resources from the host organization. In this case, we will need to negotiate for team members, unless the circumstances provide an opportunity for unencumbered recruitment. But there may be a drawback – depending on the way the team is formed, we may not inherit the best people for the team.

An alternative scenario is that we recruit exclusively for the project. If this process involves external hiring, there will be a process to follow. A third scenario is that we draw on members from the organization and also source skills or expertise from external sources. There are, of course, other situations where the establishment of the team is the subcontractor responsibility, since we have outsourced part or the whole of the project management.

The team will need to be organized, and there are different ways to do this; at one extreme we could draw up a project organization chart with clearly defined roles and responsibilities. Alternatively, we could assemble the team and let them work this out for themselves, in a relatively more emergent manner; the case study in this chapter has these characteristics.

There may be a formal initiation of the process, tied in with the planning process. For example, this could take place with the drawing together of a 'project initiation document'. And, of course, as the team develops, communication between members will increase, tasks will be undertaken, problems will emerge, and a variety of unexpected issues will need to be dealt with. Trust will build, within and outside the team, but there will be negotiation, conflict and often a need to improvise. Personalities will provide a key focus for management, and for some virtual teams, a host of other factors will need to be considered.

If the team operates in an autonomous manner, the style and speed of progress will be different from one that does not enjoy this; alternatively, the team could generate a project outcome (or means to the outcome) that does not sit well with the corporate expectations for governance. Throughout the process, the project will need support, encouragement, motivation and appropriate development.

The project will be delivered; this should be celebrated in an appropriate way and the team is likely to disband. Knowledge will have been created and hindsight will point to how things should have been done differently. Many of the team will have enjoyed working with other members; some will prefer not to work again with others.

Thus far, we have described the likely stages of the lifecycle of a project team that most of us have experienced directly. Sometimes the experience is very positive, motivating and life-enhancing; sometimes it can be awkward, difficult and life-changing. Both of these can nevertheless be ultimately rewarding, and both will certainly add to our knowledge. The stages were characterized first by Tuckman (1965: 396) and then Tuckman and Jensen (1977: 423) as:

- **Forming**: orientation, testing and dependence.
- **Storming**: conflict, polarization around interpersonal issues.

- **Norming**: overcoming resistance, 'in-group' feeling, cohesiveness, new standards and roles.
- **Performing**: interpersonal structure becomes the tool, roles become flexible and functional, channelling of group energy, structure issues overcome, providing support.
- **Adjourning**: separation, 'death of the group' feeling after the building of strong interpersonal feelings.

It is helpful to put this in a wider framework for the formation of teams and roles within the project and project management environment.

Types of team

At one level, the description of the team-assembling aspect is superficially simple and, for the experienced, largely expected. At another level, it is an inherently complex part of the project process. This is one of the areas with a high concentration of people as the engine of the project. Often we can sense when things are going well; specific combinations of people work well and the expression 'high-performing team' is a reality rather than an aspiration. However, delivering the high-performance team is challenging.

The following topic sections will explore some of the areas that we need to consider so that we can exploit an enhanced understanding in the reality of the project setting.

Project teams – some specifics and variants

We've used the terminology 'team' and 'project team' throughout this book. Since we may also see the term 'group' used in connection with people associated with teams, it is worth clarifying this point. It seems that, in respect of groups and teams, the terms are often used interchangeably and this contributes to occasional confusion between the two. Crainer (1998: 237) provided a helpful characterization for teams, which focused on the recognition that there is a common goal and that success for the individual is dependent on success for all. This also highlighted the contribution to the team of disparate and diverse individual behaviours.

Given the goal setting, ownership and dependency aspects, it seems fairly clear that in the context of genuine projects, 'team' is the most appropriate terminology. We can reserve the term 'group' to be used when we need a grouping or aggregation of things, people, or stakeholders.

We have already discussed that teams can vary in form from traditional to virtual (or disparate), as shown in Table 11.1.

TABLE 11.1   Degree of co-location for types of project team

Traditional	Co-located; close proximity of team members; interaction face to face
Hybrid	Some team members co-located, some remotely based
Virtual	Completely dispersed

Does the team formation lifecycle discussed in the previous section hold for all types of team? Let us examine this within two scenarios: one is based upon an example from the delivery of project services via a temporary international team focused for a short period, and the second is drawn from research focused on managing virtual teams.

CASE STUDY   Team formation in short-term projects[1]

Within the international development setting a wide variety of projects take place. The scale varies, as do the timeframe aspects. For example, the UNDP (United Nations Development Programme) 2014 budget, at $5,666.36m, supported projects in five thematic areas. Sixteen per cent of this budget was allocated to the theme of Environment and Sustainable Development (UN, 2014). Within this amount, $6,219,572 was budgeted for 13 projects of this type in Kenya and the average value of these projects is almost $500,000.

All projects of this scale need to be broken down into sub-projects or be redefined as programmes in order to set out manageable projects. Some aspects of these projects have a short duration, lasting perhaps days or weeks, where a team of experts are brought together specifically for the purpose of the project (or element of the project). This team of experts may in fact be a set of disparate individuals who do or do not already know each other and, owing to the timescales and nature of activities, induction opportunities are minimal.

On the basis of four different short-term projects in Africa and Asia, Pilbeam (2013) evaluated the model of coordination for these activities. This provides a useful insight into the lifecycle model of both the project and the team element. His evaluation revealed that there are four stages that comprise a 10-step model; these are adapted in Figure 11.1.

FIGURE 11.1   Four stages and ten steps

Stages		Steps
Appointment	1	Document familiarization
	2	Make contact with team (digitally)
Arrival	3	Meet the team (face to face)
	4	Establish consensus (requirements and responsibilities)
Act	5	Agree meetings
	6	Research / data collection
	7	Debrief
	8	Repeat steps 6 and 7
Account	9	Develop report elements
	10	Construct overall report

SOURCE: adapted from Pilbeam (2013)

This process is similar in many short-term review projects that need several researchers to undertake work to be completed by a deadline set by the engaging agency. Of specific interest in this example is the following:

- Sometimes the prior knowledge that a particular individual will be involved provides motivation to participate in the project (aspects of forming).

- The project specification is sometimes vague or problematic, and sometimes the team has to renegotiate aspects of the terms of reference given the particular circumstances or context of the location where the project is to take place. Time provides a constraint which limits significant changes (aspects of storming).

- The team has to get working quickly; this calls for a rapid self-induction-type period. Roles and responsibilities, agreed by the team and team leader, need to be established quickly. Team members may work independently during daytime; evenings provide opportunities to exchange information and 'get to know each other better' (aspects of norming).

- The process of building the final report for the agency benefits from initial clarity in terms of team contribution and reporting style. It is best if this is established early in the process by the team leader (concerned with performing).

- The team completes the work, leaves the country and disbands (adjourning).

- Individuals may join a future team where they will probably go through the same – or a similar – cycle (returning).

This scenario has similarities with the examples introduced in Chapter 8, concerning the media and professional services sectors. Note that, from the perspective of the individual, this reveals a sixth step in the team lifecycle process, whereby 'returning' characterizes an intent to be involved again, joining a future (related) project.

Case reflection

This scenario has a strong focus on team formation:

i   Identify the key aspects and challenges; consider the likelihood of the project having the right team.

ii Review this in relation to the project risks and consider the impact of change within the timetable.

iii Identify the likely stakeholder groups within this type of scenario; how are relationships managed?

iv Evaluate whether the characteristics of team formation in this project environment apply elsewhere.

The second scenario is based on research undertaken by Hertel, Geister and Konradt (2005), who reasoned that a five-stage model represents the lifecycle of a virtual team:

- preparation;
- launch;
- performance management;
- team development;
- disbanding.

Since establishing a virtual team is likely to bring together specialists from different locations, the first stage, 'preparation', has a focus on personnel selection, task design and reward systems. Usefully, they remark on the type of work that is suitable to be undertaken by virtual teams (ie a higher proportion of information-based work), the self-evident need for appropriate technology, and integration issues that might arise for participating individuals.

Launch activities include the initiating 'kick-off workshops', getting to know each other, and the clarification of goals and also the establishment of roles. Performance management incorporates sub-headings of leadership, communication (with respect to regulation), motivation, trust and knowledge management. This sets out performance parameters.

Team development is focused on the identification of what is required to enable the appropriate development of members of the team (and hence the team itself). Disbanding simply states the likelihood that the life of the virtual team will end as a result of the completion (or otherwise) of the project; ideally there will be some form of recognition and reintegration of teams within their 'regular' jobs.

An example provides context for this: at the end of Chapter 8 we saw a small education services company providing a form of internal project management office support though a collective or virtual form. The same company undertakes international projects using virtual teams, collaborating with educational specialists in the destination country. Ad-hoc teams also form for a specific reason (such as dealing with a potentially serious student welfare problem), and disband when the temporary project has been delivered. Since this scenario has both established and task-specific virtual teams, the path through the stages is composite but broadly consistent with the framework.

Assembling teams with the right characteristics

It is worth reiterating that one of the key project management challenges we face is putting together a good team. If our experience is with leading inherited teams or teams that include individuals that we didn't pick ourselves, we may feel that it would be very different if we have the opportunity to recruit the team in an unencumbered manner. This is a challenge faced in all sectors and project environments. Within a time-limited project, the need to get it right quickly is of higher priority.

Although it is difficult to realize the ideal recruitment aspiration, the right combination of individuals can yield a capability that would have been difficult to have anticipated. For example, consider a scenario where we are responsible for the delivery of a new multi-partner project that requires two key individuals to work within a number of associated project teams and diverse stakeholder groupings. Although there is a specification for the deliverables, the project is both time limited and budget limited; success in the project will mean that the delivered outcome will become adopted as a core operational service after the period of the project.

First, we need to search for the team. With good support for the project from the parent organization, the role profiles are established and the positions are advertised, using the appropriate channels. Ideally, one of the two individuals will have strong technical skills in a relevant area, at least one should be bilingual (speaking English and a second European language) and both need to have strong interpersonal skills and be customer focused.

Although this attracts a good number of applicants, it yields a small number of potential candidates. The two individuals (one male, one female) who join the project have profiles quite different from what had been anticipated. One has strong interpersonal skills honed in a previous role managing an IT support function; the other has strong technical and organizational skills developed though delivering consultancy assignments. Although neither is bilingual, there is a workaround for this aspect which will not compromise the work output value.

With complementary skills, character, experience and knowledge, the two individuals work together and with the project teams very effectively. The team is balanced in terms of hard and soft skills and role formation takes place quite naturally. This contributes significantly to the successful delivery of the project, with strong endorsement through the adoption elsewhere of the model developed. While we can be positive (or optimistic) about the future outcome of a project, this could not have been anticipated at the start. It raises an important question – to what extent can this be planned for? Let us consider this in the next section.

Looking for the right team

While it seems to be difficult to get exactly whom we want or predict the effectiveness of the team, it is not as difficult to reflect when the emerging team has the right characteristics. If the success of the team is associated with witnessing the delivery of outputs, measurements through the period of the project will reveal this. A sporting metaphor highlights this: through a season that is based on 30 fixtures (each one a competition between two of the 32 teams), once all of the fixtures have been completed the winners sit at the top of the table. Furthermore, the progress of teams can be seen at different stages of the season. We might not know the individuals or the coach but we can all offer a view on the effectiveness of a team.

Aside from the particular skills, knowledge and experience that an individual brings, an insight into their character and personality can also be helpful. In scenarios where we get to know an individual beforehand, when the moment comes for needing a particular role we already know something about them – about their behaviour, attitude, personality, character, and, importantly, how they get on with others. These last three things are difficult to see until the person is in the team or project environment doing it. Methods are often used to understand aspects of character and personality. An insight into these is helpful in project management.

Our first insight comes from drawing upon Barrick and Mount (1991), who showed that, within the 'big five' dimensions of personality, two of these factors were predictors of job performance (Table 11.2).

TABLE 11.2   Key dimensions of personality

Extraversion	Predictor of two occupations, 'managers' and 'sales' (1991: 18)
Neuroticism	
Conscientiousness	Predictor in all occupation groups, 'strong sense of purpose, obligation and persistence generally perform better than those who do not'
Agreeableness	
Openness	

SOURCE: adapted from Barrick and Mount (1991)

This provides some insight into the deployment of people within project environments; as 'extraversion was a valid predictor of two occupations, manager and sales', they argued that the trait would be less important in skilled or semi-skilled jobs that included 'secretaries, assemblers, accountants, engineers and architects'. There is an immediate point of reflection here; if for the engineer it is less important while being an engineer, it may be an inhibitor when they are promoted into a (project) management role that requires a high level of stakeholder engagement. This scenario would benefit from the stronger extraversion traits.

We can draw further perspectives by looking at more focused aspects of psychology to determine our own profile, as there are many mechanisms for us to assess our personality[2]; this area could provide useful information for the project management arena. Mainstream management has sought to incorporate the measurement of aspects of personality and understand how this could be a predictor of job performance in order to improve management. An industry has emerged providing personality testing relatively cheaply, at as little as $30 per candidate in 2013 (*The Economist*, 2013), and in the area of recruitment this helps an employer to generate a short list from new applicants efficiently.

The range of psychometric tests is wide; for example, Passmore (2008) devotes 15 of the 18 chapters to 'individual instruments and their use'. This includes models focusing on personality, motivation, emotional intelligence, derailing, leadership styles, resilience, stress, cultural transformation, interpersonal relations orientation and lifestyles. Looking at this from a project management perspective with a focus on team building, where we need to get the right people to undertake specific roles, such insights could provide significant value.

CASE STUDY   From functional specialist to generalist project manager

In order to provide some context to reflect on this potentially valuable area of insight, let us consider the personal journey of a member of an organization – from a functional specialist role to a generalist project manager.

Working in a marketing role for the head office of a multinational enterprise, a capable but inexperienced employee had found that their work had become quite difficult and noticed some friction between their department and the central management team. Objectives, style, roles and work outcomes were specifically in conflict with some of the established thinking, methods and processes. The experience of the incumbent paralleled that of their line manager.

During a period of high frustration and increased external personal pressures, the incumbent attempted to address some of the issues objectively by naively bringing this to the direct attention of the managing director. Shortly afterwards they were invited by a member of the corporate HRM function to participate in an extensive independent assessment, 'so that we can understand how we can support your development better'.

Subsequent to the assessment, in the follow-up meeting with the HRM representative, the individual was told that their psychometric type represented an extremely small proportion of people in management nationally, and within a short period the incumbent transferred to a different area of the business.

The line manager commented that unfortunately this was perpetuating a situation where teams lacked a balance of people, character, working style and skills, and in exasperation said that 'the problem we are creating here is that we are continuing to recruit the same type of people'. The incumbent, who commented that they 'couldn't agree or disagree with lots of the questions', was perplexed by the sequence of events.

A further dimension of this process was that the individual was fitted into a sequence of specialist positions, in part since their profile was not deemed to be suitable for the established or available roles. This seemingly poor fit was subsequently countered. Following the transfer and after undertaking a number of additional specialist roles, the organization and the individual both realized that the incumbent's best contribution was through providing a project management role comprising the delivery of a variety of diverse objectives with strong cross-functional and extra-organizational dimensions.

The most suitable role was one that required a wide variety of hard and soft skills. Ultimately the path becomes clearer; everyone learns from their experience. The assessment models play their part, but they are just one of a broader reflective process.

Reflective questions

This scenario provides an example of the difficulties associated with matching a person with an ideal (or perceived ideal) type of role:

i   To what extent is it possible to anticipate a particular type of role for an individual? What type of risks does this present?

ii What should an individual be aware of when faced with the difficulties of the type discussed in this case?

iii Consider how we can develop into a role and explore the potential consequences of a poor psychometric match

---

Two areas related to psychometric profiling are associated with Meredith Belbin and Myers Briggs. These are used quite widely and both have provided commonly used vocabulary. For each, an assessment provides the basis for the indication of preference areas.

Figure 11.2 shows the Belbin® Team Role Summary Descriptors.[3] Two are highlighted since they include traits associated with extraversion and conscientiousness, discussed earlier.

The Myers Briggs Type Indicator (MBTI®) is based on an evaluation of individual preferences across four groups (extraversion/introversion; sensing/intuition; thinking/feeling; judging/perceiving).[4] This provides a further insight into psychometric type. Both of these approaches have been used keenly and both have their critics; nevertheless, they are well worth exploring, as they can provide some useful insights that help to understand better the preferences of individuals and the performance within teams. We may find that we construct our own interpretation of teams

FIGURE 11.2   Belbin Team Role Summary Descriptors

Plant	Coordinator	Resource investigator	Associated with being 'outgoing'
Shaper	Monitor-Evaluator	Teamworker	
Implementer	Specialist	Completer Finisher	Associated with being 'conscientious'

SOURCE: adapted from Belbin.com (2014)

informed by these approaches, and this is part of a useful inventory of project management knowledge.

A spectrum of roles

Having discussed a number of aspects of management, leadership and the dynamic of individuals and teams, we will now look at some of the roles that we will typically see in the project management environment. This will enable us to build some additional perspectives on the challenges faced in recruiting the right kind of person, the emphasis or need for a specific or wide variety of skills and experience, and also to reflect that a role title could in fact mean many different things.

Although we will start with a focus on the role of project manager, we would immediately recognize that there are many different roles associated with project management. Some have the words in the role title, others do not. The following sections are based around examples drawn from a variety of sources, different geographies and sectors, shown in Figure 11.3.

We will see that the range is wide, terminology inconsistent, and there is overlap between differently titled roles. This is to be expected given the lack of widely agreed definitions between projects and programmes, as we discussed earlier. From a pragmatic perspective, this does not necessarily matter as long as the role is focused on the delivery of what is required. Sometimes role profiles and descriptions do not concur sufficiently with job requirement; this is a concern that could apply to any role; that is, it is not just problematic for project management roles.

FIGURE 11.3   Sample of roles in the project environment: intended and otherwise

Hierarchical	Directing	Managing and leading	Coordination and administration	Specialist roles	and roles undertaken in
	Program Director				Marketing
Head of Projects		Program Manager			Government
	Project Director		Project Coordinator		Retail
		Project Manager		Procurement	Arts
			Project Administrator		Manufacturing
		Project Lead		Analyst	Service

> ## Learning point
>
> The key aspect to bear in mind is that, since many projects have a significant degree of uncertainty, the role-holder needs to be aware of this. Some sectors, such as construction, know where to expect this, but uncertainty and ambiguity are a recurrent theme within many topic areas.

Recruiting the project manager: typical roles

Table 11.3 summarizes three quite distinct and eclectic project manager roles. This is based on what the organization was looking for in terms of the person, or by appraising the role from a more historical perspective.

In scenario 1, advertised on behalf of a major banking institution by *The Sunday Times* (2010), the organization was looking for a number of project managers with specific project and technical experience to join the existing team. Note that this role will focus on 'one project or programme'. This confirms indirectly a point made in Chapter 6 that project managers manage programmes.

In scenario 2, the national business support organization is looking for a project manager with an emphasis on general administration and management skills. In this type of role, the challenge is likely to lie in managing multiple stakeholder relationships, the unstated need to improvise (there will be gaps in the transition from high-level planning and funding to what is needed in terms of practical delivery) and to operate in a politically appropriate style. Of note is the two-part statement, 'a calm and efficient manner; not given to panic'.

Based on work undertaken by Walker and Dart (2011), the project manager role in scenario 3 was titled '*curator aquarium*' (superintendent of the aqueducts). The role profile adapted from this work is based upon a text written in 97 CE by Frontinus, the project manager responsible for the delivery of fresh water to Rome. This is included as an example to remind ourselves that projects, project management and project managers are not inventions of a modern era. Individuals such as Frontinus were responsible for projects in the period of the Roman Empire; of note with this one is that the post-holder appears to have needed to fulfil three roles – project manager, project champion and project sponsor.

It is also worth highlighting a number of other aspects from the work by Walker and Dart. They comment that the undertaking of complex, large-scale infrastructure projects typical of many ancient civilizations was not described and understood as 'project management', and that technologies and approaches were often adopted from other societies. They also note that the *curator aquarium* 'bore the principal

TABLE 11.3 A sample of project manager roles

Organization		Major banking institution	National support company	Roman Empire
Title		**Project Managers**	**Project Manager**	**Curator Aquarium**
Aspects of role include…	1	Joining the central project management practice – a high performing team of professional project managers with proven critical delivery skills	Knowledge required: project planning and project management; understanding of finance	Performing the roles of project manager, champion and sponsor for the supply of fresh water to Rome
	2	Supporting the delivery of a sizeable and complex investment scenario portfolio over the next 2+ years	Acting as secretary to the project steering group	Principal responsibility for ensuring the delivery of project and ensuring transfer to ongoing operational mode
	3	Focusing on one project or programme, you will work with a local business owner and sponsor; responsible for all aspects of delivery	Transnationality'; other administrative and specific management tasks	Taking responsibility for all decision making; managing all aspects of legal, procurement and governance for projects
Ideal candidate profile will…	4	Responsibilities including operational processes and technology, business change management, budget control and stakeholder coordination	Have experience of project planning work and general experience of office procedures; staff management skills	Be recommended by the emperor to the Senate
	5	Strong leadership and team-building skills; track record of managing organizational, cultural and stakeholder challenges	A calm and efficient manner; not given to panic. Able to operate at multiple levels within an organization; strong interpersonal skills	Be appointed by the Senate
	6	Bring experience in a specific technical area (eg back office, economic modelling, ERP systems)	Unarticulated: high priority is stakeholder management – build excellent working relationships with the other project partners	Deliver what is required

responsibility of ensuring the delivery and operational aspects of the supply of fresh water to Rome'. This is a wide responsibility that includes the building of an aqueduct among a number of other operational responsibilities.

They also remark on the organization in place: Frontinus was managing a programme of works including business case development, procurement and ultimate operation. Stakeholder aspects were significant, as 'success or failure had potential social and political ramifications' and it was accepted that the project manager had the right to act in a highly authoritarian style. This extended to the state having power to influence family reputation, vulnerability and potential for advancement on a different scale from what we expect today. We will discuss this further in Chapter 12.

Project directors for different situations

We can develop other perspectives on the range of roles undertaken in the project environment by comparing two project director roles being recruited in 2008 and 2009, one in the UAE and the other in the UK. Both roles were titled 'project director', but that was where many of the similarities ended; one was required to work with a development partnership concerned with raising economic performance, boosting employment and housing, and included regeneration initiatives (*The Sunday Times*, 2009).

The context of the second was concerned with the development of infrastructure that included a mixed-use development comprising buildings, boulevard, canal, bridges, hotel, transport and light rail project. This project director was needed to 'manage both the project management and delivery aspects of the development' (*The Sunday Times*, 2008).

An analysis of the style of advertisement provides an insight into the tightness of specification for the role and therefore the anticipated level of specific expertise required. For the first of these roles (project director, development partnership), just 5 out of the 180 (ie 3 per cent) words used were directly associated with project management. For the second (project director, infrastructure development), almost 20 per cent of the words used were directly or strongly associated with project management. This highlights the different emphasis at the stage of actively seeking applicants with direct knowledge of project management. Again, intuitively this is what we might expect. It reflects both the type of project and therefore the anticipated role of the incumbent, but it may also be determined by the stage of the project within its lifecycle.

A third example highlights a further variety: in 2011 (*Daily Telegraph*) a project director role, located in the Russian oil and gas sector, was described as having 'complete responsibility for the delivery of the project' and that the role would report directly to the main board. Of note with this one was that the potential recruit will 'relish the opportunity to turn around an underperforming project'. Clearly this role was required to address problems within an existing project. This last example is potentially quite different from others mentioned so far, with a different emphasis, and joining an underperforming (or failing) project will require the deployment of a different set of abilities from one concerned with the setting-up stage. Of course, it is possible that the underlying scenario is not uncommon in particular sectors, and that there is a corresponding pool of suitably experienced individuals who know how to deal with the particular set of problems.

Sector-specific project management roles

As we highlighted in Chapter 7, there are particular sectors where project management is well established as the key mechanism to deliver organizational strategy and objectives. We will focus on two of these sectors in this section, since they bring out particular emphasis that, while highly associated with these sectors, may be equally applicable elsewhere. These are informed by roles which are articulated as project management. Building on some aspects of the previous discussion regarding the Roman-era project manager, we will spend some time focusing on the construction and engineering sectors.

Engineering project management roles

Project management roles in the engineering sector require specific knowledge, skills and experience. For example, in 2012 the organization Merseytravel (*Sunday Times*) were seeking a project director to take responsibility for leading a rail procurement project valued around £300m. Regarded as a complex environment in both commercial and political terms, and a substantial project with a significant engineering component, the role sought 'extensive strategic project leadership skills and a strong track record of achievement in the rail sector'.

A perspective on the components of a project manager role in the same industry can usefully be gleaned from portals such as the Railway Career Pathways (2013). Supported by the Cooperative Research Centre for Rail Innovation, this resource provides a useful insight into the generic project management role, setting out an occupational description, knowledge, skills and attributes; much of the component descriptors are entirely similar to general project management (for example, scope, time, cost, quality and human resources), but a number of elements are considered relatively more important or specialist.

For example, individuals need 'to be able to interpret schematic drawings and designs', recognize particular working locational aspects, and work with specialist

FIGURE 11.4   Typical career path within rail industry

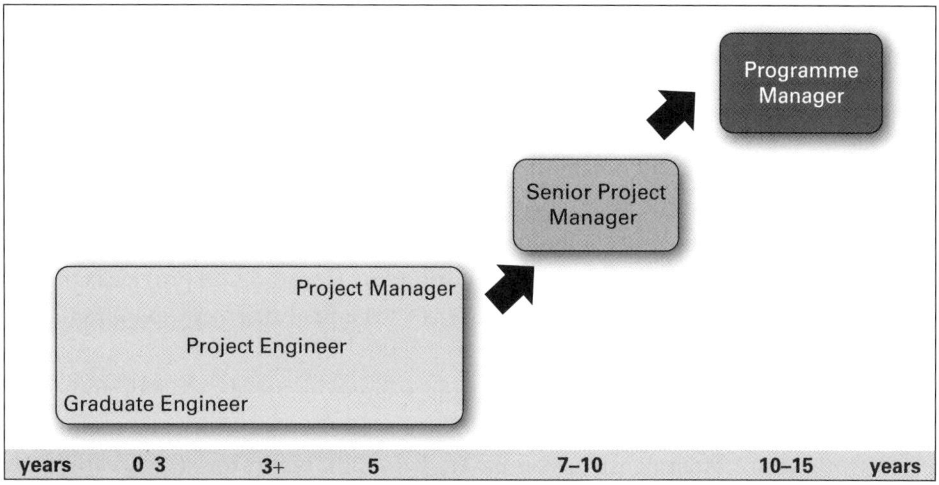

SOURCE: adapted from *Railway Career Pathways* (2013)

expertise from other project professionals. This portal also stresses the need for qualification or relevant experience in appropriate (for the role) areas such as engineering or construction. Furthermore, there is a strong emphasis on the value of a professional project management qualification or relevant vocational competence-based diplomas.

They also present the project management in the context of a potential career path within the industry, shown in Figure 11.4. This also tends to reinforce the image of professional competence and accumulation of both experience and knowledge within the sector.

Construction sector project management roles

The construction of a glass tower building such as the Shard in London, a world city, evokes a range of responses. This type of project can provide inspiration for young people to see this as an industry that provides an appealing destination for their skills, and stories about the people involved in constructing such things and their lives are inviting reading.

In 'How do I become... a construction project director' (*The Guardian*, 2013), Tony Palgrave describes his journey from 'joining the construction by accident' to the pride he felt at the end of delivering the Shard project. He also emphasized the value of working up from the bottom (in terms of career building); starting as a draughtsman, he acquired a qualification in mechanical engineering, took a role as a mechanical engineer and when dealing with a difficult aspect of a particular construction element, his employer realized that he had the capability to take on the role of project manager. He 'jumped at the chance' to be involved in the Shard project.

The feature describes some aspects of the project director role, both high and low level; the challenge of bringing together a myriad of specialists; the tight footprint in which the construction process took place; the difficult logistics, with hundreds of lorries travelling through the tight London streets nearby; and the pre-assembly, in a field, of the final 22 floors. Some similar aspects of a different story have since been told elsewhere, although on quite a different scale; the Hafod Eryri case in Chapter 1 shares a number of similarities. An aspect worth stressing for both examples, and for many others worldwide, is that of inspiration. Construction provides tangible examples of projects – from architect designs to the final delivery, operational use and, for some, the iconic aspects.

This is where project managers and project directors are developed, and some might enter the sector as school-leavers. When we refer to historical examples of projects, these are often construction based. Pyramids, walls, fortresses, cathedrals – this perpetual industry is universal and it is no surprise that, with engineering and more recently system development sectors, these provide a significant basis for the establishment of bodies of knowledge.

This reflection helps to understand why much of the project management guidance is now rooted in the language of building, engineering and systems development; it needs clear priorities, goals, rules and protocols.

A final point of reflection within this section: a key area in construction is ensuring that the project and project processes comply with building codes and with legal and regulatory requirements. Within the UK there are different families of building contracts; research undertaken by NBS in 2013 (NBS, 2013) confirmed that two of these, the Joint Contract Tribunal (JCT) and New Engineering Contract (NEC), are the most commonly used; construction project managers need to understand them sufficiently well in order to fulfil their role effectively. It is worth remarking that the same research revealed that 30 per cent of respondents reported in 2012 having at least one contract entering into dispute.

The following were highlighted as the top eight most difficult matters faced (NBS, 2013: 16):

1 assessment of delay and extension of time;
2 employer variation;
3 contractor variation;
4 scheduling and construction programmes;
5 slow pace of construction;
6 provision of employer information;
7 poor specification;
8 lateness in payment.

These relate to time, change of scope, scheduling, speed of progress, information, communication, specification and cash-flow. The research also revealed that for those involved in international work, the most challenging legal issue related to cultural differences.

Learning point

All these are challenges for construction project managers, but could also be entirely relevant for project management in other sectors. In all cases, the project manager will need to understand enough about the prevailing legal requirements, or how to understand what they need to know, by drawing upon appropriate expertise.

Construction sector: challenges typical in other sectors

Bringing together several challenging areas for project management, Figure 11.5 shows four typical steps associated with a generic new construction project. The completion of each step provides the basis to move to the next. Securing stakeholder support for the project is fundamental and universal. While seeking and securing planning permission is enacted differently in different territories, it is an entirely appropriate and necessary stage.

The need to have confirmed funding in place is paramount, and can otherwise have a detrimental effect on the start of the project. Of course, all activities will have an effect on the ultimate timeline. The diagram is intended to highlight the potential impact of slippage of these different activities; a significant proportion of the total project time will be taken up in the planning stage, which could also include feasibility work, the appointment of the design team, signing off design work, inviting tenders and appointing contractors.

If we change some of the vocabulary, this process could apply to many other areas where projects take place. In this respect the process is generic; as we discussed in Chapter 2, for a new project there will be a sequence of steps which, unless it is stopped part-way through, will ultimately deliver the outcome of the project. When it is delivered, the specific details will have been established and provide the history.

Entrepreneur as project manager

We see project management in all commercial areas and in specific roles associated with marketing, new product development, and start-up ventures. While the vocabulary will often not include the term project manager, sometimes the role is specifically set out and understood to be in the project management domain.

FIGURE 11.5 Typical challenges associated with new generic construction projects

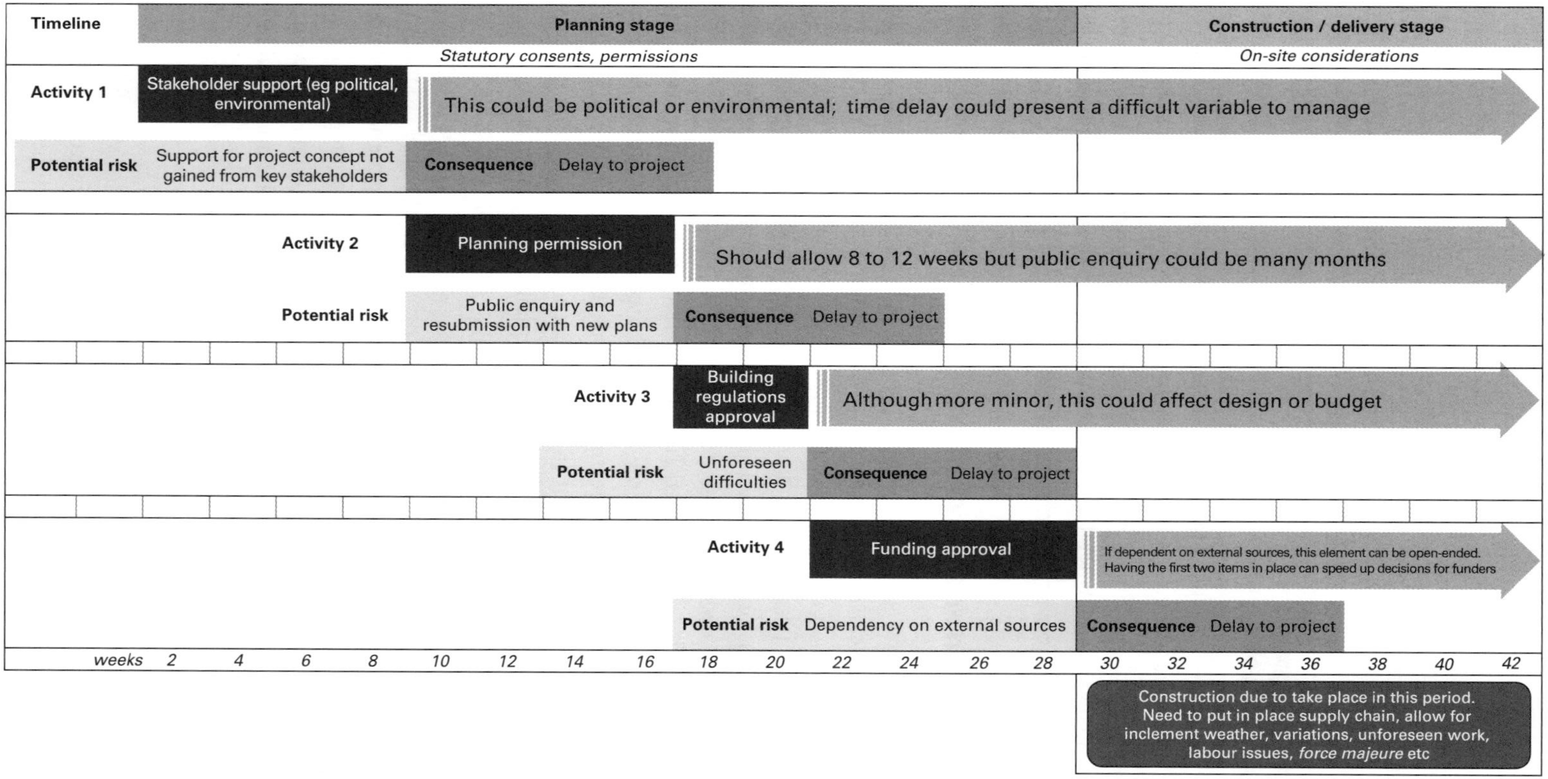

For example, a project director is required to form a new business within an existing holding company operating in the food sector. This role is located in western Africa, the parent group of companies based in the Russian Federation. Within the process of starting up the business will be a variety of steps that represent stages of a project, or of several projects, such as the recruiting of staff, assembling of resources, and establishing of organizational structures. Clearly there would be a risk-profiling exercise that would underpin some of the strategic and tactical approach.

This type of role would have a high emphasis on the establishment of strong and effective relationships with country government structures. Clearly there is an associated need to work with a variety of stakeholder groups.

We introduced in Chapter 1 the notion of projects going through a sequence of gates, where success at each stage is not guaranteed. This is highly relevant in the world of the entrepreneur, as the terms 'stop', 'go' or 'maybe' would be used in connection with things such as ideas, business plans or requests for funding. It is a new activity; there will have been an idea, followed by a period of planning; the assembly of resources; organization of the human resources team; understanding exactly what the stakeholder landscape looks like, including customers, suppliers, business support, and government, including standards bodies. It could be a long list.

Entrepreneurs and project managers are very closely related. We could argue that they are the same thing, but the vocabulary conveys, in some respects, different images. Regarding entrepreneurs as risk takers needs to be conditioned; good entrepreneurs understand the risks but recognize that it is impossible to undertake something without taking one. They look to succeed. Project managers have to do the same, though the risk profile will vary across the different types of project that they are expected to deliver. Certainly, the 'first-timer' project will have significant uncertainty and therefore a risk profile that reflects this. An entrepreneur's new-start business venture is likely to be a first-timer project.

Furthermore, it is likely that an entrepreneur will need to pursue opportunities without having control over all of the required resources; they may need to borrow them from somewhere.[5] Secondly, the integration of strategy, the funds, people, developing the business model and taking on the risk is needed to transform the idea into a viable business (Barringer and Ireland, 2012). The stages of the business formation process provide a further example of project lifecycles.

This is true in many geographies and cultural settings. For example, consider the entrepreneur in Mexico. Described as a country with businesses that have a paternalistic style, is strong on family models and where collectivism is stressed, but also where 'business and government offices open and close at different times' (David, 2005: 267), the entrepreneur will have challenges that reflect this specific context. The Mexican government has sought to promote entrepreneurship as a means of generating growth in the economy, and businesses 'have grown at an impressive pace, making the country a new destination for venture capital firms...' (Guest commentary for CNBC.com, 2012). Mexico has a number of strengths here; nevertheless, challenges still arise (EY, 2013) in relation to areas such as:

- Funding; entrepreneurs report difficulty with access to finance.
- Declining performance in terms of innovation (measured in numbers of patents registered).
- Complicated and expensive indirect tax structure.
- Low participation in secondary and tertiary education despite growth in government spending on education.

EY (2013) also highlight that the formation of a buoyant venture-capital ecosystem is inhibited in some respects by cultural issues. Although the availability of both venture capital and bank credit is weak, this contrasts with seed and pre-seed funding, for which the availability is likely to be higher (and the source of finance could be from friends or family).

Consider these two factors from a project management perspective. An entrepreneur in the real-estate market can build a business plan and develop the associated financial forecasts. The plan will likely include aspects relating to marketing, sales, management, and other relevant or critical areas. This planning will inform the financial aspects of revenue and costs. In many geographies, the securing of funding will present a challenge, but if it is especially difficult to source, this presents a significant risk to the viability of the start-up project. Where commercial (bank) options are limited, this increases the likelihood that funding will be sourced from family or friends. This is not the same as a commercial process; the entrepreneur project manager will need to approach this with a different style and emphasis, and there may be limits on the potential achievement of financing that is influenced by the cultural setting. Stakeholder relationships will be paramount.

A start-up activity is a project; an entrepreneur is faced with dealing with all stages of the lifecycle of a new-start business, undertaking activities associated with almost every project management topic. Markets may be underdeveloped, providing both opportunities but also risk of failure; weak incentives for entrepreneurial activity and limitations of financing force improvisation; with limited initial resources, the need to build a capability to deliver business objectives forces the entrepreneur to bring in appropriate expertise on a low-cost or borrowed basis. The need to undertake roles in the business informs the structure. In all of these challenges the entrepreneur needs to innovate and work within a wide stakeholder landscape. They need to get best value from all of their resources and ensure that they comply with what is necessary. They are seeking to succeed.

For the entrepreneur, the perpetual uncertainty, the need to establish cooperative partnerships, recognize constraints and be innovative are some of the same traits characteristic of a good project manager. We could argue that this is also true the other way round.

We will next consider how we should seek to develop a project capability by drawing upon Chapters 1–11, considering the emerging factors that influence contemporary thinking, and by using the past to look towards the future.

Summary

This chapter has explored the important aspect of teams within project environments; we have reflected upon the project team within the project environment and the lifecycle of the team, both in more traditional and virtual forms. This has included a consideration of the challenges associated with establishing the ideal team.

We have examined a sample of roles within the project environment in order to understand better the holistic nature of providing solutions to projects in different environments. By reviewing some sector-specific scenarios, we have considered the generic components and reflected on the wider applicability.

Notes

1 This case study draws upon information from the following sources:

Pilbeam, C (2013) Coordinating temporary organizations in international development through social and temporal embeddedness, *International Journal of Project Management*, **31**, pp 190–99

UNDEF: Projects: retrieved on 25 October 2014 from http://www.un.org/partnerships/approved_projects.html

UNDP: Our projects, (30/09/2014), retrieved on 25 October 2014 from http://open.undp.org/# 2014

UNDP: Our projects – Kenya, retrieved on 25 October 2014 from http://open.undp.org/# 2014/filter/focus_area-4/operating_unit-KEN

2 For example, Eysenck and Wilson, G (1975); Jarrett (2011).

3 Further information can be sourced from http://www.belbin.com/

4 Further information can be sourced from http://www.myersbriggs.org/

5 This is based on the Stevenson and Janillo definition quoted in Barringer and Ireland (2012: 32).

References

Barrick, M and Mount, M (1991) The Big Five personality dimensions and job performance: a meta-analysis, *Personnel Psychology*, **44**, pp 1–26

Barringer, B and Ireland, R (2012) *Entrepreneurship: Successfully launching new ventures*, Pearson Education, Harlow

Crainer, S (1998) *Key Management Ideas: Thinking that changed the management world*, 3rd edn, Prentice Hall, London

Daily Telegraph (2011) Advertisement for Project Director, 19 January

David, F (2005) *Strategic Management: Concepts and Cases*, Pearson Education, Harlow

The Economist (2013) Emotional breakdown: Can leaders be identified by psychometrics? 6 April

EY (2013) The EY G20 Entrepreneurship Barometer, retrieved on 22 October 2014 from http://www.ey.com/Publication/vwLUAssets/EY-G20-country-report-2013-Mexico/$FILE/EY-G20-country-report-2013-Mexico.pdf

Eysenck, H and Wilson, G (1975) *Know Your Own Personality*, London, Harmondsworth

The Guardian (2013) 'How do I become… a construction project director', 19 March

Guest commentary for CNBC.com (2012) Move over Brazil: why Mexico's entrepreneurs are prime for investment, 19 September

Hertel, G, Geister, S and Konradt, U (2005) Managing virtual teams: a review of current empirical research, *Human Resource Management Review*, **15**, pp 69–95

Jarrett, C (2011) *The Rough Guide to Psychology*, Rough Guide Reference Series, Rough Guides, London

NBS (2013) National Construction Contracts and Law Survey, 1 October, retrieved on 22 October 2014 from http://www.thenbs.com/pdfs/NBS-NationlC&LReport2013-single.pdf

Passmore, J (2008) *Psychometrics for Coaching*, Kogan Page, London

Railway Career Pathways (2013), retrieved on 20 October 2014 from http://www.railcareerpathways.net.au/career/project_manager

The Sunday Times (2009) Advertisement for Project Director, 11 October

The Sunday Times (2008) Advertisement for Project Directors, 13 July

The Sunday Times (2010) Advertisement for Project Manager, 25 April

Tuckman, B (1965) Development sequence in small groups, *Psychological Bulletin*, **63** (6), pp 384–99

Tuckman, B and Jensen, M (1977) Stages of small-group development revisited, *Group & Organization Studies*, **2** (4), pp 419–27

Walker, D and Dart, C (2011) Frontinus – a project manager from the Roman Empire, *Project Management Journal*, **42** (5), pp 4–16

Develop the capability

Introduction

In order to build insights into capability building, this chapter is intended to bring together the thinking and reflection that has taken place during the previous formative development of concepts in the project and project-manager-related arenas. This will help to inform the development of high-level perspectives important to anyone with a responsibility for delivering projects.

It will also include a small number of additional topics, such as leading change, that are more appropriately introduced at this stage of our reflection. As these will be linked to concepts already developed, the reader is encouraged to consider these through a strategic lens.

Drawing on sources that have evaluated the characterization of success in projects and project management environments, this analysis will be used to frame the further development of holistic and strategic thinking. The chapter will look to the past in order to inform the future; project management is not a new concept within civilizations that have thousands of significant historical project artefacts.

The last section will consider how unpredictable changes in technology, more predictable changes in demographics and reactive political circumstances will likely affect one of the world's oldest activities. This will be concluded by a reflective summing-up of the subject from the perspective of the person, from where the reader will be encouraged to apply, learn, develop and contribute to the delivery of successful projects on a global stage.

Context

In our journey so far, we have explored topics that are either dedicated to project management, incorporated from other management disciplines, or are intended to help extend our perspectives and encourage the development of higher levels of reflection in the arena of delivering projects. Part One had a strong focus on approaches more traditionally involved with project management. For example, in Chapter 1 we introduced the notion of projects (what they are and what they might not be) and project managers, and the close relationship between projects and risk.

Reflection included the discussion of project processes, lifecycle, the inherent complexity within projects, the importance of stakeholders and change aspects.

Chapter 2 included an introduction to the conceptual phase of the project lifecycle and highlighted that this is where we might get involved in projects. The development of feasibility analyses and business cases would prompt the first of several questions: why, who, what, when and how will it be delivered? The chapter also encouraged us to acknowledge that there may be much that we do not know regarding the project, and that we should prepare for assumptions and expect constraints.

The emphasis in Chapter 3 was on planning, the need to understand and incorporate stakeholder perspectives, and wherever possible seek clarity in terms of what and when required, breaking things into manageable activities and using analytical approaches when appropriate. This prompted the planning of time, resources and costs, and incorporating quality as a dimension of the specification. The value of planning was recognized and that it can be difficult to get right.

Part Two was concerned with developing more realistic perspectives; Chapters 4 and 5 focused on the activities that would ideally take place in delivering the projects planned. This opened up some practical considerations associated with all of the topics already discussed in Part One, and encouraged us to explore the demands, pressures and consequences. Within this phase of a project, several of the topics were introduced as borrowed from general management.

Increasingly we drew upon skills, knowledge and experience gained from elsewhere, either within the project's host (parent) organization, or from experience we have otherwise developed in our lives. We concluded Part Two by examining the learning that could take place within the project environment. For many, a reviewing process had been taking place throughout the lifecycle of the project; for some, this might take place at the end. This process is a further area where relatively more corporate mechanisms are already established, such as the important area of auditing. Our discussion sought to delineate project reviews and to focus on the creation of valuable insights presented.

In Part Three we acknowledged that delivering successful projects is challenging. From our latter discussion in Part Two we saw a spectre of project failure; in response to this, we might turn to further formalized developments through adopting practitioner approaches, based on the assumption of logical sequence and control within the lifecycle, or through the adoption of relatively radical lighter models that have emerged since 2001.

We saw that these are not mutually exclusive; rather, this affects the acknowledgement that project management does not come in just one size – it is contingent. We have subjected the project management vocabulary to aggregation and considered the impact in terms of people, teams and locations. This has included the project itself, since in aggregated form it becomes a programme or an ingredient of the subsequent aggregation into portfolios.

Although this follows different formulae, depending upon the organizational context, we acknowledged that the core unit is the project, and the core person is the project manager. While we maintain these as core terms, vocabulary is in turn one aspect of the next area considered, that of language, communication and culture. This extension of our view of projects as global vehicles brings a host of additional considerations for the management of projects, and has taken our discussion well beyond idealized project lifecycles and naïve expectation. This led us to the final set of topics, concerned initially with management and leadership but also with the challenge of building teams.

Undertaking projects from a holistic perspective

Reviewing a small sample of project management roles highlighted the variety of activities that constitute project management. Projects are not about one person; they are about people, all of whom need to know enough about their role and contribute to delivery of capability. Projects are about all of these things, including:

1 being creative, open to new ideas and concepts;
2 realizing that there are some fundamentals such as risk, change, stakeholders;
3 questioning and being constructive;
4 considering the broader picture;

5 balancing analysis with action-orientation;

6 acknowledging that we will not know everything;

7 developing perspectives of success and failure not previously considered;

8 understanding the value of constructively reviewing activities and progress;

9 balancing formalization and informalization in respect of planning and management;

10 developing good observational and project intelligence that informs our judgement;

11 understanding the term project in the context of programme and portfolio management;

12 acknowledging that many projects will be international in some respect;

13 being able to manage and lead synergistically and promote wide appropriate involvement;

14 recognizing that projects are challenging team efforts that benefit from insights into organizational behaviour;

15 understanding that project management roles sit within a spectrum of people activities;

16 building strategic perspective informed by observation of experiences from elsewhere.

These 16 points summarize many aspects of a personal journey in developing an understanding of project management. A challenging aspect of this comes from the realization that while project management is generic, it is also not generic. Aspects of a particular role in a particular sector will provide a context demanding emphasis in certain areas. This is encapsulated strongly in the two different project director roles discussed in Chapter 11. Role A suggested that a wide range of insight and knowledge would be required. Role B, required to lead the development of infrastructure, needed technical and sector-specific insights that would enable the project director to be effective immediately.

That is not to say that project director A would not be effective immediately, nor that project director B would not require insights into the other areas we have discussed; it is rather that each role will be different.

The 16 points are summarized in Figure 12.1, which highlights the challenge faced in developing an effective project management capability. We need to know about all of the areas, and more too – when we factor in more specialist knowledge areas associated with particular sectors, this reveals that this is not one but many roles. Like an iceberg, each segment breaks into further sets of knowledge, skills, traits and competences. How much do we need to know about each one? This

FIGURE 12.1   Ingredients in the development of project management capability

1	Being creative, open to new ideas and concepts	5	Balancing analysis with action-orientation
2	Recognizing fundamentals of risk, change, stakeholders	6	Acknowledging we will not know everything
3	Questioning and being constructive	7	Develop new perspectives of success and failure
4	Considering the broader picture	8	Constructively reviewing activities and progress
9	Balancing formalization and informalization in respect of planning and management	13	Managing and leading synergistically, promoting wide appropriate involvement
10	Developing good observational and project intelligence to inform judgement	14	Recognizing that projects are challenging team efforts that benefit from insights into organizational behaviour
11	Understand projects and the context of programme and portfolio management	15	Understand that project management roles sit within a spectrum of people activities
12	Acknowledge that many projects will be international in some respect	16	Build strategic perspective informed by observation of experiences from elsewhere

usefully draws out a further skill for the person involved in managing or leading projects: knowing how to deal with a particular gap. This is about making a decision as to whether to:

- understand it fully;
- understand it sufficiently;
- delegate to an expert.

The key word is balance. We learn how to balance time, benefit, cost and risk. For example, when a project involves the need for a contract, we may need to investigate this further. We can expend significant time on this, but there may well still be a risk that we do not know enough to follow the most appropriate course of action. There is a time to acknowledge the value of an expert and defer to their judgement or to use their capability formally.

A further example is concerned with the degree of formality within a project. How much planning do we do? Which method should we use? Are we over-planning? Conversely, ask the question from the opposite perspective. The answers to these questions will be increasingly evident when we have considered the type of project, stakeholder landscape, risks, and evidence of benefit by looking elsewhere for insights. It is vital to look at the project from a longitudinal perspective and to recognize that there are lateral aspects which may be phase specific. Figure 12.2 shows how the relative importance of each might move throughout the life of the project, reflecting changes in emphasis of aspects such as goals and objectives, stakeholders,

FIGURE 12.2   Change in emphasis though the project lifecycle

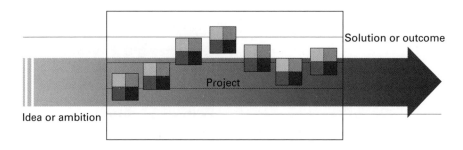

Solution or outcome

Project

Idea or ambition

capability or phase. The same consideration will apply to the 16 summary points. For a creative arts project the balance will be different from a financial sector information technology project. The effective project manager understands this aspect. It is like playing the right ones from a hand of cards.

This balancing will reflect the society in which the project will take place. We argued in Chapter 9 that projects frequently have some international component and in Chapter 10 we considered the benefits that can be gained from cultural (in terms of negotiation) and gender (in terms of leadership) diversity.

When we aggregate people into teams, we hope that they will perform on the basis that 1 + 1 = more than 2, that is, their output is greater than the sum of the individual parts. In project environments where success depends on the team, if we bring together people who do not have the right characteristics, 1 + 1 still equals 2. Worse, it could be less than this. A relatively homogenous team may lack the necessary difference to make the whole more than the sum of the parts. With a more heterogeneous group, there are more opportunities for positive interaction, to generate a third substance. The combination of different chemicals provides a useful metaphor – in a laboratory, adding sodium to water produces a lot of fizzing. Generating the right reaction between two or more people can really make a difference.

Delivering projects in a strategic style

From the start of our project management journey, we have built from the 'bottom up': introducing the notion of projects, project management and project managers, the empirical ingredients such as risk, project lifecycle and associated stages, the acknowledgement of dealing with the needs of multifarious groups of stakeholders, and the aggregation and deployment of soft skills has led us to acknowledge the need for appropriate emphasis, focus and balance. It also highlights, by aggregating all of these areas, the need for taking a strategic perspective for project management.

Delivering a course titled 'strategic project management' immediately prompts a question – are we managing strategic projects or are we project managing strategically? Both. And more, too. As we saw from the review of sample job roles and by reflecting upon numerous examples, the scope and scale of projects vary dramatically, but the challenge may be high in all of them. We need to think about and deliver projects from a broad perspective. We need to act strategically in delivering projects.

We will focus next on two key areas. Firstly, orientation towards projects: this helps to reflect on the appropriateness of taking a particular approach, anticipating the response, increasing the likelihood of getting it right. Secondly, we will focus on change; we have already highlighted that change is both a driver for a project and also essential to manage during the lifecycle. In this section we will reflect on change as a key component of project leadership.

Project societies

In discussing projects and the value that they create, we also considered their role as the modus operandi of organizations. In addition to organizations that are oriented towards projects, project-based businesses are increasingly common in many sectors; we can heighten this train of thought to consider the extent to which societies or economies are also becoming increasingly project based. This poses some questions; in a society where hierarchy is acknowledged as being relatively more common (accepting the discussion regarding power and distance), introducing flat project structures could provide some tensions or be inappropriate. Correspondingly, it is likely that the project will take place in keeping with the cultural basis of the territory – we discussed the nature of cross-border projects in Chapter 9.

However projects are delivered, the growth in their contribution to economies is effective in two ways: projects contribute to economic activity and this is reflected in a growing proportion of a workforce engaged in the activity. For example, changes have been discussed in relation to Australia, which has a project-based or project-oriented environment (Crawford, French and Lloyd-Walker, 2013). This dimension will become increasingly important. We have discussed that technology and globalization have in part driven so far the use of virtual teams; the nature of demographic changes coming will provide further stimulation to working environments where short-term working becomes increasingly commonplace.

As projects are becoming increasingly 'centre stage', this leads to lateral discussions regarding career paths and the associated challenges facing project workers. For example, where projects are temporary organizations with staff leaving at completion, planning career development has a different meaning when compared with more traditional, relatively stable workforces.

Leading change

Change is something that can provoke a strong reaction, though sometimes the reaction will be expressed silently. Since people are not sure what it will mean to them, resistance to change comes from three sources (Piderit, 2000):

- cognitive (the cause of the resistance is largely understood);
- emotional (resistance is largely through an emotional reaction);
- behavioural (a behavioural reaction to the change).

A brief example: there have been many complaints over a protracted period about the increasingly outdated system in use. The project provides a new system. Towards the point of replacement, the users start to defend their 'old system' when they realize that they will have to change from the one they disliked to the new one. It is a curious but often seen reaction. This may be cognitive; it may involve emotional responses and can provoke some unusual behaviour.

When we consider the term 'change' within organizations or management, a number of scholars such as Kurt Lewin come to mind. Concerned with planned change, and associated with the emergence of organizational development, this school has been delineated from 'emergent change' (Burnes, 2004). Planned and emergent change are both particularly relevant to projects; the project will change something and the change is therefore planned; it is emergent since, especially with genuine first-timer projects, aspects of the outcome will be difficult to predict. While the planning will help us to visualize the intended outcome, the impact of this and the associated change is often difficult to predict.

As a practitioner who became initially embroiled in project management largely by circumstances rather than design, I recall the moment when I was first introduced to *Leading Change* (Kotter, 1996: 21). The eight-stage process seemed to fit almost exactly the experience gained during the implementation of both a new system in a multinational enterprise and also within a government sector multi-agency deployment of strategic change that incorporated technology adoption and deployment:

- establishing a sense of urgency;
- creating the guiding coalition;
- developing a vision and strategy;
- communicating the change vision;
- empowering broad-based action;
- generating short-term wins;
- consolidating gains and producing more change;
- anchoring new approaches in the culture.

Such was my reaction to this that I still feel it has the right ingredients for anyone involved in a project, especially where their project takes the organization or stakeholders to a different destination from where they are currently. This process exudes leadership. We should seek to use such a framework, as it provides the basis for harnessing the leadership qualities that we discussed in Chapter 10.

Project success factors

Although failure and success were discussed in Chapter 6, this section highlights reflective perspectives developed from research regarding success in projects. A key conclusion drawn earlier, and often seen in this research, is that success is a difficult thing to define and correspondingly difficult to measure. Within the area of defence research and development projects, Dvir, Raz and Shenhar (2003) looked through the eyes of the stakeholders' end-user, project manager and contracting office, to highlight that success was based upon a proper definition of project goals and deliverable requirements.

Jugdev and Muller (2005) acknowledged that success is a complex and ambiguous concept that changes through the lifecycle. They suggested that project managers should:

- establish critical success factors at the outset of the project;
- understand who are the stakeholders and determine a success category for each;
- avoid using single-point indicators of success – ensure that indicators cover both efficiency and effectiveness;
- remember that success measures change over the project lifecycle;
- develop and maintain good and effective relationships with key stakeholders.

Cooke-Davies (2002) highlighted eight factors critical to project management success, of which six correlated with on-time performance, two with on-cost performance, one critical to project success and three with consistent corporate success.

An analysis by Ika (2009) summarized the change over time in expectation in terms of measuring success over the following time periods:

- 1960s–1980s   Period 1
- 1980s–2000s   Period 2
- 21st century   Period 3

This highlighted that the iron triangle of time, cost and quality remains a success factor in all periods, but that in each the number of criteria increased. In period 2, client satisfaction, end-user satisfaction and benefits to stakeholders and project personnel were added. By period 3, this also included 'strategic objectives of client organization and business success'. This highlights the challenge of meeting increasing expectations, discussed in Chapter 6.

Shenhar *et al* (2001) proposed a four-part framework that is sufficiently robust to provide the basis for measuring success in a contemporary scenario based on:

- project efficiency;
- impact on the customer;
- business success;
- preparing for the future.

They make the point that a mindset focused on completing the work efficiently without an effective outcome may lead to disappointing business results.

If we are genuinely building a project management capability, we need to be mindful of all of these characteristics of success, suggestions for practice and reflection on the continually changing expectations of stakeholders. There is one further aspect worth reflecting on here. Technology has provided a big change in the interaction between customer and supplier, leading both to the opportunity to provide a good value product with high-quality service (such as online retailers) and to delivering service standards that contribute to high levels of dissatisfaction, such as that provided by the UK energy suppliers (*Daily Telegraph*, 2014). This presents a paradox: a good experience in one area and a poor one in the other. Yet in projects the expectation continues to rise. There is context for communicating the success of projects to a broad audience.

CASE STUDY   The case of cricket

Success and the luck of the ball[1]

For an estimated one-sixth of humanity, a World Cup semi-final cricket match is the most important thing to watch; estimates for the game in 2011 between India and Pakistan put the audience at over one billion people. It is a sport where Sri Lanka sits high in the world rankings. For many others, though, cricket is an impenetrable event that in England can only take place in fine weather. But it is business to those organizations involved in serving up a tasty spectacle to global audiences: tournament events, cup competitions to be organized, teams, fans, marketing, the media, stakeholders aplenty.

The Ashes Test series between England and Australia is about passion, with the winning nation enjoying the warm glow of victory until the next set of matches. For a cricket stadium, hosting a Test match can bring significant financial well-being. In 2013 Trent Bridge, the home of Nottinghamshire Cricket Club, was the stage for one of these encounters.

Lisa Pursehouse, the chief executive, described how 'from the moment we got the gold package we never stopped'. Many activities needed to be in place to ensure that everything that could be right would be for the event. This was the culmination of a master plan that had seen the stadium transformed into one of the best outside London, convincing the cricketing authorities that Trent Bridge could provide an unforgettable experience for millions of fans. Of course, that could be affected by the weather.

Over the five-day match the weather was fine. A different problem emerged: England were in a winning position with a high likelihood that the game could be completed by day three (of five). Although this would delight the English fans, it would have a significant adverse impact on the business not only at Trent Bridge but for restaurants, hotels, transport firms and shops in the area. An Australian player, Ashton Agar, came to the rescue, with a second chance when the umpire[2] gave him 'not out'. The Australian team fought back and the game was played out over the full five days, broadcast globally. This was a delight for the fans and the associated businesses. On this occasion England won.

One of the winners from this game was Trent Bridge. The annual report and accounts for Nottinghamshire Cricket Club (2013: 26) reported subsequently: 'Had Agar been given out stumped there was a strong possibility that the Test Match would have been completed in three days and the Club would have reported a financial loss for the year.' Instead, the club reported record total income and an enhanced reputation.

Hosting an Ashes Test match is a considerable undertaking in terms of planning, resourcing and managing an array of business-as-normal and project activities. The English weather would feature in a risk analysis, but no amount of planning can possibly predict the playing out of the game. Luck can play a significant role in the success or failure of events. However much we do not want to use it, the expression 'with luck' is pertinent in project environments.

Case reflection

This scenario highlights that an effective project capability may not be enough to guarantee success:

i What strategies can be deployed to overcome this?

ii By considering comparator scenarios, what perspectives can be drawn in terms of meeting stakeholder expectations?

iii What are the challenges inherent within any business case modelling this type of activity?

iv Evaluate the risk profile in relation to both the scenario introduced and any additional proposals discussed in questions i to iii.

Learning point: acknowledging the role of 'luck'

While this may seem like anathema to some of us, luck may be an ingredient in the success of some project activities. This perhaps reflects the limit of our project management process power, where we can influence but not guarantee precise project outcomes.

What the future holds

For anyone involved in forecasting, the best place to start to predict the future is by looking at what happened in the past and also by understanding better the factors that will influence what we want to predict. In the deployment of project management, a pattern has emerged. Firstly, the use of the hard skills has been stable for several decades. Accredited training and development schemes help to maintain a critical mass of knowledge, skills and vocabulary. This is influenced by the sector in which the project takes place and the character and experience of the person involved. For example, an analytically minded person will probably have a preference for planning, in contrast to someone who is action oriented.

This stability is not matched by the expectations of stakeholders, nor in terms of recognizing that a wider and better balanced set of project management skills and approaches is now essential. The fundamental principles, however, are largely unchanged. As we saw in the Roman Empire project manager example in Chapter 11, the same core activities take place, and these are subject to similar constraints. Of the five key areas compared in the research, 'outsourcing' is shown in Figure 12.3:

FIGURE 12.3   Comparison of selected practices: Roman and contemporary period

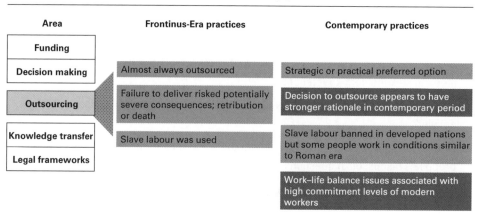

SOURCE: adapted from Walker and Dart (2011)

different eras, similar considerations. We could reflect on the rise of 24-hour, 7 days a week communication in the context of work–life balance.

It is worthwhile reflecting on a further example: in his work on Victorian London projects, Hughes (2013) reviewed the historical aspects of sanitation projects. He discusses the underlying scenario in the 1840s and the experience of London with cholera epidemics on three occasions in the same century, noting that the smell from the River Thames was so bad that it was not possible to work in areas of the Palace of Westminster. The overriding need to do something provided a strong driver for the sanitation project, which had programmatic aspects. This saw the emergence of the Institution of Civil Engineers (1846), and of associated contracts where the relationship with stakeholders was managed in a relatively holistic way. All of these characteristics (or equivalents) are relevant to a 20th-century project.

The sewers that Joseph Bazalgette designed were intended for a population of 3.5m, roughly 30 per cent greater than the population at the time (*The Economist*, 2014). By 2014, London had a rising population of 8.4m and an upgrade project could be under way by 2016. Technology enables the process to take place in a more efficient manner, but there will still be problems to address and a need to innovate, and stakeholders will present a challenge within the project management. History repeats itself.

Projects are about people; people will change

Advertising reveals much about the changes in some societies; continuing advances in technology have changed some aspects dramatically, leading to disconnection between generations and within demographic sectors. We live in a digital world, jobs have changed and the world will continue to change. Yet we still need sewers; we still need buildings; we still need infrastructure. There will still be entrepreneurs and the successful ones will manage their projects well.

In 'Management intuition for the next 50 years', McKinsey put forward an assessment of the dynamism in emerging markets, changes from technology and connectivity, and ageing populations (*McKinsey Quarterly*, 2014) – all of these will collide, leaving us to contemplate the nature of this increasingly volatile world. Whatever the future actually holds, there will be lots of change; change tends to cause, or is caused by, projects. It is likely that project management approaches need to be nimble to stay relevant. The fundamental principles remain, but they will be acted out by new generations of people who are used to a fundamentally different style and means not only of communicating, but of doing things.

One final point to raise is the consideration of globalization, international aspects and cultural dimensions. With a shift in economic emphasis from the west to the east, the cultural landscape will change the project landscape. Project management styles and expectations may well change, perhaps shifting from the individual towards the collective. The profile of stakeholder power is likely to change, for the reasons just discussed and because we cannot anticipate future changes.

Project management has to listen, observe, analyse and reflect. It needs to continue to ask the important questions: why, what, when, who and how? As a metaphoric bridge between strategy and operations, project management can remain as important as the physical form.

Summary

The summing up of this chapter is largely about bringing together the topics covered in all the previous ones. We have reflected upon all the topics and the need to maintain balance in our approach and style of project management in relation to the particular type of project and the stakeholder context.

We have considered some of the key factors associated with bringing success to project environments and acknowledged that the form of this can never be guaranteed. Often the best we can do is influence outcomes. As we have developed our insights, we have become better able to apply the right approach in the right way at the right time.

As we look to the future, we are certain that it will be uncertain; things will change and the need for projects is guaranteed. Enjoy the feeling of anticipation, use your insight and overcome the challenges – deliver your projects well. Celebrate and look forward to the next.

Notes

1 This case study draws upon information from the following sources:

The Hamilton Spectator (2011) Cricket World Cup may be 10 times Super Bowl audience, 1 April, retrieved on 27 October 2014 from http://www.thespec.com/sports-story/2200505-cricket-world-cup-may-be-10-times-super-bowl-audience/

International Cricket Council Reliance ICC T201 Ranking (27 November 2014), retrieved on 27 November 2014 from http://www.icc-cricket.com/team-rankings/odi

Nottingham Post (2014) Notts Cricket Club delight at 2013 profits but are not resting on their laurels, 16 January

Nottinghamshire County Cricket Club (2013) Annual Report & Accounts

2 The umpire is a referee; 'not out' means the player (and on this occasion the match) continues.

References

Burnes, B (2004) *Managing Change: A strategic approach to organisation dynamics*, Financial Times Prentice Hall, Harlow

Cooke-Davies, T (2002) The "real" success factors on projects, *International Journal of Project Management*, **20**, pp 185–90

Crawford, L, French, E and Lloyd-Walker, B (2013) From outpost to outback: project career paths in Australia, *International Journal of Project Management*, **31**, pp 1175–87

Daily Telegraph (2014) Energy suppliers: the ultimate guide to price and service, 18 September

Dvir, D, Raz, T and Shenhar, A (2003) An empirical analysis of the relationship between project planning and project success, *International Journal of Project Management*, **21**, pp 89–95

The Economist (2014) London's sewers: smelling sweet, 20 September

Hughes, M (2013) The Victorian London sanitation projects and the sanitation of projects, *International Journal of Project Management*, **31**, pp 682–94

Ika, L (2009) Project success as a topic in project management journals, *Project Management Journal*, **40** (4), pp 6–19

Jugdev, K and Muller, R (2005) A retrospective look at our evolving understanding of project success, *Project Management Journal*, **36** (4), pp 19–31

Kotter, J (1996) *Leading Change*, Harvard Business School Press, Boston, MA

McKinsey Quarterly (2014) Management intuition for the next 50 years, September

Piderit, S (2000) Rethinking resistance and recognizing ambivalence: a multidimensional view of attitudes toward an organizational change, *Academy of Management Review*, **25** (4), pp 783–i94

Shenhar, A, Dvir, D, Levy, O and Maltz, A (2001) Project success: a multidimensional strategic concept, *Long Range Planning*, **34**, pp 699–725

Walker, D and Dart, C (2011) Frontinus – a project manager from the Roman Empire, *Project Management Journal*, **42** (5), pp 4–16

GLOSSARY

activity duration   The time expected for a particular activity to take place.

actual   A known amount or value.

actual cost   The known cost.

adjourning   A key stage associated with the lifecycle of teams.

agile approaches   The term given to iterative processes based on flexibility and interaction.

analogous estimates   Estimating based on prior experience or analogous scenarios.

APM   Association for Project Management.

APMP®   An APM certification qualification.

Atern®   An agile approach.

audits   Often describes an inspection or investigation of an undertaking.

baseline   Used to describe a reference point or level.

body of knowledge   A set of terms, concepts, approaches and activities associated with a professional domain.

bottom-up   The planning process takes place unconstrained by a target (or limited by a certain) amount.

business case   A justification for undertaking a project (or programme).

cause–effect–cause analysis   A problem-solving method based on progressively pursuing causes and effects.

CBS   Cost breakdown structure; a process of breaking down the cost into smaller components to develop or understand the structure.

change   As relates to the project process and the impact of the project.

change control process   A means of controlling change management within the project process.

change management   A means of dealing with changes (often in terms of expectations) within the project process.

closure   Associated with the completion of a project.

competence area   In relation to the individual, these are often grouped in terms of technical, behavioural and contextual characteristics.

complexity   A measure of the difficulty with analysing or understanding something.

conceptual phase   A discrete phase within some project lifecycle models.

conformance   Stated requirements to which the project must conform.

cost estimation   The process of estimating likely and unknown costs associated with a project.

cost planning   The area of identifying the costs of resources needed for the fulfilment of a project.

critical path   The longest sequence of dependent activities that each need to be completed for the project overall to complete.

critical path analysis (CPA) The analysis process associated with determining the critical path.

cultural intelligence Intelligent behaviour in relation to specific cultures and adjustment capabilities.

decision trees An analytical technique based on separating activities into logical branches sequences (like a tree).

earned value A measure of progress; the value of completed work.

emotional competence (EQ) A group of competencies associated with dimension of leadership.

EST Earliest start time. Associated with network planning and analysis.

EVM, earned value management Management through measurement of earned value against a baseline plan.

execution or delivery phase A discrete phase within some project lifecycle models.

external dependencies A item that is outside the control of the project manager or project management team.

feasibility The testing of an idea or concept; an analysis of possibility, practicality and viability.

forecast An estimate for an unknown amount or value.

forming A key stage associated with the lifecycle of teams.

forward pass The process of working through a network diagram, from left to right.

functional organization An organizational form based on functions such as marketing, finance, human resources.

Gantt chart The name often given to a time-planning bar chart.

gates A checkpoint (stop, go, or other action) between phases or other subdivision of the lifecycle.

group A collection of items or people with some underlying structural logic.

GVT Global virtual team; a globally dispersed team.

handover Associated with the acceptance, transfer or commissioning of the outcome of the project.

heavyweight matrix Often associated with a project management organization where staff are seconded to the project.

hybrid project team A project team with some co-located, others remotely based.

intellectual competence (IQ) A group of competencies associated with dimension of leadership.

IPMA International Project Management Association.

ITT Invitation to tender.

lean medium A communication medium that has 'least common denominator' characteristics; ie the medium reduces the content to its leanest form.

liability creation Although projects create value, in the longer term the need for renewal (eg in the form of refurbishment) causes a liability.

lightweight matrix   Often associated with a project management organization where staff participate in the project in addition to their normal work.

LST   Latest start time. Associated with network planning and analysis.

management review (report)   A report that provides a strategic perspective or draws attention to specific critical items, especially with external dependencies.

managerial competence (MQ)   A group of competencies associated with dimension of management.

milestone   A significant event or specific goal.

MNT   A multinational team.

network analysis   An analytical method associated with time and resource planning.

network diagram   A diagrammatic representation of project activities, durations, sequence and relationships.

norming   A key stage associated with the lifecycle of teams.

OBS   Organizational breakdown structure; a process of breaking down the organization into smaller components to develop or understand the structure.

opportunity cost   The cost of pursuing one thing to the detriment of something else that could have been developed or undertaken.

optimism in estimating   Sometimes expressed as optimism bias; a positive expectation that actuals will be achieved at least as well as estimates.

outsource   A process of buying-in or subcontracting services.

outturn   The cost value at completion of the project (or stage of project).

PBO   Project-based organization; one in which the project is the primary means of delivering the product or service.

PBS   Product breakdown structure; a process of breaking down the product into smaller components to develop or understand the structure.

performance   Delivery to stakeholder expectations.

performing   A key stage associated with the lifecycle of teams.

pessimism in estimating   A conservative approach to planning; an expectation that actuals will exceed estimates.

phase   A subdivision of a lifecycle.

PIR   Post-implementation review; a review undertaken after the implementation of the project.

planned cost   The estimated cost.

planned value   In EVM, the total planned activities at planned cost.

planning phase   A discrete phase within some project lifecycle models.

PMI   Project Management Institute.

PMO   Project management organization; the organization of the project in terms of its management.

PMO   Project management office; sometimes referred to as a project support office.

PMP®   A PMI certification qualification.

portfolio   An aggregated group of programmes (and therefore projects).

PPP Public–private partnership; a long-term contract between a government and private entity for the provision of a public service.

Prince 2® A project management approach.

programme A combination of projects plus other organizational or project-like activities.

progress reviews Activities that take place over the duration of a project, at key stages or otherwise, formally or informally.

project A temporary group activity that produces something unique.

project autonomy The degree of independence or freedom.

project board The element of the project management organization that has a more strategic emphasis.

project budget A statement of the costs planned for the project.

project charter A document developed to inform or support the delivery of a project.

project domain The field, region or world constituted by the project.

project governance Relevant organizational or specific policies, regulations, procedures or associated rules deployed in project environments.

project initiation document A document developed to inform or support the delivery of a project.

project lifecycle A basis for articulating the different phases within a project.

project management A set of activities associated with the fulfilment of a project.

project management team The key delivery element within the project management organization.

project manager The person with the responsibility for the project.

project organization An organizational form that is based on delivering projects.

project parent A host organization or managing body that has ultimate responsibility for the project.

project selection criteria Criteria that enable the selection of projects, often on the basis of competing business cases.

project sponsor A representing senior executive who ensures support for business case, changes and other appropriate forms of commitment required.

psychometric profiling A technique used to help understand better psychometric styles and preferences.

quality assurance role A role that is sometimes deployed with a key focus on the quality aspects of a project.

quality planning The area of identifying and planning the aspects associated with the quality expected with the fulfilment of a project.

resource management The area of managing the resources identified and planned for the fulfilment of a project.

resource planning The area of identifying and planning resources needed for the fulfilment of a project.

responsibility matrix A tool that can help allocate roles and responsibilities.

reverse pass The process of working through a network diagram, from right to left.

reviews Associated with an assessment intended to make value-adding changes.

RFQ   Request for quotation.

RFT   Request for tender.

risk   State of being uncertain.

risk identification   Proactively seeking to identify risk.

risk management   The process of managing risk.

risk mitigation   A process of controlling or responding to identified risks.

risk profile   Identifying and grouping relevant risks, likelihoods and impacts.

risk response   Possible or proposed response to risk identified.

risk response strategy   Strategy adopted to respond to risks identified.

risk scoring   Reflecting the likelihood of risk events by assigning a judgement.

scope   The extent of the project (in terms of requirements, solutions, resources) relevant for the delivery.

self-organizing team   This may be relevant in certain project environments where the process or outcome of the project is difficult to define.

sequential approaches   Following project lifecycle processes in a logical sequence; also known as waterfall approaches.

service level agreement SLA   A basis for the agreement of a specified level of service between two parties.

shared risk   This is often associated with the sharing of risk between the client and the supplier.

slack   The difference between the latest start time and earliest start time.

spectrum   Used to highlight a wide range of types or possibilities.

stakeholder   Groups or individuals who affect, or are affected by, the project.

stakeholder envelope   The stakeholder expectation or impact boundaries within which the project takes place.

stakeholder oven   A metaphoric expression that highlights the potential feelings experienced by project managers during the lifecycle of the project.

stakeholder strategy   An approach to enable the successful development of effective relationships with project stakeholders.

storming   A key stage associated with the lifecycle of teams.

team   A focused group of people with common goals and where success for one depends on success for all.

termination   Associated with the completion of a project.

termination phase   A phase within some project lifecycle models.

time-planning bar chart   A representation of activities and their respective sequences and durations in bar-chart form.

top-down   The planning process takes place constrained by a target (or limited by a certain) amount.

traditional project team   A project team co-located with close proximity of team members.

triple constraints   Often used to mean the time, cost and quality constraints.

uncertainty   Reflecting doubt.

value capture Stakeholder groups gaining value from a project that has been undertaken.

value creation Projects provide a process that creates value and benefit.

value lag The timing difference between the creation of value and its capture by stakeholder groups.

variance The difference between an estimate and an actual; this could relate to costs, schedules, or other project progress measures.

virtual project team A dispersed project team.

waterfall approaches Following project lifecycle processes in a logical sequence; also known as sequential approaches.

WBS: work breakdown structure A process of breaking down an activity into smaller components and understanding the structure.

INDEX

Italics indicate a figure or table.